Suddenly, from both sides of the road, came a steady stream of tracers from enemy machine guns. Bullets hit Hawkins's truck and practically shot the engine right out of it. The vehicle stopped dead. Before he could try to get it off to the side of the road, all hell broke loose. Hilburn ground his truck to a halt and, diving for a ditch, yelled back to me that the road was blocked. By this time, Williams and I had done the same thing. Small-arms, machine-gun, and mortar fire started sweeping the road. Amid complete chaos, troops piled off of vehicles and yelled for their buddies and units.

The ditch on the right (east) side of the roadway was fairly deep and provided excellent cover and concealment. It sloped up to a railroad bed with a set of narrow-gauge tracks. The slope offered good firing positions. On the left side of the road was a very shallow depression, along with a few scattered trees and telephone poles. It provided much less protection, but it had to be manned to cover the enemy approaching from the west. . . .

By Bruce H. Norton
*Published by Ivy Books:*

FORCE RECON DIARY, 1969
FORCE RECON DIARY, 1970

*With Donald N. Hamblen:*
ONE TOUGH MARINE

*With Maurice J. Jacques:*
SERGEANT MAJOR, U.S. MARINES

*With Len Maffioli:*
GROWN GRAY IN WAR

# GROWN GRAY IN WAR

Major Bruce H. Norton,
USMC (Ret.)
and
Master Gunnery Sergeant
Len Maffioli, USMC (Ret.)

IVY BOOKS • NEW YORK

Copyright © 1997 by Bruce H. Norton and Leonard J. Maffioli

All rights reserved under International and Pan-American Copyright Conventions. Published in the United States by Ballantine Books, a division of Random House, Inc., New York, and distributed in Canada by Random House of Canada Limited, Toronto.

http://www.randomhouse.com

Library of Congress Catalog Card Number: 96-95499

ISBN 0-8041-1599-0

Unless otherwise noted, all photos are from Leonard J. Maffioli's collection.

This edition published by arrangement with Naval Institute Press.

Manufactured in the United States of America

First Ballantine Books Edition: August 1997

10  9  8  7  6  5  4  3  2  1

*This book is lovingly dedicated to Darice, Bruce II, and Elizabeth, who make it all worthwhile*

*And to the thousands of Korean War POWs who never returned home—you are not forgotten*

# Contents

List of Maps                                    ix
Foreword                                        xi
Preface                                         xiii
Acknowledgments                                 xvi
List of Abbreviations                           xviii

 1  Memories of Youth                            1
 2  Boot Camp                                   20
 3  War in the Pacific                          36
 4  Return to War                               58
 5  Inchon, Seoul, and Beyond                   71
 6  Task Force Drysdale                         87
 7  Capture                                    104
 8  Our Welcome to Kanggye                     122
 9  Reeducation, Chinese Style                 139
10  A Cultural Affair                          155
11  The Move South                             167
12  Escape                                     183
13  Welcome Back                               200
14  The Aftermath of Korea                     210
15  Looking for a Home                         217
16  New Posts and Stations                     232
17  My Third War                               245
18  Fair Winds and Following Seas              272
Epilogue                                       290

# Contents

Appendixes 291

Bibliography 304

Index 307

# Maps

Western Pacific operations, February 1945      45

Iwo Jima, U.S. Marine Corps amphibious landings, 1944      49

Peninsula of Korea      76

Area of operations, 1st Marine Division in North Korea, October–December 1950      92

The battle around Hagaru, North Korea, 1950      95

The route of U.S. prisoners of war from Kanggye to Chunchon, North Korea, 1951      113

Da Nang and surrounding area, Quang Nam Province, South Vietnam, 1967      250

Battle areas during the Tet Offensive, South Vietnam, 1968      258

# Foreword

LEN MAFFIOLI ALWAYS impressed me favorably with his enthusiasm and spirit. His account, through the medium of Maj. Bruce H. Norton, U.S. Marine Corps (Ret.), reflects these attributes greatly.

Len's story is most interesting, and mostly new to me because Len and I saw each other only occasionally over the years. At Kanggye, Len was one of the POWs on whom I felt I could rely, and did. My attempts to give some guidance to the other POWs was never favorably received by our captors, to say the least.

Len's version and mine of the events of the night of 29 November 1950 agree, essentially. As it was a polyglot group—U.S. Marines, British Marines, and U.S. Army soldiers—it was difficult to organize the resistance. But we were able to hold the enemy off until well after midnight. Then, Frank Noel, an Associated Press photographer, came up the road from the south. He had been captured, and the Chinese (Communists) had sent him in to demand our surrender. After talking to many of our men, and confirming that we were almost out of ammo, I went down the road to talk to the Chinese. I surrendered after asking that our wounded be cared for and released, to which they agreed. Many of our wounded survived and were picked up by the Marine regiments to our north as they made their way south to Koto-ri and then Hamhung.

Len's recounting of events after they were separated from us to go south for release was fascinating to me. Their ultimate escape was miraculous. Their rescuers in the tanks must have been astonished and the POWs delirious.

The remainder of Len's career, and his approach to new challenges, exemplify the versatility and drive he possessed. He obviously sought to improve every organization to which he was assigned: tank unit, recruiting station, or embassy security guard.

This Marine's story is a well-written, intriguing tale of a man who is devoted to the Corps and to his fellow Marines.

*Lt. Gen. John McLaughlin*
*U.S. Marine Corps (Ret.)*

# Preface

*As a rule it is easy to find officers, but it is very hard to find*
*noncommissioned officers.*
—Napoleon I, 1809

"THE OLDER I get, the better I was." This phrase is often spoken among veterans, and many nod their heads in silent, smiling agreement. As Marines get further away from their wars, they often tend to make them more as they wish they had been, rather than how they really were. This is not the case with M.Gy.Sgt. Leonard J. Maffioli's story.

After finishing my fourth book, *Sergeant Major, U.S. Marines*, I had no interest in working on another Marine's life story anytime soon. Throughout the time-consuming research and the writing itself, which is a joy, there remains the urge to superimpose my values on those of my subjects, which is unfair to them and to me.

I changed my mind after meeting Len Maffioli and listening to him talk about his military experiences: the island-hopping that took him across the Pacific and onto the fire-swept beaches of Iwo Jima; his participation in the Korean War as a member of the ill-fated relief column known as Task Force Drysdale; his subsequent capture, six-month internment and his escape from the Chinese; and his tour of duty, seventeen years later, during the Tet Offensive in Vietnam. I knew that his thirty-three years of service to Corps and country would prove to be much more than an enlightening and educational patrol through Marine Corps history.

There is a saying that "bad wars make for good Marines." Combat experience cannot cure a man of bravery, but it certainly can provide him with an inventory of "lessons learned"— many the hard way—and all of them to be remembered.

The lessons learned by Len Maffioli during three wars, particularly during his time in Korea as a prisoner of war, should be of particular interest to every Marine and military historian.

Seeing combat for the first time on Saipan, Tinian, and Iwo Jima in the Pacific during World War II, Private First Class Maffioli learned the horrors of war quickly. Enemy mortar and artillery fire did not discriminate against age, rank, or service.

Five years later in Korea—the amphibious landing at Inchon, the retaking of Seoul, and the 1st Marine Division's attempt to reinforce itself near Koto-ri—was the second war in which Maffioli, then a corporal, was thoroughly challenged. His most difficult test came at the hands of the North Koreans and, later, the Chinese Communists, who tried to break his spirit. Although humor and acrimony might be used in describing the conditions of brutal confinement that Len Maffioli, his fellow Marines, and Allied soldiers were forced to endure, there was nothing remotely amusing about surviving in a North Korean hellhole where four of every ten prisoners died.

Maffioli is one of only eighteen U.S. Marines ever to escape from the Chinese Communists. He is living proof of the outstanding quality of training and esprit de corps that are integral parts of being a U.S. Marine.

Seventeen years later, then, M.Sgt. Len Maffioli took his many "lessons learned" to Vietnam. From 1967 to 1968, as the operations chief of 1st Tank Battalion, he witnessed a war quite unlike any he had seen before—a war where politics and tactics changed as rapidly as the seasons.

Following his twelve-month tour of duty in Southeast Asia, Len Maffioli continued his career as a Marine noncommissioned officer for eleven more years. He was with the Marine Security Guard in Saudi Arabia and Afghanistan and served as a Marine recruiter in the United States before he retired in 1979.

The story of Master Gunnery Sergeant Maffioli—this extraordinary record of small discoveries and survival—is an effort to document accurately the thirty-three-year career of a professional Marine staff noncommissioned officer. His service to Corps and country was nothing less than exemplary.

—*Maj. Bruce H. Norton, USMC (Ret.)*

# Acknowledgments

THE BIOGRAPHY OF Len Maffioli would have been impossible to write without the help, patience, and cooperation of Col. Richard D. "Mic" Mickelson, USMC (Ret.), Carlan F. Mickelson, and Crystal M. Lottig. I also extend my great appreciation to all of them. I particularly want to thank Ethel Kanner Maffioli for having the foresight to save all of her son's letters to her during World War II, the Korean War, and the Vietnam War. And to my wife, Darice, for providing me the most valuable gift of all, the quiet time required for writing this book, I offer my deepest gratitude.

—*Maj. Bruce H. Norton, USMC (Ret.)*

AMONG THOSE TO whom I am deeply indebted for their assistance, and especially their patience with my seemingly endless telephone calls asking that they jog their memories once more, are Andrew "Chief" Aguirre, CWO-4 James "Gunner Jim" Carroll, USMC (Ret.), M.Sgt. S. W. "Bill" Phillips, USMC (Ret.), SFC Saburo "Sam" Shimomura, USA (Ret.), and Kenny Williams. A special thanks to Lt. Col. Martin Wisda, U.S. Army, of the Department of Defense Prisoner of War/Missing in Action Office (DPMO) and Lt. Col. Johnie E. Webb, Jr., U.S. Army (Ret.), of the Army's Central Identification Laboratory, Hawaii (CILHI), for their assistance with the information concerning the "Missing in Action-Unaccounted for" American personnel of the Korean War. And last, but certainly not least, my thanks go to my loving wife, Donna Moore Maffioli, for her patience, encouragement, and countless hours spent helping me tell this story.

*—M.Gy.Sgt. Len Maffioli, USMC (Ret.)*

# Abbreviations

| | |
|---|---|
| ADC | assistant division commander |
| AFEES | Armed Forces Examining and Entrance Station |
| AFQT | Armed Forces Qualification Test |
| AP | Associated Press |
| ARVN | Army, Republic of Vietnam |
| ASP 1 | Ammunition Supply Point No. 1 |
| B/31/7 | Company B, 31st Battalion, 7th Infantry Regiment (example) |
| BNR | bodies not recovered |
| CCF | Chinese Communist Forces |
| CILHI | Central Identification Laboratory, Hawaii |
| CMC | Commandant of the Marine Corps |
| CO | commanding officer |
| COC | combat operations center |
| CP | command post |
| CPV | Chinese People's Volunteers |
| CPVA | Chinese People's Volunteer Army |
| CTZ | Central Time Zone |
| DESFEX | desert firing exercise |
| DI | drill instructor |
| DMZ | Demilitarized Zone |
| DofNE | duration of the national emergency |
| DOW | died of wounds |
| DPMO | Department of Defense Prisoner of War/Missing in Action Office |
| EOD | explosive ordnance disposal |

| | |
|---|---|
| FMF | Fleet Marine Force |
| G/3/1 | Company G, 3d Battalion, 1st Marine Regiment (example) |
| G-2 | Intelligence Section (division level) |
| G-3 | Operations and Training Section (division level) |
| G-4 | Logistical Section (division level) |
| HBT | herringbone twill |
| HQ | headquarters |
| HQMC | Headquarters Marine Corps |
| H&S | Headquarters and Service Company |
| KCS | Kit Carson Scout |
| KIA | killed in action |
| LCM | landing craft, mechanized |
| LCVP | landing craft, vehicle, personnel |
| LSD | landing ship, dock |
| LST | landing ship, tank |
| LVT | landing vehicle, tracked |
| MACV | Military Airlift Command, Vietnam |
| MAF | Marine Amphibious Force |
| MAG | Marine Aviation Group/Military Advisory Group |
| MARS | Military Amateur Radio System |
| MCD | Marine Corps District |
| MCRD | Marine Corps Recruit Depot |
| MIA | missing in action |
| MLR | main line of resistance |
| MOS | military occupational specialty |
| MP | military police |
| MSG | Marine Security Guard |
| MSR | main supply route |
| MT | motor transport |
| NCO | noncommissioned officer |
| NCOIC | noncommissioned officer in charge |
| NKPA | North Korean People's Army |
| OIC | officer in charge |
| OP | observation post |
| OQR | officer's qualification record |
| PIO | public information officer |

| | |
|---|---|
| POL | petroleum, oils, lubricants |
| POW | prisoner of war |
| PX | post exchange |
| RCT | regimental combat team |
| ROK | Republic of Korea |
| RPG | rocket propellant grenade |
| R&R | rest and recuperation |
| RS | recruiting station |
| RSLA | Recruiting Station, Los Angeles |
| RSS | recruiting substation |
| SATR | supported arms training regiment |
| SNCO | staff noncommissioned officer |
| SRB | service record book |
| SSDC | Southern Sector Defense Command |
| T/E | table of equipment |
| TI | technical inspection |
| TVTBn | track vehicle training battalion |
| UCMJ | Uniform Code of Military Justice |
| UN | United Nations |
| USAID | U.S. Agency for International Development |
| USIA | U.S. Information Agency |
| USMC | U.S. Marine Corps |
| USMCR | U.S. Marine Corps Reserve |
| VA | Veterans Administration (now, Department of Veterans Affairs) |
| VC | Viet Cong |
| XO | executive officer (second in command) |

# =1=

# Memories of Youth

THE DOMINICO MAFFIOLI family immigrated to the United States in 1914 and settled down in the Hibbing, Minnesota, area. My father, Carl Charles Maffioli, was born in 1899 in the town of Bardello, Lombardy Province, Italy. He was one of six children born to Dominico and Rosa Maffioli.

As head of a large family in a poor village, Grandfather Dominico knew his future lay not in Italy but in the United States. He first came to work in this country in 1910 and worked at a variety of odd jobs. He enjoyed some success as an estate caretaker and later as a miner in Hibbing, where he worked for four years to save enough money to return to Italy and collect his family. On his return to Bardello, he learned that two of his sons had died in accidents: one drowned, and the other fell from a swing and broke his neck.

My mother, Ethel Kanner Maffioli, the second of three children born to Harry and Mary Skelly Kanner, was born in Hoboken, New Jersey, in 1898. Harry's parents had come from Germany and Mary's from County Cork, Ireland. Harry Kanner, a carpenter by trade, moved his family from New York to New Jersey and then to Missouri before finally settling in Denver, Colorado, in 1917.

My father was fifteen years old when he arrived in the United States. He worked at a number of odd jobs before enlisting in the U.S. Army in 1918. After completing basic training, he was enrolled in advanced training when the war

1

ended. He was stationed in Denver, Colorado, at the time, and that was where he met and fell in love with my mother.

My parents were married in Denver in 1919. When my father was discharged from the army, he took a job as a delivery man for a dry-cleaning company. Because he still had trouble reading and writing English, my mother accompanied him on his route and helped him to read maps and street signs.

In 1921, my sister, Marion Rose, was born in Denver. The family moved to California that same year and settled first in the San Francisco Bay area. My father again found work in the dry-cleaning and laundry business and worked his way up from route salesman to manager before owning his first small dry-cleaning store. With only a grade school education, but having a keen business sense, he owned and operated the largest dry-cleaning plant in northern California by the age of twenty-nine, as he realized the American dream that had brought him to this country.

Within a couple of years—and especially after learning about California's job opportunities and mild weather—both sides of my parents' extended families moved to the Berkeley/Oakland area of northern California. Family gatherings, particularly Sunday dinners, became a wonderful tradition because the families lived within a few blocks of one another. Of course, when my father's family was hosting the dinners, the food was Italian, served northern Italian style, dishes I love to this very day.

My mother's sister Lillian married Leonard Hubberts, whom she met in Berkeley, and her brother James also settled in the Berkeley area, where he met and married Elizabeth Orr. When I was born on 1 July 1925, my two uncles actually drew straws to see whose name I would carry. Leonard won, and I was named Leonard James Maffioli. Two years later, Leonard and Lillian had twins, James and Jane. My family lived close by, and my sister and I spent as much time at the Hubberts' house as we did at home.

My father's dry-cleaning business was largely a wholesale operation, and the 1929 stock market crash left him with thousands of dollars worth of uncollectible bills. Like tens of thousands of others throughout the country, he lost his business overnight.

After the loss of our family's source of income, we made a series of moves. We left our beautiful home in the Claremont Hills section of Oakland for rental flats and small houses in Emeryville, Santa Rosa, San Jose, Hanford, and Los Angeles—wherever my father could find work or manage dry-cleaning and laundry plants. An ambitious, hard-working, and proud man, my father was never out of a job for more than a few days and never considered accepting any type of welfare or other public assistance. In 1935, my brother, Carl Charles Maffioli, Jr. (known as "Sonny"), was born in San Francisco, and, a year later, we moved south to San Diego after a brief stop in Los Angeles. (That same year, my father's sister, Angela, married John Paoletti of Oakland, and the following year, they had a son, named Dominic after his maternal grandfather.)

A beautiful city, San Diego had a population of about 135,000 at that time. It was a "Navy town" with several large bases, including the U.S. Naval Destroyer Base at Thirty-second Street, the U.S. Naval Training Center, and the U.S. Naval Air Station on the island of Coronado, along with dozens of naval ships anchored in the San Diego Bay. When the fleet was in, the city bustled with activity, but when the fleet left for maneuvers, it was quiet, with only the shore-based sailors left to patronize the local bars and locker clubs on Broadway and Market Streets.

We started life anew in a pretty, Spanish-style home located on Twiggs Street in the Old Town section of the city. I went to Fremont Grammar School, which because of our frequent moves, was the eighth grade school I attended. Less than a mile from the school, across the railroad tracks and a stretch of tidal mud flats, was the U.S. Marine Corps Base that trained recruits in "boot camp"—a place that, later, would have a profound impact on my life.

I enjoyed the usual boyhood sports of sandlot football and softball, bicycle riding, and bay and ocean fishing. On occasion, a friend and I rode our bikes to the waterfront and fished for mackerel from the Broadway and Navy Piers. Other times, we rode over to the sleepy town of Pacific Beach and fished on Mission Bay or in the ocean.

One day, a friend asked if I would like to go with him to the dump at the Marine Corps Base on the following Saturday morning. Not having anything better to do, I accepted his invitation, but I had no idea what he was talking about. When Saturday arrived, we walked over to the base parade deck, known as the "grinder." We watched the Marine recruits mercilessly marched up and down the parade deck by their drill sergeants, and I could see why they called that place the grinder. Finally, my buddy led me to a remote area at the corner of the base. He began rummaging through a large pile of discarded Marine Corps trash as he looked for treasure.

"Once in a while," he said, "if you're really lucky, you'll find a real campaign hat, or maybe a broken bayonet."

We didn't have any luck on that first trip, but, later on, we managed to scrounge some real "artifacts" that we proudly showed off to our friends at school.

Several months later, this same buddy and I went down to the Fisherman's Wharf area and met up with a man named Tony. He owned a small rowboat, complete with a jury-rigged sail, that he rented at twenty-five cents per hour. (Tony didn't seem to care to whom he rented his boat or how old they were.) We had scraped up fifty cents, and Tony agreed to rent his boat to us for a two-hour sail.

We managed somehow, by rowing and manipulating the sail, to get the boat out to the middle of San Diego Bay, just offshore of the Naval Air Station on Coronado. We were laughing and having lots of fun when we suddenly noticed a destroyer bearing down on us as she turned around Point Loma. The destroyer gave us a loud blast from her signaling horn. We barely got out of her way, and her passing wake nearly swamped us. This was great fun, of course, and our early luck with the destroyer made us as cocky as neophyte sailors. We thought we had mastered the skill of sailing until we noticed an aircraft carrier headed in our direction.

Unlike the smaller destroyer, she wasn't coming on fast, but it was obvious that she wasn't going to get out of our way, and we knew she couldn't swerve. We panicked. As we frantically tried to row in one direction, the sail pulled us in another. We tried waving off the carrier, but her horn started blasting us with its earsplitting sound. We just managed to get off of her port beam as she steamed by.

The carrier started backing down to tie up at her pier on Coronado. The naval officers on the bridge were looking down at us, swearing and shaking their fists, while the sailors and Marines on the stern and in the gun tubs were cheering us. We maneuvered our boat close enough for some of the crew to throw down cigarettes and matches. We thought we were big shots, and, on that very day, I do believe I formed my opinion of the U.S. Navy.

At age twelve, I had a brand-new bicycle and took on the responsibility of a paper route. I rode over to the Marine Corps Base in the evenings, parked my bike, walked through the two-story Spanish-style barracks, and hawked my papers. My young and impressionable eyes took in the cleanliness and uniformity of everything: the orderly and clean living spaces, the drum-tight bunks, the spotless '03 Springfield rifle slung at the foot of each Marine's rack, and the foot-locker aligned below it.

About this time, the San Diego–based Marines were ordered into China to help safeguard the Shanghai International Settlement. My sister Marion knew a Marine who was leaving for China, and she and I went to the base and watched the Marines board the trucks that would take them to the Navy Pier and the transport ships waiting for them. Khaki-clad, with full packs, and wearing campaign hats and polished, high-top dress shoes, they were an impressive group to a young kid. I guess that was when I was hooked—I knew that someday I wanted to be a Marine, too.

Our house was located at the bottom of Presidio Park hill, and we played in a large grassy area of the park close to home. The Serra Museum was located close by, and its tower offered a commanding view of the beaches and Mission Bay and eastward into Mission Valley. Behind our house was a deep canyon that ran for about a quarter of a mile, parallel to Juan Street, to the foot of what is known as Mission Hills. The canyon was covered with sagebrush and cactus, and it was an excellent place to hunt for small game. I had received a .410-gauge shotgun as a gift on my twelfth Christmas and used it to bag quail and rabbits, which my mother prepared and cooked for the family.

In 1939, our family moved from our rental house in Old Town to a wonderful home that my parents purchased in Bay Park Village, which was only a few miles north of Old Town but on the eastern shore of beautiful Mission Bay. By then, I had graduated from Fremont and was enrolled at Point Loma, a junior-senior high school.

I began to form new friendships with the kids of Bay Park— friendships that lasted until we entered the service. There were three Alford brothers; Art was my age, Don was a year younger, and the youngest, Gene, was sometimes allowed to tag along with us. Dave Wilkinson was a year older than me and his brother Bud a year younger. Farris Kolbeck, whose father owned a large truck and trailer repair service, and I would be the only two boys in our gang to graduate from high school in June 1943. Also, there was Robert Royal ("Bob") Sullivan, the only member of our gang who would not return from World War II. He was killed in action while serving with the U.S. Army during the liberation of Europe. Before the war, we had all lived within a five-block radius in Bay Park Village.

Unfortunately, within a year of our move, my parents separated. My father took a room near his plant, and my mother and we kids stayed in the new house. This predicament was to have a profound effect, not only on my schoolwork but also on my behavior. There was always something to do in our new surroundings. We lived less than a quarter mile from Mission Bay, which, at high tide, came up to a small seawall bordering the Pacific coastal road, Highway 101. During extremely low tides, it was possible to walk nearly all the way across the bay, except for swimming across a few narrow channels. Some of us did this a few times, but we learned to be cautious about stepping on the numerous small stingrays that lay on the bottom of the bay.

One day, one of my buddies came up with the idea of building a clubhouse out in the water on Mission Bay. Bill

White, who was a few years older than most of us, owned an old car. To complete our plan for our clubhouse, we drove in Bill's car out to an "oil well" in the hills above Morena Boulevard, where Clairmont is now located. We kids called it an oil well, but it wasn't. Whoever was drilling never really struck anything to the best of my knowledge. We "borrowed" some long, heavy planks and hauled them, a few at a time, to the bay. After scrounging some smaller planks and working many hours during weekends, we finally completed a pier-type structure that ran out into the bay. There was just one small problem; our pier didn't run all the way to the shore, and we had to wade or swim out to it, depending on the tide.

We still needed a clubhouse. After a few days of cruising around, we found just what we were looking for, a wooden outhouse, the forerunner of today's portable john, but it was the property of the California Highway Department. Nonetheless, we waited until nightfall and then carried the outhouse down to Mission Bay, waited for high tide, and then floated it out to our pier. With considerable shoving, pushing, and pulling, we managed to get it onto the end of the pier and marveled at our accomplishment. Someone found a potbellied stove that we installed with some additional pipe. We finally had a comfortable gathering place. Often, we took our sleeping bags out to the clubhouse on a Saturday and spent the night on the pier.

The end of our clubhouse came during the winter of 1940, when San Diego experienced a particularly bad rainstorm and the wave action on Mission Bay worked against our pier. The outhouse and pier couldn't stand up against Mother Nature and were washed away. Several days later, we found a few planks, but that cast-iron stove is probably still there. In years to come, the Mission Bay State Park would be developed, the bay would be dredged here and filled in there, all to build the foundation for future hotels and resorts. According to a current map, our pier was on the southern tip of what is today the park's Leisure Lagoon.

While attending Fremont Grammar School, I had behaved myself fairly well and managed to stay out of trouble most of the time, but a few of my antics displeased my teachers. They usually resulted in trips to the principal's office, where justice was administered with the principal's leather trouser belt. I got my share of deserved licks. When I complained about them at home, my mother had said, "Why can't you be a good boy, like the others?" and my father had added, "He probably didn't give you enough of what you deserved." There was little sympathy for wise guys in the Maffioli household.

Point Loma High School was a different matter. After my parents separated, my grades began to fall because of inattention to my studies and I was reprimanded for "sassing back" my teachers. I could do my schoolwork with little effort if I put my mind to it, but there were too many distractions. One day, a teacher was explaining to our class how dangerous it could be to drop items in the school hallways. As an example, she told about a pencil stub that someone had dropped and which she had slipped on. Her feet shot out from under her, and she hit the deck—hard.

This particular teacher must have tipped the scales at more than 275 pounds, if she weighed an ounce, and my reaction to her story was to mutter that I bet her fall had really shaken the building. Some of my classmates heard my comment and began giggling. The teacher also heard it and pointed to the door. I was out, headed for the vice-principal's office. Now, this guy had a well-deserved reputation for being mean. He kept a small horsewhip in his office. For my indiscretion, I received five lashes, along with the admonition that he didn't want to see me in his office ever again.

Not long afterward one of my buddies pinched a package of chewing tobacco from a five-and-dime store and gave me a chaw (my first and last) just before we entered the classroom. For those who are unfamiliar with the acquired art of chewing tobacco, the rules are simple—you can chew the stuff for only a finite period of time before you have to spit out the tobacco juice. I couldn't leave the classroom, so I slid out from behind my desk, made my way to an open window, and spit. The third time I did this, the teacher told me to keep my seat. After a few minutes of chewing, I couldn't hold in the tobacco juice any longer and dared not swallow it. I stood up. The teacher told me to sit. I tried to mumble that I had a mouth full of chewing tobacco and, despite her warning, I ran to the window to spit it out. By that time, I had swallowed about half of it, and I barely made it outside the classroom before I began to heave my insides out. This breach of classroom etiquette cost me another trip to the vice-principal's office and another five whacks with his whip.

Somehow, I managed to survive the seventh, eighth, and half of the ninth grades before school officials decided that I might do better elsewhere. In fact, they were adamant—using the term *expelled* and telling me specifically not to return to Point Loma High.

I enjoyed much of junior high school, particularly the sports, where I tried out for Class C track. Also, I did well in ROTC (Reserve Officer Training Corps). I passed all of my inspections and liked the field campouts. I even enjoyed the glee club and drama classes; I sang solo for a Christmas program and played the role of Joe Harper in *Tom Sawyer*. But, in retrospect, these were subjects taught by teachers I liked. It was the boredom of the heavy-book studies that turned me away from being a serious student. Fortunately, Bay Park Village was located on the border of two school districts. So, rather than tell my parents that I had been expelled from school, I announced that I had grown tired of Point Loma and had the opportunity to attend La Jolla, another junior-senior high school.

I'm sure my father assumed that I would take over his dry-cleaning business when the time came for him to retire. He began my apprenticeship early by having me sweep out the plant on Saturday afternoons when the crew had finished for the day. As a teenager, I wasn't really interested in the business, but my father was the boss and I did as I was told. When I was fourteen years old, I had to start working regularly on Saturday afternoons. Transportation was a problem. Unless I got up early and rode to work with him, it took me several hours to get to East San Diego via bus and streetcar.

Work cut into my recreational time and left only Sundays for relaxing, but I quickly learned the various jobs associated with the dry-cleaning business. In a few months, I was able to run the dry-cleaning room, with two huge washers and a large extractor, by myself. The main part of my job was operating the "still," which distilled the cleaning fluid, a benzene-type petroleum solvent. Once a week, usually on Saturday afternoons, the still had to be cleaned thoroughly, which meant I had to empty the heavy tub of about twenty gallons of damp filter powder used to absorb dirt and impurities from dirty clothing. Periodically, a buddy and I hauled the powder out to the city dump. The dump master liked to see us coming. He'd have us throw the goo on top of whatever he might have a difficult time burning. That benzene fluid definitely made things burn.

Our Bay Park gang usually managed to stay out of trouble, but we did get into mischief once in a while. One Halloween night, we manufactured a man-sized dummy and dressed him up in a shirt and bib overalls. We then suspended him from a tree limb, which hung over Morena Boulevard, and waited until we saw a car heading in our direction. When the unsuspecting driver reached a predetermined spot on the road, we dropped the dummy from the limb and it landed directly in front of the oncoming car. We had never heard such tire screeching and swearing, especially when the driver discovered that the victim was a dummy. The second time we tried it, a lady got out from behind the wheel and explained to us that her husband was a heart patient and our practical joke could have killed him. Realizing that out stunt was fun but stupid, we left the dummy by the road and walked off.

We had another stunt that we performed down by the bay when traffic was particularly heavy on Highway 101 and we were dressed in our bathing suits, dripping wet from swimming. One of our guys lay down on the shoulder of the road. We covered him from head to toe with a beach blanket and then pretended to be crying as we stood over his "body." When cars began to stop and people asked what had happened, we told them that we'd been swimming and our buddy had drowned or that he had been hit by a car, depending on how imaginative we felt at the time. Standing around the "deceased," we listened to their gasps and sympathetic remarks until we heard the sound of sirens in the distance. Then, the "dead" one suddenly jumped up and grabbed the blanket and we'd all run like hell across the highway. One Sunday, a police car rolled up unannounced, and that was our last performance of that trick.

I got along much better with the teachers and school officials at La Jolla High School. Although I made a few new friends there, I still ran with the Bay Park crowd most of the time. Once again, I became active in the glee club and ran in a few Class C track meets, but my after-school work schedule kept me from getting enough training and I had to drop out of track a second time.

In 1940, I was fifteen years old and becoming interested, as do most boys, in cars. My father had taught me the mechanics of driving at the age of twelve, and I had driven him all the way from San Diego to Oakland to visit relatives when I was thirteen. Automobile traffic wasn't particularly heavy, and there weren't too many policemen patrolling California state highways. My father finally relented and bought a 1937 Ford coupe, with the understanding that I would work off the purchase price at his dry-cleaning plant on Saturdays and during school vacations. To obtain a driver's license in California, one had to be at least sixteen years old, but that was not a problem—I drove without one. I managed to get by for nearly a year before a traffic cop nabbed me and gave me my first ticket. In traffic court, the judge admonished me and advised that I get a learner's permit. I considered this an insult because I had been driving for almost four years, but I did as I was told and got the permit.

From then on, my main interest in life was that car. The same held true for my friends. We worked on cars—fixing them when they broke down and constantly looking for new gadgets to put in or on them. The first necessity was always a set of dual, straight-through mufflers, the forerunner of the glass-pack exhaust system. Depending on the length of the muffler, the sound resonating from beneath the car ranged from a sharp crack to a low, deep rumble. "Smitty" mufflers, manufactured and installed by the Smithy Muffler Company, near downtown San Diego, were considered by many to be the best. The V-8 engines, like the one in my Ford, sounded pretty fair, but the "straight sixes" (six cylinders) sounded the best when dual mufflers were mounted to the exhaust manifold, which was split in half.

We "hopped" the cars up the best way we knew, saving our money for such items as Edelbrock intake manifolds and dual carburetors. This newfound freedom to travel wherever we wanted also led to the inevitable drag to see "who could beat who"—whose car was the hottest? One weekend, we might travel to the nearby Laguna Mountains, a particular favorite during the winter months when there was usually some snow, and another weekend might find us at the beaches, always popular during the summer months. Pacific Beach became a favorite hangout for us—Bay Park was short on girls our own age, but "PB" seemed to have plenty of them. Although we enjoyed lots of impromptu beach parties on the north side of Crystal Pier, there was no prettier place in California than the La Jolla Cove, where the high school crowd always hung out.

I can still recall the moment we heard the news. It was Sunday, and the gang was at the Wilkinsons' to decide what to do that day. Someone had his car radio on, and the announcer broke into the program to declare that Pearl Harbor had just been bombed. We stood around, stunned but not realizing the magnitude of what we had just heard. Unlike many Americans, we did know one thing—San Diego was a Navy town and there was always a lot of Navy news in the papers. We knew where Pearl Harbor was, and it was a lot closer to San Diego than to the rest of the country.

The changes in our seaport town, in the people, and in our daily lives were immediate. The next day, school officials herded us into the auditorium, where we listened to President Roosevelt ask Congress for a declaration of war against Japan. Barbed wire was strung along our beaches; our schools practiced air raid drills; blackouts and rationing of certain materials, gasoline, and food became a way of life. At La Jolla High School, we were organized into classes and taken by our teachers across the road and behind the school buildings to practice hiding in the nearby hills. As soon as gas rationing began, I volunteered to be an air raid messenger. I was given extra gas coupons, had blackout lights installed on my car, and had a special sticker displayed on the windshield that allowed me to drive during blackout conditions.

I was not taking any college preparatory courses at La Jolla because I thought that I wasn't going anywhere but into the dry-cleaning business once I graduated from school. In mid-1942, as a result of the already increasing labor shortage, the local high schools announced a program that allowed students to attend school for half a day and to work at a job during the rest of the day. With so many young men either enlisting or getting drafted, the country's work force was greatly diminished. My father immediately jumped at this opportunity, and I reported to work at his plant each day at noon. I had no reason to complain; I had a car, plenty of gasoline, and I earned a decent salary, but I didn't like the business any better than I had before. It just wasn't close to my heart, and I soon realized that I didn't have the "business head" my father had. I could learn to do various jobs, but the administration end of it didn't come easily.

My father had taken on a partner, and together they built a brand-new dry-cleaning and laundry plant located at Thirty-third and University Avenue in East San Diego. They called it Cabrillo Cleaners and Laundry, and business was booming. There were a lot of U.S. Army units in and around San Diego; in fact, the soldiers brought their uniforms in from as far away as Campo in the easternmost part of the county. And, of course, more and more Navy ships and sailors began to arrive in San Diego. My father's company had landed the contract for the Marines stationed at Camp Elliott, which was located on Kearney Mesa, where the 1st Marine Division was training.

From time to time, my father's business had trouble with the labor unions that wanted to organize the employees. Although the plant paid better than union wages, the labor unions occasionally organized picket lines to parade in front of the plant. I recall one particular day when some of the pickets threatened to come into the plant and "tear up some of the clothes." My father picked up the telephone, called the commander's office at Camp Elliot, told him about the union's threats, and reminded him that the plant was full of Marine uniforms. A colonel said he would take care of the problem. Forty-five minutes later, two trucks loaded with Marines rolled to a stop in front of the plant. The Marines hopped off the trucks and fixed bayonets to the business end of their rifles. Marching back and forth at "port arms," they forced the men on the picket line off the sidewalk. The pickets disbanded, the Marines stayed on the scene for several hours, and there were no more problems with the local labor unions. This incident was just one more plus in my book for the U.S. Marines—I could see they didn't fool around and took a most direct approach in solving a problem.

Now that all of the Bay Park gang owned cars, we were chasing the girls and Pacific Beach was our happy hunting ground. The summer months were particularly good, with beach parties, and cookouts. There were also the Friday night trips to Tijuana, Mexico, only twelve miles south of San Diego. The people were always friendly to us, and the bartenders served alcohol to anyone who looked, even remotely, to be over sixteen years old. A greater temptation in Mexico was marijuana. The attendants in nightclub men's rooms readily offered it for sale. We had been told that it was "bad stuff," and we steered clear of it. Also, we didn't want to run the risk of getting caught with it when we crossed the border into California.

The individuals who made up the Bay Park gang were really a good bunch of guys. Although I'm sure our neighbors got tired of the sounds of loud mufflers and screeching tires, not one of us was ever arrested for a felony or even a misdemeanor. By the time we all left to join the different services, all we had were traffic tickets—dozens of them, thanks mainly to those Smitty mufflers.

Wartime conditions continued to change the city of San Diego. Barrage balloons, suspended above the city, were manned by U.S. Army crews, with heavy winches, located in numerous downtown parking lots. The balloons were positioned to help prevent the possibility of enemy low-level bombing. A huge steel-mesh camouflage net was strung over the entire aircraft plant where the B-24 Liberators were being built at an ever-increasing pace. All homes and businesses had to be "blacked out" during air raid alerts, and anyone caught showing any light faced a stiff fine.

Early in 1942, the Japanese-American students—our long-time friends and neighbors—had disappeared. They had been hustled off to relocation camps far away from the coastline. In many cases, there had been rumors that shortwave transmitters were found in their homes, but this was pure fabrication caused by panic, fear, racial hatred, and just plain maliciousness.

As soon as they turned seventeen years of age, some of the members in our gang tried to enlist, but usually their parents refused to sign the consent papers necessary for induction. I told my parents that I would like to enlist, but my father was adamant that I would first have to graduate from high school and "get that piece of paper" (he never could remember the word diploma). He had been denied an education, and he knew the importance of getting as much schooling as possible. My father now realized, and probably had for a long time, that I really didn't care too much for the dry-cleaning and laundry business. I loved my father dearly, as I'm sure he loved me, but I had trouble working for, or with, him. Our temperaments were too much alike—he often flared up and chewed me out for something, then he forgot all about it within minutes. In turn, I got angry and threatened to quit. He shouted back, "Go right ahead," and then I cooled off. These daily occurrences were not making for a harmonious working environment.

My high school graduation day finally arrived on 19 June 1943. My record at La Jolla was better than at Point Loma—I had been expelled only once for "cutting brodies" (making circles in the muddy school parking lot) with my car, while half the school hung out the windows cheering. When the vice-principal expelled me, my father found out about it and called him. He promised the vice-principal that I would be a changed lad if he allowed me back in, and he did. With the fear of God put into me by my father and the threat of losing my car, I returned to school with a new attitude.

I graduated just twelve days shy of my eighteenth birthday, and I knew that, within five days of that date, I was required by law to register with the local Selective Service Board. What I did not know was that, once I registered, I would no longer be able to join the branch of service of my own choosing but would have to go through the Selective Service process. I had envisioned lounging around on the beach at La Jolla Cove on the weekends while working at my father's plant, but the United States government did not entertain those same ideas.

During the first week of August, my sister Marion married Marine 1st Sgt. Stanley C. ("Scotty") Scott, whom she had dated for more than a year. A number of times, Stan had brought some of his Marine friends to our house. I had listened as they told stories about their travels around the world. It was fascinating stuff, and I became convinced that the Marine Corps might be just what I was looking for. I went down to the local recruiting station and was told that, because I had registered with Selective Service, I would have to wait for the draft.

About this time, my life took another turn. I had finally quit working at the dry-cleaning plant, and a good friend and former classmate, Bob Hasha, suggested that I consider a job at Consolidated-Vultee Aircraft Corporation's factory at Lindbergh Field, where he was employed. It was fairly easy for me to get hired because of the labor shortage, and I managed to get assigned to the department where Bob worked.

Shortly afterward, Bob introduced me to Phyllis Mathis, who lived in Pacific Beach and was a recent admission to La Jolla High School. She was absolutely stunning. We started going steady almost from the start.

Curious about the possibilities of becoming a Marine, I wrote a letter to the Marine Corps Base and asked if there was some way I could sidestep the regulations imposed by Selective Service and enlist in the Corps. The response, quick and short, stated that I would have to wait for the draft. The letter was signed by a first sergeant, who suggested that I take his letter along when I went to the induction station and perhaps a Marine liaison sergeant could help me.

In mid-October, my long-awaited draft notice arrived and I went to the personnel office at the aircraft plant to tell them that I was going to quit. One of the women who worked in the office explained that, because of my job at the plant, I rated a six-month deferment and the plant would help me to stay on. "Deferment, hell," I said. "I want to go. I've been waiting for months just to serve." By the look on her face, I could see the personnel office didn't get this kind of reaction often.

Early on the morning of 19 October, I reported to the local draft board and climbed aboard a dilapidated Greyhound bus for a three-hour trip to Los Angeles. The bus companies must have been having a serious problem obtaining parts, but, after several hours, we pulled up at the front of the induction center in downtown L.A. On the bus were all sizes and shapes of men, ranging in age from eighteen to thirty-five. Some demonstrated a good deal of bravado, but others seemed to be scared. There was only one thought going through my mind—to find that liaison sergeant, do some fast talking, and get myself into the U.S. Marines.

The induction center was jammed with what seemed to be hundreds of potential draftees. The first event of the day was to get us all to sit down and take a written examination, known as the mental test. To me, it appeared to be designed so that it would ensure few failures. Next came our physical examinations. Our clothing was taken away, and we spent the next several hours running around in our underwear. Fortunately, the place wasn't too cold and some warmth was generated by so many men, but some of them certainly could have used a bath.

The last event of the day was the announcement of each man's classification. To my shock, it was also announced that all eighteen-year-olds found fit for general duty (no serious mental or physical problems) were to go to the U.S. Navy that very same day. I had just been herded into the Navy line when I spotted the Marine sergeant standing by his desk, in full dress blues but with only one leg! (I found out later that he had lost his leg while fighting on Guadalcanal.) Clutching my letter from the San Diego Marine Corps Base in one hand and my examination results in the other, I left the line and walked over to him. I handed him my letter and began to explain that my brother-in-law was a Marine first sergeant and he and his pals would kill me if I came home as a sailor. With tears in my eyes, I pleaded with him to help me.

The sergeant grabbed my induction papers, crossed out the word "Navy," and circled "Marine Corps" on the form. Just about this time, a Navy chief petty officer spotted me and came over to tell me to get back into the Navy line.

The Marine looked at the chief and said, "This kid's Marine family, chief—he's going into the Corps."

The chief muttered something like, "Hell, then, you can have him."

That was all it took. I was going to be a Marine.

We were sworn in less than an hour later, and only two of us were selected for the Corps. By coincidence, the other kid had also gone to La Jolla High School and I knew him. His father was an active-duty Marine major and had arranged for his son to be sworn into the Marine Corps regulars, rather than start his service as a reservist. I was sworn into the U.S. Marine Corps Reserve, and my papers were stamped with the acronym DofNE, which meant duration of national emergency. I could not have cared less—I was now a Marine.

The ride home was much more quiet than our earlier one that day. Some of the men were in a state of shock. A few had made it into the Navy, but most ended up in the Army. As for myself, I had orders that directed me to report to the Marine Corps Base at San Diego for recruit training in exactly two weeks, 2 November 1943.

When I arrived home, I began spreading the news. Marion and Scotty were very happy for me, but my mother cried a little at the thought of her son having to go off to fight in a war. I called my father, and he didn't have too much to say, other than wishing me "good luck." My father and I had remained on good terms after I quit working for him and I stopped by to see him from time to time, but things were different now. I told him that I would see him before I left for boot camp and would, of course, stay in touch by mail and, when I got the opportunity, by telephone. I got my affairs in order around the house, arranged for my mother to keep and use my Ford, and stopped by to say farewell to friends and neighbors, some of whom seemed quite pleased that I was leaving for Marine Corps boot camp.

I saw Phyllis as much as possible, mostly on weekends because she was still in school. She promised to write regularly and to visit me at the base if she could. But, 2 November came faster than I had anticipated. I packed my ditty bag with the barest of necessities and wore old clothes, on the advice of my brother-in-law. I walked through the main gate of the Marine Corps Base, gate No. 3, which today is located in front of the Headquarters and Service Battalion command post. The sentry on duty directed me to the Receiving Barracks, and I crossed the threshold to a career of service to my country that would last for more than thirty-three years.

# =2=

# Boot Camp

No MATTER HOW many times new Marine enlistees are told how tough boot camp is going to be, few are prepared for the sudden shock of leaving the normalcy of civilian life and entering the strange new culture known as the United States Marine Corps. I, too, thought I was prepared; Scotty and his Marine buddies had laid it on pretty thick, and with pleasure, when they saw that I was in need of discipline. Yet, in my first letter home, a one-page missive hurriedly scrawled to give my mother my mailing address, I wrote, "Boot camp is tough—tougher than I thought!"

I was at the Receiving Barracks just long enough to turn in my orders before being pointed in the direction of a tent camp located on the far side of the parade deck, where the modern recruit barracks stand today. Several other guys were waiting around, and it wasn't long before forty or fifty of us were trading stories and wondering what was to come. Standing outside the canvas tents, we were waiting for a troop handler when we began to hear derisive hoots and howls—yells of "You'll be sorry" and other such comments—from passing "salts" who probably had not been there more than a week or two themselves.

We were assigned cots and footlockers. Early the next morning, a corporal called us outside and arranged us into some semblance of a formation. He asked if anyone in the formation was unable to read or write English. Two brothers, both in their twenties, from the Appalachian region of West Virginia raised their hands. They were dismissed from the formation to be assigned to a remedial reading class. I was astonished. Born and raised in California, where school attendance is mandatory until the age of sixteen, I hadn't realized that, in some parts of the country, unfortunate kids were not even getting basic education in reading and writing.

Within minutes, a troop handler had us go inside to surrender all personal possessions other than pens, pencils, and shaving gear. One character thought that he should keep his switchblade knife, which he referred to as an "East Dallas Special," because he "might need it overseas." It was quickly scooped up, as was a deck of cards belonging to a self-proclaimed card shark, who had visions of relieving his fellow privates of their pay.

We fell in again, outside the tents. Along came one of the sharpest-looking Marines I had ever seen—the epitome of a Marine, in a starched and neatly pressed cotton khaki shirt, field scarf (tie), sharply creased green trousers, and leather shoes shining like mirrors. He introduced himself as Cpl. V.L. Billingsley, our drill instructor (DI). He then made a profound statement: "You can give your soul to God, boys, because your ass belongs to me for the next seven weeks."

When we had partially recovered from the shock, he told us that we were now Platoon 960 of 1943, and that our address was Recruit Depot, Marine Corps Base, San Diego 40, California. We were sixty-three boots whom Corporal Billingsley would mold into basic Marines in less than two months.

There was no doubt in my mind that this guy was for real and that he meant business. He was not some parent or schoolteacher who was simply going to tell us to be good, and I didn't even want to entertain the idea of what the consequences might be if we crossed this individual.

We were marched to the barbershop and quickly shorn of our locks. There we experienced an age-old favorite joke of the barbers, but one that none of us had ever heard. One of the recruits in our platoon sported a handsome pair of muttonchop sideburns. When he sat down in the barber's chair, the barber asked him if he would like to keep them. Caught off guard, the recruit said, "Golly, sure I would." The barber then shaved off the sideburns and handed them back to the startled recruit. We all snickered.

Because I was thin-faced and my ears stuck out prominently, I had always tried to let my hair grow down over my ears to take attention away from them. When the barber was through with me, I looked like I had sprouted a pair of wings on my head, but none of the other recruits looked very pretty either. Many had scars on their heads that they probably never knew about or had long since forgotten.

Two assistant drill instructors, Privates First Class Jones and Smith (not their real names), joined Corporal Billingsley. Jones looked and sounded like a foreigner. He wasn't a bad sort, although he didn't have a great deal of patience. Smith was a stocky, solidly built bastard who had played football somewhere and liked to think he was a gridiron hero. He was a real SOB who knew he was in a position to throw his weight around. In the coming weeks, we would learn that he was the one who did the thumping, hitting, and shoving or otherwise abused his authority. The members of the platoon had no use or respect for Smith whatsoever.

The next event of the day was receiving our first uniforms, the HBT (herringbone twill) utilities known as dungarees. For headgear, we were given pith helmets, which we wore for almost the entire seven weeks. The dress uniforms would come later, including the garrison caps to be worn with utilities, khaki for summer and green for winter. The popular utility cover, called the gung-ho cap, had not yet reached the Corps. The field shoes, above-ankle height, were of a rough leather that we would polish until they shone. Later on in our training, we would receive brown dress shoes.

Corporal Billingsley formed us into squads and, because of my Junior ROTC training in high school, assigned me as one of the platoon's squad leaders. The position was a decided advantage, as I watched the others try to learn their left from their right to the satisfaction of our drill instructor. My knowledge of how to conduct the manual of arms was an added bonus. As is usually the case, the first few days of close-order drill were tedious and frustrating (particularly so for Corporal

Billingsley) until the platoon finally caught on and began to respond as a unit.

The academic instructors ran us through general classification testing and screening, and I scored well on the reading and vocabulary portions, average on mathematics, and poorly on the pattern analysis. Mechanical aptitude was something I simply had not been born with, even though I enjoyed tinkering with automobile engines. Surprisingly, the results of our testing and screening came back quickly; in my second letter home, I mentioned that I had been selected for tank school as a crewman.

My brother-in-law Scotty, as the first sergeant of a motor transport company assigned to the 4th Marine Division, which had formed at Camp Pendleton, had suggested that I consider a future in a motor transportation outfit, but tanks sounded more glamorous to me. By the end of the fifth day, we had been issued full equipment, including the new M1 Garand rifle, complete with bayonet. I would carry that service rifle through three campaigns and turn it back in, two years later, to the armory.

A day or two after getting our equipment, we were herded over to sick bay for the first of a series of eight or nine inoculations—the dreaded shots. Neither the Navy corpsmen nor anyone else seemed very concerned about the aftereffects of those shots. It was "line 'em up, stick 'em, and get 'em outside." Several hours later, while we were standing in line for noon chow, one of the recruits in our platoon fainted. The recruit standing next to him took one look, and he dropped alongside the first one. Before it was over, more than ten recruits were lying on the grass. The drill instructors dragged them aside, waited for them to come to, and then took them back to sick bay. A few remained there for several days. We all had sore arms for the next few days—typhoid and cholera shots were famous for long-term discomfort—but the aftereffects were particularly felt during the manual of arms, as we moved that nine-pound M1 rifle from shoulder to shoulder. Two weeks later, we returned to sick bay for the remainder of our shots and suffered sore arms again.

By the end of our first week of training, we were ready for a break and glad when Sunday rolled around. Corporal Billingsley had indicated that we might be rewarded with some free time. There was church call in the morning. It was mandatory for each recruit to attend one of the services offered: Protestant, Catholic, or Jewish. I attended the Catholic mass and went to confession and communion, something I had strayed from during my later teenage years. My mother was overjoyed when I reported this in one of my letters. We had the remainder of that Sunday for leisure time, and most of us took the opportunity to write letters to family and friends.

One day during the second week, our platoon was delivered to the depot's dental section, a day that I had been dreading and one that I will never forget. I knew I had cavities; my teeth had needed attention for some time, but trips to the dentist had been few and far between during the depression years. In fact, I can't remember ever having gone to see a dentist when I was very young. Later, when I was old enough to go on my own, I never seemed to keep my appointments.

But, on this day and within a period of two hours, the Navy dentist drilled and filled nine teeth! I was a nervous wreck—he must have used some type of local anesthetic, but he didn't use enough. I was squirming around in that chair like a skittish monkey. The dentist kept telling me to move my tongue, until I finally asked, "Where the hell do you want me to put it?" He reminded me that I was speaking to a naval officer, but I guess he considered the circumstances because I never heard anything more about it.

Our training continued with a daily regiment of calisthenics in the morning, followed by hours of close-order drill, the manual of arms, and study periods devoted to such subjects as military courtesy, customs, and traditions, in addition to discipline, interior guard, first aid, field sanitation, and personal hygiene. Classes on the nomenclature, functioning, field stripping, and care and cleaning of the M1 service rifle were also a daily ritual.

There were rifle inspections daily. When our platoon did not perform to the satisfaction of one of our drill instructors, we had to double-time out to the far reaches of the base, commonly referred to as the boondocks. This was a sand dune area south of the grinder (parade deck), where today Lindbergh Field's runway No. 27 and Harbor Drive are located. We ran with our M1s at port arms and, when ordered to "hit the deck," dived, rifles first, and buried them in the sand as we hit the ground. Then, we had to run back to our tents and start cleaning our dirty weapons—again.

I remember one day when our platoon was standing "at ease" on the grinder as we waited for a formal rifle inspection to begin. Hearing two fighter planes buzzing around overhead, I looked skyward to see two P-38s dogfighting over Point Loma. A few seconds later, they collided in midair. We watched two parachutes pop open, and both pilots began to drift down toward the ground. Their planes had been high up when they struck one another, and it seemed to take a long time before the pilots disappeared from view.

The next day, I was able to get a copy of a San Diego newspaper and there, on the front page, was the story of the accident. One of the pilots had drifted out to sea and was picked up by the Coast Guard. The other pilot was not so fortunate. As he was descending in his chute, his plane circled back into him and cut off both legs at his knees. He had bled to death before he ever hit the ground on Point Loma, according to the newspaper story.

At the end of our second week, our platoon was allowed to have visitors. My father surprised me by being the first to visit me. He brought along a fine box of chocolates. There were no restrictions on such gifts, but we were required to share our spoils with, first, the drill instructors and then the other recruits in the platoon. Needless to say, candy and other goodies didn't last very long.

I had hoped that Phyllis would come to visit, but she didn't. The lack of any letters from her was a problem that I was anxious to solve.

As our training continued and we learned what the drill instructors expected from us, our lives got a little easier, although there seemed to be no pleasing that bastard Smith. He continued to rant and rave and, on occasion, take a swing at us when he could get away with it. He had a bad habit of challenging recruits. When he pushed or shoved someone, ostensibly to correct a body position, and was challenged, he said, "C'mon, try it, whataya gonna do about it?" No one was foolish enough to swing on Smith, not only because he was physically strong but because none of us wanted to risk a court-martial.

We eventually learned that both Jones and Smith themselves had completed recruit training only a few weeks before our platoon began training. This was a common practice that resulted from the great number of recruits and the shortage of stateside personnel for DI duty. (In fact, when our platoon graduated, one of the men in our platoon was retained at the base as a drill instructor.)

Corporal Billingsley had a method of dealing with the fights that broke out within the platoon. Carrying two sets of large-size, well-padded boxing gloves, he summoned the offenders behind a hootch (hut), gathered the platoon around them, and the fight was on. The gloves guaranteed that no one got hurt, but a lot of pride was wounded.

We had a kid from Ohio whom we called "Big John." A large, sort of slow individual, Big John frequently had trouble keeping up with the rapid-fire pace of boot camp. To make matters a little worse, a kid from Texas ("Tex") was always threatening to whip someone's ass, mainly Big John's because of the punishment the platoon received as the result of his mistakes. One day, Corporal Billingsley got tired of Big John's antics and took him and Tex behind the hootch. He told Tex to "knock some sense" into Big John but, to everyone's surprise, Big John cleaned Tex's clock. It was Big John's shining moment, and Billingsley never bothered him after that fight.

There were plenty of penalties for minor infractions of the rules. Generally, I was able to keep my nose clean, but I was caught several times. We were normally allowed to smoke during breaks. One day, Jones saw me toss a cigarette butt away without field-stripping it as we had been taught to do—shredding the paper from the unsmoked tobacco until the butt became a speck of paper. (There were no filters in those days.) This indiscretion resulted in my having to get a length of thread and tie a matchstick to one end and a needle to the other. I was told to scout the area for cigarette butts until I had collected one hundred of them, then report back to Jones and count them out, one by one. Another minor infraction resulted in my having to scrub the deck of the head (bathroom) with a toothbrush. This laborious and time-consuming chore, which I never completed, took up a great deal of my "free" time.

Some of the more embarrassing punishments, which I was fortunate to escape, were meted out for referring to one's rifle as a gun. This serious offense resulted in a recruit having to march around with his rifle in one hand and his penis in the other, as he proclaimed loudly, "This is my rifle [displaying the weapon], and this is my gun [displaying his manhood], this is for fighting, but this is for fun." The luckless culprit rarely repeated his mistake.

Another humiliating punishment was used on those individuals who displayed improperly scrubbed underwear. The DIs referred to these as "hash marks" or "mustard stains" and ordered the offender, carrying his skivvies, to parade around in front of the platoon and announce, "I have mustard in my drawers." Again, this error was rarely repeated.

One morning during our third week of training, we had just been dismissed from formation and were walking between some huts when I heard the sound of an aircraft and then some crashing noises. As I started to run away from the sound, I glanced over my shoulder and saw the nose of a B-24 Liberator bomber plowing through a row of wooden air-bedding racks. The props of the plane were chewing right through them. They looked like toothpicks flying through the air. The B-24 finally slowed to a stop, its right wing not more than fifty feet from our hootch, which was the last one in a row.

The pilot emerged from his plane with his .45 pistol in one hand and a carrying case in the other. He looked around and saw that he was still on government property, which I guess made him feel a little more secure. By this time, recruits from the platoon were gathering around to see what had happened. Some said that when they first heard the sound of the crash, they dove under their bunks and started praying, not knowing what was happening.

A group of officers and MPs (military police) arrived

almost immediately, and our platoon was called out to cordon off the damaged aircraft. We had our rifles and bayonets but no ammunition. Our platoon stayed in position until shortly after dark, when it was determined that no one was trying to steal the plane. The MPs took over the job of guarding the B-24. We learned from them that the case the pilot had been carrying contained a new type of bombsight, which he was required to protect at all costs. The following day, a crew from Consolidated-Vultee came over and dragged the plane back to their factory, which was located next to the base. It took a few more days for a hole in the chain-link fence to be repaired.

We figured that we had been extremely lucky. The story was all over the base that, the year before, a bomber had tried to take off but had plowed into a mess hall where recruits were eating. Three Marines were killed. Not long ago, I ran across a magazine article that told the story:

On Monday, May 10, 1943, the first of three XB-32s to leave the Consolidated-Vultee factory at Lindbergh Field in San Diego crashed, killing the pilot and three Marines on the ground.

Observers said the plane seemed to accelerate slowly. With the end of the runway coming up fast, the pilot, Richard A. McMakin, was obviously having a hard time taking off. Two bystanders thought they saw the wing flaps in the up position as the aircraft passed them. The pilot rotated the nose in a last effort to take off and dragged the tailskid in a violent trail of sparks and dust.

The XB-32 left the end of the runway at 135 MPH and raced into the barracks at the Marine Corps Base (now the Marine Corps Recruit Depot). Dust and smoke boiled up. The plane skidded along the ground, leaving pieces in its wake. After what was left of plane # 1141 stopped, the crew members who were able scrambled out. Six of them were injured. The crash killed McMakin.

Investigators considered a wing-flap failure the most probable cause.

In addition to McMakin, three Marines were killed, and 63 were injured with 10 of those hospitalized. (Lt. Edward L.

Leiser, "Wing and a Prayer," *Traditions, San Diego's Military Heritage* 1, no. 10, 1995, 3. Reprinted with permission of Heritage Press & Publications, San Diego, Calif.)

One day, one of our drill instructors told us that the grandmother of another DI had died. The DI could be granted leave to attend her funeral, but he lacked the necessary funds to do so. This announcement was terminated with the statement, "Now, we all know that it's against regulations for that Marine to accept any type of loan or donations." As was expected, the platoon got together and chipped in, at least a buck per man. The money was placed in an envelope with the man's name on it and surreptitiously left under his pillow by the next recruit catching "house mouse" duty (making up the DIs' bunks and cleaning up their hootch). It could have easily totaled a month's pay or more for the DI in "mourning."

The way I remember it, each DI had one relative die while we were at boot camp. This deplorable practice had been in existence for a number of years, I later learned, and probably continued for many more. I talked with former Marines who claimed that they had really "cleaned up" during their four-year tours of DI duty.

At the end of our fourth week of training, we were transported to the rifle range, located at Camp Matthews on Torrey Pines Mesa, the present site of the University of California, San Diego. We were glad to get away from the base and anxious to start firing our M1s and see how well we could do as new Marine riflemen. The DIs had been talking about the rifle range during the preceding week, and our ability with the M1 played an important role in our chances for promotion. They told us that 50 percent of the platoon would be promoted to the grade of private first class at graduation.

Unfortunately, when we arrived at the range, so did the fall rains. Hardly a day went by without at least some drizzle. We had to lie on our ponchos, or even in the mud, at the "snapping-in" and firing ranges, but we fired as long as our targets were fairly visible.

Many of the recruits in our platoon came down with severe colds, coughs, and running fevers, which the DIs called "cat fever." They told us that we could go to sick bay for treatment, but if we lost more than a day or two of training, particularly during firing week, we would be dropped from the platoon and recycled through another platoon. None of us wanted to stay in boot camp any longer than necessary, and few, if any, went to sick bay for relief.

We spent our first week on the range snapping-in, sometimes called dry-firing, and firing the small-bore .22 rifle to help us learn the complexities of aligning the rifle sight. I had owned a .22 rifle since I was fourteen years old and had no problems with learning how to shoot the M1. We also fired the Colt .45-caliber semiautomatic pistol and the new M1 carbine for familiarization—called "fam-firing."

We discovered that the rifle range was a good place to meet visitors because we had more leisure time on the weekends. After cleaning our rifles on Saturday mornings, we were free until early Monday morning.

My pal, Bob Hasha, brought Phyllis to Camp Matthews to see me on Saturday afternoon. It was her first visit. She hadn't written, and I was beginning to wonder where this romance was headed. Bob told me that he was just about to leave for the army, and, of course, he took some good-natured razzing from me. Some of my fellow recruits overheard him and looked at him as though he were some kind of alien.

My mother, sister, and Scotty, came up the following day, and Scotty took us all to the Staff Noncommissioned Officers' Club for lunch. This was quite a treat for me, as a private, to be in an SNCO club.

We also had more free time in the evenings while we were on the rifle range. A few civilian caterers were allowed within the camp—the forerunners of today's "roach coaches," or catering trucks. We were allowed to patronize them, and the gentleman who sold ice cream always had the longest line of recruits waiting near his truck.

When we started live firing on Monday of our second week, we alternated between shooting and taking turns pulling down and scoring targets in the impact area, known as the butts. Scoring targets was interesting work, and some guys took a perverse pleasure in waving a "Maggie's drawers," the red flag that signaled a miss at the target. Of course, there was absolutely no humor at all in the situation when we saw that flag in front of our own targets while firing. One thing that really surprised us was the unmistakable sound of rounds going directly overhead—and not too far overhead at that. The sound of a bullet is more like a sharp crack of a bullwhip, rather than the whizz or zing heard in the movies. This was also good training because it taught us exactly what the real thing sounded like.

We fired Monday through Thursday, with Friday scheduled as a prequalification day. This was the last chance to get our rifle "dope" straight—windage and elevation adjustments that would bring the bullets onto the target. It was also the only time when we did not field-strip our rifles after firing. They were left alone, with only a clean patch being run through the bore and without any change being made on our sights.

Our anxiety and stress on the night before shooting for record were heavy. All we talked about was how well we thought we'd do the next morning. Although there wasn't very much interplatoon competition in those days, Corporal Billingsley let it be known that he did not expect to take any harassment from the other drill instructors for returning with a low percentage of qualification when the shooting was over.

My main concern was my off-hand position when firing at the 200-yard line—it wasn't good. I wasn't very big, still skinny and without muscular arms, and trying to keep a steady hold on that nine-pound rifle wasn't easy. Still, I had done well all week in the sitting position on the 300-yard line, and I had fired several "possibles" at the 500-yard line, in the prone position. On Saturday morning, we moved to the range for the final time. Our ability to shoot would determine what type of shooting badge, if any, each of us would wear on our uniforms.

On qualification day, I shot well at the 300-yard line and fired another possible on the 500-yard line. As I had feared, my off-hand position was lousy and kept me from firing as an "expert rifleman." I missed the qualifying score for that category by only a few points and fired as a "sharpshooter." Our drill instructors were happy. The platoon had done well, and we didn't have to march the ten miles back to the base, a fate suffered by those platoons with a certain percentage of non-qualified shooters.

We had no sooner returned to the depot when Scotty came to visit and told me that his outfit was getting ready to ship overseas. He had checked with headquarters at the base and learned that I was slated for transfer to Camp Elliott to wait for the next tank crewmen class to begin. He asked, "What do you want to do, Len, hang around the States or go over and fight the Japanese?"

I didn't hesitate. I told him I wanted to go and fight, the sooner the better. Scotty said he'd see what he could do to make that happen with a change of orders, and then he said good-bye.

The last week of training involved a great many administrative details, in addition to getting ready for graduation, having our final fittings for uniforms, and squaring away our living areas for the next group of recruits. One afternoon, we received the long-awaited announcement of who had made the promotion list. I was pleased to hear my name called out as one of those who would leave the base as a new Marine private first class.

Each recruit on the promotion list was issued one red chevron to be worn on the green dress coat for graduation and some red thread to stitch the chevron in place. This came as quite a shock—some of the recruits had never threaded a needle, let alone sewn anything. We were told to sew our chevrons on the left sleeves of our coats. The stripes for the other articles of clothing would be issued to us before we left the base, and we could sew them on later. The reason for this was the wartime shortage of material—a Corps-wide problem when new stripes were issued for promotion.

We never learned whether or not it was on purpose, but the DIs gave us no special instructions on exactly where to place the chevron on the coat sleeve. I knew damned well it was not supposed to look like the letter "V," but several guys went right ahead and spent a lot of time sewing, only to have their coats resemble those of British soldiers. The DIs raised hell when they saw them, and those Marines corrected their mistakes immediately.

* * *

Graduation day finally arrived, fifty-one days after I had reported for training, on 23 December. The ceremony was simple—no band, no parade, and no visitors. After a final rifle inspection, we were dismissed to pick up our orders and told where to meet the transportation that would take us to our next duty station. I don't recall that any leave was granted, but my orders stated that I was headed to Camp Elliott, less than ten miles from home. And, my mother still had my car.

We were assigned to a "casual" outfit and marched to a separate part of the base. Four other Marines from the platoon also had orders to Camp Elliott, and we learned that we would be taken there the next day, Christmas Eve.

While we were enjoying a little rest at the casual company area, a group of us were called outside at 1600 and notified that we had been selected to stand guard duty that night. Piling into a truck, we had no idea where we were going until we came to a stop at the U.S. Naval Destroyer Base at Thirty-second Street and were assigned walking posts. Mine turned out to be on a pier alongside a Navy cargo ship said to be full of various types of deteriorating ammunition from the Pacific area that had been brought back to the States for disposal. It was considered dangerous, and the Navy wanted no one nosing around, although there was a crew on board the ship. I was posted at 1800 and told I'd be relieved at midnight. A six-hour watch was no problem, and I had little choice in the matter. I was less than eight hours out of boot camp and still "Sir-ing" everything that moved.

It was cold on that pier. Fortunately, I was wearing my green dress uniform, complete with overcoat. Except for inspections, this was the only time during my entire career that I wore my overcoat. I lugged it around the world in the bottom of my seabag until it went out of style and service.

Midnight came, no relief showed up, and I was getting hungry and groggy. I had been up since early that morning for my big day. By 0200, I was actually walking in my sleep and damned near walked off the end of the pier. A sailor, on watch on one of the ship's upper decks, yelled down and told me to come aboard for a cup of hot coffee. I was reluctant to do so.

General order number five, "not to leave my post unless properly relieved" (as well as all the rest of them), had been drilled into me. He yelled again, "Hell, those guys have forgotten all about you, c'mon aboard."

By this time, I'd really had it, and I did as he suggested. One of the stewards gave me at least two cups of good, strong Navy coffee, along with a sandwich, and I had a chance to rest my bones. Less than half an hour later, I was back walking my post and thinking that the Navy wasn't half bad after all.

Near 0600, a Jeep appeared with the corporal of the guard and my relief. The corporal posted the new sentry, and I hopped in the Jeep for the ride back to the guard shack. I asked the corporal why I had been left on post all night—for twelve hours—and he virtually repeated what the sailor had said, "They forgot about you and that post. Sorry."

I got a ride back to the base, where my buddies were waiting for me and the transportation that would take us to Camp Elliott. Our wait wasn't long, and, by noontime, we had reported in at Camp Elliott and turned in our orders and service record books. We were assigned to quarters, issued bedding, and told to find an empty rack. It was Friday, 24 December, and, of course, we were wondering what our chances were for weekend liberty. I asked a sergeant, and he said, "Sure, everybody's got the weekend off for Christmas."

One of my buddies and I went to the administrative office. A clerk typed up our liberty cards and told us to be back no later than 0600 on Monday morning. I found a telephone and called home. My mother said that she would pick me up at the main gate in an hour. We got cleaned up, pressed our greens and fresh shirts, and headed for the main gate. Both of us were pretty tired, and I was particularly dead on my feet after being up for more than thirty-six hours, but the adrenalin rush that came with the thought of my first liberty as a Marine kept me going.

We were two blocks from the gate when we saw a Marine major approaching us on the same side of the street. My buddy whispered, "Here comes an officer, what do we do?"

During recruit training, we had never had the opportunity to salute an officer because there were never any around. The only ones that had been close enough to salute were inspecting officers while we were in formation. Of course, we had practiced the proper method, but this would be the first time for both of us. I whispered back, "We've got to salute."

When the major was about six paces away, we threw two perfect highballs and said, "Good evening." The major returned the salute with a "Good evening, boys," and passed by. We had done it, and it was an incident that I'll never forget. We had been on our way to our very first liberty and had saluted our very first officer—a major in the Women's Reserve!

My mother was waiting at the gate with my car, and my buddy caught a bus headed in the opposite direction. I drove home, where Marion, Scotty, and my brother Sonny were waiting to celebrate Christmas Eve. I lasted as long as I could. Excusing myself a few hours later, I hit the rack and slept for the next twelve hours.

# =3=

# War in the Pacific

I REPORTED BACK to camp Elliott on Monday morning, 27 December 1943. My five mates from Platoon 960 and I were assigned to a casual company, then steered to another barracks and assigned racks and issued bedding. Our new living area needed some squaring away. The beaverboard huts had been used by a Marine Raider outfit that had returned to the States for deactivation. The walls were marked with holes because the Raiders had used them for target practice with their K-bar knives.

Our first duty was to go to the police shed and draw street brooms, one each. Those brooms were the biggest damned things I had ever seen. The brush part was almost as wide as I was tall, and it was all I could do to get the broom started down the roadway. We were kept at it for three days, and we swept every street within a three-block radius. Next, we were sent to officers' quarters, where we were told to get busy cleaning up the officers' huts and shining their shoes. Christ, I thought, here I'd joined the Marine Corps to fight and I'd ended up being a street sweeper and a shoe-shine boy. Even our DIs had shined their own shoes. Now, the best I could hope for was that the tank school I had been assigned to would start soon or that Scotty would be able to get me up to Camp Pendleton.

On Friday, 31 December, I was wondering what my chances were for New Year's liberty. I was daydreaming about getting into my car and heading toward the beach to see my girlfriend, Phyllis. We had gotten together for a short time on Christmas

Day and had exchanged gifts, although I don't recall what they were.

My dreaming was rudely interrupted by someone yelling, "Hey, Maffioli, the first sergeant wants to see you, right away."

Hurrying over to his office, I wondered if I was in some kind of trouble. The sergeant was reading a piece of paper in his hand.

He glanced up at me and asked in a loud gruff voice, "Who do you know?"

I didn't understand what he was asking and said, "I beg your pardon, sir."

He repeated, "Who do you know?"

I replied that I didn't understand what he was asking, and he said, "I've got a set of orders here, transferring you up to Camp Pendleton. I'd give my left nut [grabbing his crotch for added emphasis] to get into the 4th Marine Division—they're mounting out for combat soon, and I'm stuck here at this post troops outfit!"

Suddenly, it hit me. My first sergeant brother-in-law had been able to arrange for my transfer. I played dumb, though, and expressed surprise, without letting on that I knew anything about how this miracle had occurred.

The "Top" told me to be out in front of his office at 0800 the following Monday morning, and a car would take me to Camp Pendleton. So, once again, I was free for the holiday weekend, and I made the most of it.

On Monday, the driver dropped me off in front of division headquarters, and I reported for duty. My orders were quickly endorsed, and I was assigned to the 4th Motor Transport Battalion. Transportation was arranged, and a Jeep took me to battalion headquarters, where I was further assigned to Headquarters and Service (H & S) Company, 1st Sgt. Stan Scott's company. My brother-in-law was now my first sergeant. This situation would result in a great deal of razzing and unsolicited remarks directed my way during the coming months.

Scotty met me at company headquarters and then called a corporal to escort me to my new barracks. Now, of course, he was First Sergeant Scott, rather than Scotty.

I spent the next few days getting acquainted with my surroundings and drawing my "seven-eighty-two" gear, equipment needed for the field and signed for on a Form 782, hence the name. The 4th Motor Transport Battalion was located in 14 Area of the camp, not far from the back gate and adjacent to the Naval Ammunition Depot at Fallbrook. As a new kid on the block, I also caught my share of guard duty.

I had been in the company for three or four days when First Sergeant Scott had a close friend, M.Sgt. Lloyd Stearns, an old-time truckmaster, take me out into the hills in a 2$^1$/$_2$-ton, 6 × 6 truck. We drove into some low hills, and he began giving me instructions on the finer points of driving that monster truck. He went through all facets of the proper shifting of gears, double-reduction, double-clutching, hill climbing, and descending. We were out driving for a good four or five hours. When we returned to the motor pool, I was still behind the wheel. By then, I had a good basic knowledge of how to handle the truck. That lesson had been my motor transport school!

Camp Pendleton was bustling with activity, and the troop areas seemed to be bursting at the seams. The 4th Marine Division was getting ready to embark, and the 5th Marine Division had recently formed and was in training. With post troops added, there were at least 45,000 Marines and Navy corpsmen at Camp Pendleton.

We had truck convoys rolling down to the San Diego docks day and night, and I was soon doing my share of the driving. We caught liberty when the opportunity presented itself, but there were certainly no normal working hours, including the weekends.

On 6 and 7 January 1944, the slower Navy LSTs (landing ships, tanks) and LSDs (landing ships, docks) left port and were joined on the 13th by the remainder of the forward echelon of ships sailing from San Diego. The Marines on board had not been told where they were going. Not until they passed Hawaii would they know that they were headed for Roi-Namur in the Marshall Islands. The 4th Division was the first and only Marine division to mount out directly into combat and the first to capture Japanese-mandated territory. It secured its objective in a shorter time than it took for any other important U.S.

operation since the Japanese attack on Pearl Harbor in December 1941.

As badly as I wanted to go, I had joined the division too late. Our trucks and drivers were needed to haul the remainder of the division's gear to the docks. As it turned out, the objective islands in the Pacific were so small that all of the division's motor transport capability was not needed.

Some of the convoy trips to San Diego proved interesting. Because of gasoline rationing, traffic was never heavy. In the larger convoys, the truck platoon and section leaders had red lights and sirens on their Jeeps, and they had the authority to block major intersections so that the trucks could roll through without interruption. Convoy discipline was somewhat lacking on the return trips, however, especially if we were allowed to straggle back to Camp Pendleton. It was not unusual to look in the truck's rearview mirror and watch trailing vehicles peel off, bound for various destinations. Military Jeeps and trucks belonging to the other service branches could be found parked in front of bars and restaurants throughout downtown San Diego. The extensive military presence was just too much for anyone to be overly concerned with minor violations of the rules.

One evening, after I had driven from Camp Pendleton to San Diego, I parked my truck in front of my mother's house, barely a half-mile from the main highway. I hopped into my car and drove to Pacific Beach to see Phyllis. Several hours later, I returned to my truck and started back to camp. I reasoned that my stopover was legitimate because I would be off duty when I returned to Camp Pendleton. As I was driving up Rose Canyon, the driver in a car directly behind me began to honk his horn and flash his lights. I pulled over to the side of the road, and the car pulled in behind me. In the car was my first sergeant. He chewed me out like I was a two-week private and told me his interpretation of the "misuse" of government property. I hadn't known that he and my sister had driven down from Oceanside to spend the night with my mother. I had been in too much of a hurry to notice his car when I returned to the house, but he had certainly noticed the Marine Corps truck parked in front of his mother-in-law's home. Scotty had fallen asleep while waiting for me to return, but the rumble of the truck starting up had awakened him. His dressing-down when he caught up with me was sufficient to keep me from ever repeating that stunt.

One day, not long after, I was driving a platoon from the 4th Division's Scout Company to Harbor Drive, where the division would board a ship headed overseas. There were some rugged characters in the platoon. The gunnery sergeant in charge, a grizzled old-timer, sat up in the cab beside me. As we drove through the coastal town of Cardiff-By-The-Sea, I heard a popping sound coming from the rear of my truck. The "gunny" stuck his head out and then looked back at me and said, "It's just my boys having a little target practice." They were shooting at the shore birds along the beach!

We had just passed the celebrated Beacon Inn, and I was having visions of us all landing in jail. Less than a mile down the road, a Marine Corps sedan pulled alongside my truck. A colonel in the back of the sedan began gesturing wildly for me to pull over. He got out, said that he saw Marines firing from the rear of my truck, and asked my destination. After I told him where I was headed, he said that he would follow us and conduct a weapons inspection to find out who did the firing. Of course, I claimed no knowledge of what had happened and the old gunny feigned complete surprise.

As we continued down the coastal highway, the gunny took a long drink out of his canteen and then asked me if I wanted a swig. Assuming the canteen was full of water, I thought his gesture thoughtful and took a healthy gulp. I almost choked— the canteen was filled with gin. I knew that I was carrying "dangerous cargo," but realizing the hazardous duty these men faced, I understood their cavalier attitude.

Shortly afterward, a cleaning rod poked through the flap between the truck's cab and the cargo compartment. A voice asked, "Hey, Gunny, you wanna clean your carbine?" He declined, saying he hadn't fired his weapon, and then the voice said, "We're all set back here."

When we arrived at the docks, the colonel held his rifle inspection. When he could not find a dirty weapon, he went on his way.

We finally got the remainder of the division's gear and personnel loaded. On 4 February 1944, we sailed for Maui, Territory of Hawaii, which was to be the wartime home of the 4th Marine Division. Maui was—and still is—a beautiful tropical island, but we hadn't come for the attractions. We had plenty of work to do—running convoys to the docks at Kahului and back to our camp located between Makawao and Haiku. The area had been pineapple fields until the Seabees arrived and built huge tent camps.

The division arrived during the latter part of February, and regular training and operations were quickly resumed.

Each Marine was allowed one day of liberty per week, normally not on a weekend because the islanders liked the place to themselves on those two days. They were friendly, though, and we became good friends with many of them. There wasn't too much to do on liberty unless one was a beach bum. Beer was not very plentiful, and what was available locally was so "green" that it often wasn't drinkable. Primo and Royal were the two most popular brands; occasionally, the camp slopchute (snack bar) served Iron City Pilsner made in Pennsylvania.

A few months after our arrival on Maui, my brother-in-law was transferred to one of the battalions in the 14th Marine Artillery Regiment (14th Marines), and a young first sergeant named John Claunch, whom everyone called "Jake," assumed Scotty's duties. From the start, Scotty had helped me to become a Marine. That was a debt I could never hope to repay. I would miss his sage advice, but, more important, I would miss his genuine friendship.

One afternoon after I returned to the motor pool, I walked over to the company office and asked Jake if I could use a typewriter to write a letter to my mother. He was agreeable, and I sat down and began to bang out the letter. I had taken two years of typing class in high school. Although I was no speedster, I could usually manage about forty words per minute with a fair degree of accuracy. I should have known that Jake had an ulterior motive in letting me use the typewriter. He stood in the background for a few minutes and then exclaimed, "Ha, you're just what I've been looking for—I've found my new company clerk!" I was reassigned the following day and ended up with three new jobs: company clerk, company runner, and the company executive officer's driver.

Despite the occasional boredom of being a company clerk, the job definitely had its advantages. My liberty day was changed to that of the executive officer. On most days off, all he wanted from me was to be dropped off at the Maui Country Club for a game of golf, followed by drinks with his fellow officers. His routine gave me the use of the Jeep for the rest of the day until it was time to pick him up. Liberty expired at 2000, and there was a strict curfew, even for civilians, at 2200. Overnight passes were all but impossible to come by.

It became apparent by the tempo of activity around the camp that the division would soon be headed for another operation. Landing exercises increased, and the camp began to buzz with rumors that soon became reality. In mid-May, we sailed for Pearl Harbor to load up on provisions and to load LSTs before heading west for the Marianas—and Saipan, my first amphibious operation and my first battle.

D-day for Saipan came on 15 June 1944. At dawn that morning, I had my first glimpse of a battle area. Much of the island was burning. Carrier aircraft were relentlessly bombing and strafing, and naval ships and boats were blasting away with their deck guns and rockets. The sound was almost deafening.

I was on board the USS *John Land* (AP 167), a new troop transport commissioned that year. We were several miles offshore when H-hour began and waiting anxiously for news of the landing to come over the ship's intercom. Shortly after 0900, we received the news. The beaches were said to be lightly defended, but enemy artillery and mortars were taking a heavy toll, with some landing craft being hit before they could make it to shore.

Late that afternoon, it became apparent that my company was not going ashore that day, but we were treated to a bit of action when the alert to "general quarters" was sounded, along with instructions for all embarked troops to clear the decks and go below. Fortunately, I was on guard duty and remained topside. Within a minute or two, every ship in the area began firing its guns skyward when a Japanese "Betty" bomber appeared. We were one of the last ships on the line. As the Betty headed out to sea, our crew on the stern's 5-inch gun had the last shots at it. Sure enough, the fifth round hit the plane, which caught on fire and started down. A big cheer went up from the crew and guards when we saw it. The next morning, the young members of the gun crew, proud of their achievement, stenciled a Japanese flag on the barrel of their gun.

On D + 1, the *Land* pulled in closer, and word was passed that we soon would be going ashore. Because of the barrier reef that protected the shores of Saipan, we would have to go down cargo nets to reach the waiting LCVPs (landing craft, vehicle, personnel) and LCMs (landing craft, mechanized) and transfer at the reef into the "alligators" (amphibian tractors, or amtracs) that would take us ashore.

Someone assumed that, as the company runner, I would carry any and all extra gear with me—the Jeep would come ashore later. I was loaded down with my pack and equipment, my rifle, and the company mailbag, along with other gear. Just before I began to climb over the ship's railing to catch the net, the battalion executive officer, a rather portly individual, ordered me to take some of his gear because he didn't think he "could make it down the net with all this gear." I draped what I could around my neck and waist and started down the net, all 130 pounds of me, plus 60 to 70 pounds of additional gear. The sea had grown to large swells, and the sailors in the landing craft below were having a difficult time keeping their boat close to the ship. I was convinced that if I fell, I would go straight down through the deck of the boat. Somehow, I managed to make it, although it was my first time down a cargo net. (Because of the shortened duration of basic training and my quick transfer to the division, I had never had any net training, wet or dry.)

Our alligators ground ashore midway between Charan-Kanoa and Agingan Point, the 4th Division's landing area, while the 2d Marine Division landed farther north.

My first taste of battle left a lasting impression. Many of our dead had not yet been picked up; one of the first dead Marines whom I saw was a major lying motionless in the sand not one hundred yards from the high-tide line. He wore no rank insignia, but the number stenciled on the back of his dungaree jacket indicated his rank. Not far inland was a Japanese field hospital with the dead bodies of their bandaged infantrymen still on litters. Bombing and shelling had torn the hospital to pieces. Weapons, equipment, and medical supplies littered the area.

A bunch of us, mingling around near the beach, waited for orders on which way to go. The word came to dig in until a suitable command post (CP) could be found for our unit. I thought the order was dumb and was looking around in the hope of finding some kind of souvenir, when suddenly someone yelled, "Jap plane coming" and people started scrambling for cover. I looked up and was shocked to see a Japanese Zero fighter, not more than sixty or seventy feet above us, coming straight down the beach with its machine guns blazing. The tracer bullets were a different color than ours, and, as I dove for cover, I saw the red "meatball" painted on the fuselage. I don't know why I thought I had enough time to dig in at that moment, but I literally tried to burrow into the sand. The Zero's bullets hit fairly close and wounded a couple of Marines farther down the beach, but they had done no other real damage. This was my first time under fire—the first time I had been shot at—and I had my first real look at the enemy. As the plane zoomed by, I could plainly see the pilot in the cockpit. I never again disregarded the order to dig in—ever.

Our battalion CP was finally set up at the base of Fina Susa Ridge, about fifteen hundred yards inland. Over the hill to the southeast, Marines were still fighting to take Aslito airfield, the major one on the island. The weather was hot and humid, and the stench of decaying bodies was indescribable. To add to the sickness, large, black blowflies, which normally inhabited the sugarcane fields, covered the human remains, both Japanese and American. The recovery of our dead took priority. They were removed to an area that would become the 4th Marine Division's cemetery and placed in separate graves plotted and numbered by survey parties with Graves Registration personnel. The enemy dead were scooped up when transportation and Japanese prisoners became available, trucked to an area near the beach, and dumped into common graves scraped out

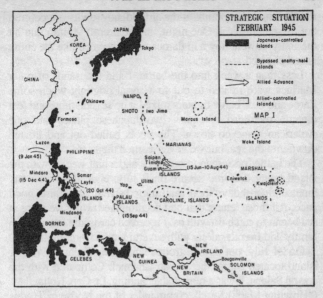

Western Pacific, operations, February 1945. (Source: Whitman S. Bartley, *Iwo Jima: Amphibious Epic* [Washington, D.C.: Historical Branch, G-3, Headquarters Marine Corps, 1954], inside back cover.)

by bulldozers. These graves were the width of the 'dozer blade, five or six feet deep, and twenty or thirty feet long.

Our company trucks had been landed, and they continued to supply us. I had an immediate problem in performing my duties as clerk/runner, however, because not all of our Jeeps had come ashore. Until I finally found a usable Japanese bicycle, I had to walk everywhere my duties took me. I wanted to commandeer one of the Japanese motorcycles that had been found, but that never happened. Within a short time, my bike gave out and I returned to walking.

One of my duties was to sound the headquarters siren whenever the alert sounded, which occurred fairly often, especially at night. A Japanese Betty bomber, dubbed "Washing-Machine Charley" because of the noise of its unsynchronized engines, came over the island several times. The bombardier usually aimed his bombs at the airfield, now under our control, but he seldom hit it. One night, an antiaircraft 90-mm gun hit the Betty. It went down in flames, and it seemed like the entire island cheered.

Less than a week into the battle, I and thousands of other Marines were treated to our first aerial dogfight when some Zeros and U.S. Navy fighters mixed it up several thousand feet directly overhead. We saw two Japanese planes and one American plane go down. The pilots bailed out and floated down into the sea, but we never learned their fate.

The battle for Saipan lasted three and a half weeks, with the island being declared secure on 9 July, eight days after my nineteenth birthday. Soon, mail started arriving at a fairly good pace. All those letters that had accumulated while we were at sea began to catch up with us. I received cards and letters from family and friends, along with several letters from Phyllis.

On 24 July, our assault troops landed on Tinian, a smaller island located across the Saipan Channel. Compared with the one on Saipan, it was a remarkable landing. Lt. Gen. Holland M. ("Howling Mad") Smith, commander of the Northern Troops and Landing Force, later referred to it as the "most perfect" amphibious operation in the Pacific War.

The Japanese commander on Tinian had assumed that any large-scale landing attempts would have to be made at Tinian Town, which had harbor facilities, located at the southwest end of the island. He had concentrated the bulk of his troops there. On the west side of the island, near the northern tip called Ushi Point, were two small beaches—one only 60 yards wide and the other no wider than 120 yards—only 1,000 yards apart. The Japanese commander had determined that it would be virtually impossible to land any large number of troops there. Several days prior to the landing, however, amphibious reconnaissance Marines from the V Amphibious Corps had landed in rubber inflatable boats at night and concluded that a large amphibious landing could be made. They also found the beaches to be lightly defended. The important contribution of the reconnaissance Marines to this landing cannot be overemphasized.

Early on the morning of the 24th, the 2d Marine Division off-loaded from transports onto landing craft several miles off

Tinian Town and, as a tactical feint, started toward the harbor area. The Japanese commander fell for it and consolidated his troops for the attack. Almost simultaneously, the 4th Division Marines started landing on the two narrow beaches, dubbed White Beach 1 and 2, and faced light to moderate resistance. Within nine hours, the entire division had landed.

The battle for Tinian lasted for nine days. The island was declared secure on 1 August, but the mop-up continued for several weeks. During this time, the 2d Marine Division suffered a considerable number of casualties.

Although he was then with the 14th Marines, Scotty and I managed to get together a few times while we were on Tinian to swap news from home and tell some war stories. Scotty had injured his foot during the campaign and was scheduled for further transfer to a hospital when he returned to Hawaii.

The 4th Division boarded transport ships and began the long, slow sail back to Maui. It had been rumored that we would stay on Saipan, which was to be used as a rear base, but the 2d Marine Division had been chosen for this duty, much to our relief.

Back on Maui, our division joined much needed replacements, resupplied, and resumed training. On 16 December, almost a year to the day after I had received my warrant to private first class, I was promoted to the grade of corporal.

In January 1945, the 4th Division boarded ships again. Following a week at Pearl Harbor, we sailed for what was to be the bloodiest campaign in Marine Corps history—the battle for Iwo Jima. D-day was 19 February; within two days, the volcanic beaches were so littered with wrecked landing craft and amtracs that we could not get our motor vehicles ashore.

I was on board the USS *Sanborn* (APA 193), which carried, among other units, the 3d Battalion, 25th Marine Regiment. The battalion commander, Lt. Col. Justice M. ("Jumping Joe") Chambers, would earn the Medal of Honor within four days of landing. We watched as some of his men went down the landing nets into landing craft. Many of those boats were damaged by enemy gunfire before returning for another load of Marines, and some never returned.

The transports served as secondary hospital ships. On D + 1, our ship pulled in closer to the beach to take on more casualties; we had been taking them on board since shortly after the initial landing. By nightfall, we had at least a dozen landing craft circling our ship and requesting that we take their wounded. We couldn't help them because our sick bay was already full. The tables in the officers' wardroom were being used as operating tables, and the wardroom and passageways were jammed with casualties on stretchers.

Late that afternoon, the call had gone out for volunteers among the Marines who were still on the ship to help with getting the stretchers on board and to assist in handling the steady flow of casualties. Most of us were thoroughly frustrated that we had not gone ashore and were anxious to help in any way we could. I volunteered immediately and carried stretchers for eight hours straight. I managed to get a little sleep and was asked to help out in the passageways by assisting the wounded waiting for wardroom tables. I lit cigarettes for some, brought water to others, and helped out in any way possible. Then, a doctor asked me to join him in the wardroom. I held one Marine's arm while the doctor snipped off several fingers that had been mangled by a hand grenade. I cut open green dungarees to expose all types of wounds and watched in amazement as the doctor treated the injuries.

I will always remember how calm most of the patients were, even those with the most serious wounds. One strapping young Marine had had a tourniquet left on his leg too long. The doctor told him, "Son, I'm very sorry, but I'm going to have to take that leg off."

The kid looked up at him and asked, "Did you say just the *one*, Doc?"

When the doctor replied "Yes," the kid said, "Thank God, I was afraid I was gonna lose them both!" These were Marines!

On D + 4, 23 February, we had pulled in very close to the shoreline. We were between two battlewagons that were pounding away with their enormous 16-inch guns. The concussion from the guns was unbelievable and the noise deafening. I was taking a breather on the top deck and watching through binoculars as some tanks advanced toward a ridge. Someone yelled, "Hey, they're up on Suribachi!"

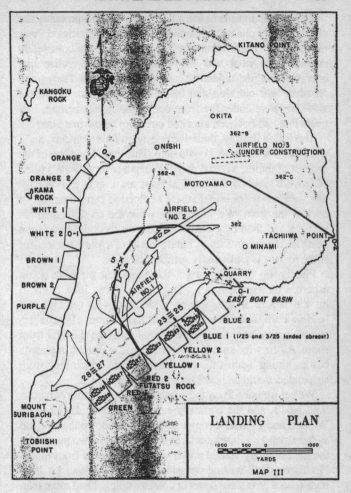

Iwo Jima, U.S. Marine Corps amphibious landings, 1944. (Source: Whitman S. Bartley, *Iwo Jima: Amphibious Epic* [Washington, D.C.: Historical Branch, G-3, Headquarters Marine Corps, 1954], inside back cover.)

I looked up in time to see a flag being raised—probably the second, larger one that became the subject of Associated Press photographer Joe Rosenthal's famous photo. I was completely engrossed in what was happening and didn't realize that everyone else had suddenly scattered below decks. I saw some splashes near our ship and heard clinking sounds off to the side. We were under fire from one of the Japanese shore batteries that had not been knocked out. I got below in a hurry.

The following day, the call came again for volunteers, and I went down to see how I could help. This time, I had one of the saddest of duties, a burial detail. We had several DOWs (died of wounds) on board. They had been sewn up in canvas bags and were ready for burial at sea. I helped to carry them up on deck at the stern. We stood there while the chaplain said his prayers, and then they were slipped over the side. I had seen death and burial on Saipan, but the burial of a Marine at sea, for some reason, is particularly somber and sad.

Finally, on D + 7, we got the word that we were going ashore. I transferred to a landing craft with my Jeep, ready to hit the beach. It was littered with destroyed vehicles and landing craft, and I was shocked at the number of casualties still waiting to be transported to the safety of the ships far from shore. As the wind shifted, the eerie sound of dozens of plasma bottles hitting against the rifle barrels, from which they were suspended, could be heard up and down the beach.

We set up our CP on the southeast edge of Motoyama airfield No. 1, and the company executive officer, 1st Lt. Fred Winker, and I found a convenient ready-made bunker for use as our small HQ (headquarters). About the time we moved in, the mail delivery started and it was great to hear from home. Phyllis was still writing occasionally, but two other La Jolla high school girls were better at corresponding. I had more than my fair share of mail to answer when I found the time to write.

One letter that I received was extremely distressing—my father had suffered a heart attack and had been hospitalized for a while, then ordered to get bed rest for several months. His business partner, Don Dix, had been drafted into the Army in 1943, and the workload had fallen on my father. He had tried to find a good manager to help out, but things at the dry-cleaning plant weren't going well.

On D + 13, a B-29 bomber, the first to land on Iwo Jima, made an emergency landing on airfield No. 1, close to our bunker. As soon as the plane had rolled to a stop, a bunch of us ran over to it and waited for the crew to hop out. The crewmen appeared and started telling us how they had left a Japanese city burning the night before during their incendiary raid. One of them asked, "Where's the front line around here?"

A Marine replied, "Oh, about a hundred yards over that way," as he pointed toward the other end of the island. This was a gross exaggeration, but it made those airmen scramble.

One day, my buddy, John ("Hook") Grant, and I were out in the Jeep when we noticed the entrance to a cave. We walked in a little way and saw that the cave opened up into a large room carved out of sandstone. In one of the corners, a ramp led down to another room of the same size, ten feet below the first room. We went into the second room, only to find a third level that was at least forty or fifty feet underground. This third room was full of dead Japanese soldiers. A favorite trick of the Japanese was to sneak out of their caves at night and retrieve their dead, perhaps to keep us from getting a correct count.

Hook and I had started searching for souvenirs in the third room when we heard voices, speaking in Japanese, that were coming from an even lower level. There were live Japanese below us! We ran up the two flights as fast as possible. We were getting into the Jeep when we spotted some engineers in the process of sealing cave and bunker entrances. We told them what had happened, and they said that they would take care of it. About then, we realized just how stupid we had been—we could have been killed by the Japanese or sealed in their cave by our own troops. That was our last cave trip.

Not long after, Grant and I were again out in the Jeep to deliver a message to another Marine unit located near the base of Mount Suribachi. As we drove along the road, an artillery round landed not far behind us. We were passing through the bivouac area of an infantry outfit, and the round had exploded close to the troops. I sped up, but a second round landed on the road and exploded fairly close by. A third explosion made us realize that some Japanese gunner was firing at us. Giving that Jeep as much gas as I could, I tried to put some distance between us and his gun.

Grant was showing more than a little concern. He yelled, "If you can't get this Jeep moving any faster, I'm gonna have to leave you!" He was ready to bail out of the Jeep for the closest cover, but we rounded a bend and the shelling stopped.

One day, I was sent to the 4th Marine Division cemetery to check on some casualties with the Marines at Graves Registration. Dozens of bodies were laid out in neat rows. The registration personnel were searching them for dog tags, identification cards, or other personal effects. Theirs was one of those "terrible job—but someone has to do it" situations. They worked quietly and methodically and made every effort to determine the identity of the dead. If they found no tags or card on a body, they searched the clothing for a stenciled name.

I noticed one Marine captain lying there who looked like he was merely taking a nap; he had recently died, and there were no visible wounds on his body. Noting that the name on his dungaree jacket was Irish but not a common one, I returned to our CP and asked our battalion commander, Maj. Mike Danneker, if he had known that captain. Danneker replied that the dead Marine had been one of his best friends.

The heavy casualty count continued to grow. When the battle for Iwo Jima was over, the 3d, 4th, and 5th Marine Division cemeteries would have more than six thousand graves.

The Japanese were running out of troops, and Iwo Jima was declared secure on 16 March. As usual, someone forgot to tell the Japanese, and the mop-up operations continued while the divisions prepared to leave the island. The 4th Marine Division was one of the first to go, but our outfit, Motor Transport, was one of the last units to board the waiting ships. This was only right—last in, last out—and we had taken few casualties compared with those of the Marine infantry units, which had been all but decimated.

As we were packing up our company gear, Sergeant Claunch told me to make sure that I got my Jeep safely back to Maui. Then, he left the beach to catch a ride out to his designated transport ship. I had gotten all of my gear together and loaded it into my Jeep because I knew that I would be on the same vessel as the Jeep, the USS *Hercules* (KA 41), one of the Navy's larger cargo ships.

I drove to the beach to catch a landing boat or anything else that could ferry me and the vehicle out to the ship, but it seemed as though every craft was either loaded or committed to a full load. I drove up and down the high-tide line with no success. Late in the day, I decided to look for a place to spend the night and ended up sleeping in the Jeep. Early the next morning, I continued my searching routine but with the same results—all available landing craft were loaded.

Then, I became hungry and realized that I was out of chow. The day before, I had thought that I would be on board ship and hadn't planned on needing extra rations. I drove up to the level area of the island. As I began looking for something to eat, I ran across an Army ration dump. I drove into the compound, and a "doggie" (U.S. Army) lieutenant walked up to the Jeep and asked what I was doing. Identifying myself, I explained that I needed some chow. He looked down at the markings on the Jeep's bumper and said, "I don't know where you got the Jeep, but the 4th Marine Division has left the island. Even Graves Registration is gone—I can't give you anything." Then, he walked away.

A soldier walking post nearby had overheard our conversation. He walked up to me and said, "Marine, I'm going to turn my back and I won't know what you do." I grabbed a case of rations and got the hell out of there. Thanks to the Army.

Getting back down to the beach, I saw an LCM loading equipment and drove up to it. A chief petty officer was in charge of the loading, and I explained to him that I needed a lift out to the *Hercules*. He said he thought he had a full load, but I watched until the LCM was ready to shove off. There was a small space near the bow that I thought would accommodate my Jeep. When I asked the chief, he said, "I don't know, but go ahead and back your Jeep on. If it gets damaged, don't blame me."

I backed the Jeep on board. As the ramp closed, it bent the bumper a little, but I didn't care. I had the ride I needed. The LCM carried me out to the ship, and we lifted anchor the following morning. To this day, I believe that I was probably the last Marine from the 4th Division to leave Iwo Jima.

No one who ever fought on Iwo Jima, and who was fortunate to have left the island alive, will ever forget the absolute carnage and total destruction that he witnessed or the determination of our Japanese enemies. Of the twenty-one thousand Japanese troops on the island, fewer than one hundred were ever captured. The rest either had died in battle or had committed suicide in their caves, rather than surrender.

The trip back to Maui was the best time on board ship that any of us had enjoyed. The *Hercules* was a huge ship, but on board were only fifty Marines, mostly drivers of the vehicles on board and several from my company. The captain was a fine gentleman, apparently very understanding. At the evening meal, he announced that, although it was a long-standing naval regulation not to serve alcohol on board Navy ships, he was going to overlook that regulation because of what we had all been through. Every evening, the crew members and passengers were each allowed one can of beer.

Those beer-hounds who really enjoyed their brew immediately sought out those who didn't care and began trading for the beer. A buddy of mine, Cpl. William ("Heavy") Howells, who tipped the scales at close to 250 pounds, liked his brew and tried unsuccessfully to talk me out of mine.

We were allowed to sleep in any compartment we desired, as long as we stayed out of the cargo holds, but we could go below and check on our vehicles. I kept a cot in my Jeep and often used it to sleep on the ship's weather deck. The ride to Hawaii was long but a comfortable one.

When we arrived at Maui, the whole island turned out to greet us. There were banners strung across highways, hula shows, and parties, and each Marine received a copy of a welcome home message. While we had been gone, the island legislature had petitioned the military government at Pearl Harbor for our return. The islanders were great people. I made many friends among them and had dinner in the homes of several, including the Silvas of Lower Paia and the John Helms family of Puunene. Helms worked for the large sugar factory at Spreckelsville.

Life again settled down to the routine replacement of personnel and equipment and more training. Much to the benefit of the new replacements, the Marine Corps studied its "lessons learned in combat" and never stopped training. We had a little more time off now, even an occasional Saturday.

Scotty had been flown to Hawaii from Tinian. He was now back in the States and getting medical treatment for his injured foot. Letters from home brought me up to speed on his recovery. Phyllis finally wrote the "Dear John" letter that I had been expecting. She merely stated that she thought it best that she didn't write any longer, whatever the hell that meant.

In the middle of July, my mother sent some magazine clippings that explained what had happened to Phyllis. She had entered a local beach beauty contest and had won. This qualified her for the Miss San Diego contest, and she had won that, too. Before it was over and before I could get home, Phyllis had entered the Miss America Beauty and Talent Contest in Atlantic City, New Jersey. She made it all the way to first runner-up to the winner, Bess Myerson. In my opinion, Phyllis was much more beautiful than Bess, but, unfortunately, she lacked the necessary talent to win. Bess played the violin. There was little wonder why I had been "aced out" by a bunch of draft-dodging young stallions who made a habit of hanging around beauty contests. As the French say, "C'est la vie."

On 6 August 1945, the B-29 bomber *Enola Gay* dropped a single bomb on the city of Hiroshima, and the world changed forever. Three days later, another atom bomb fell on Nagasaki, and that was the end of the war for the Japanese. We celebrated all over the island, and, of course, the rumors began immediately that we would start heading back to the States. When it was all sorted out, a point system had been devised, in which points were awarded for each serviceman's months of service overseas, each campaign, wounds, and so forth. Those Marines not having enough points to go home would be formed into military police battalions and other similar units and sent off to Japan and China as occupation troops. I had enough points at the time to get back to the States but not enough to be discharged. Small aircraft carriers began arriving at Kahului harbor and, as early as 6 October, some Marines departed Hawaii for San Diego. It was now only a six-day trip because zigzagging to avoid Japanese submarines was no longer necessary. The first troops from the 4th Marine Division arrived in San Diego on 12 October.

We knew that, as service and supply troops, we would be going home last, but the word kept changing as to exactly when our ship would come in. In my letters home, I changed our departure date three times. Finally, at the end of October, we got the word that the USS *Fanshaw Bay*, a CVE (carrier), was scheduled to take us home, and we pulled into San Diego six days later. There was a Navy band playing, dancing girls were doing their stuff, and lots of wives and sweethearts were there to greet the ship. Unlike other units, however, we did not parade up Broadway but boarded trucks that took us directly up the coast to Camp Pendleton. During the trip home, the point system had been altered and I had acquired enough points to be discharged.

At Camp Pendleton, the processing began immediately. Marines were either transferred to new locations, based on the needs of the Corps, or discharged after being sent to large processing centers nearest their homes. In addition to Camp Pendleton, as I recall, there was a large center for Marines located at the Naval Training Center, Great Lakes, Illinois, and another one in Florida. The administrative process required a few weeks—there were physical examinations to be done, allotments to be stopped, and all pay matters to be cleared up before we were mustered out and could collect travel pay. Our green dress uniforms were collected, and we wore dungarees. When our greens were returned, an emblem depicting a golden eagle had been sewn above the right breast pocket. This insignia, commonly referred to as a "ruptured duck," indicated that the wearer had been discharged.

We were granted liberty while we waited, but we were encouraged to be available for all of the necessary classes designed to help Marines back into civilian life. On 23 November 1945, exactly two years and twenty-one days after I had reported for active duty, I received my discharge papers and started to leave Camp Pendleton. I was about halfway to the main gate when I realized that my M1 rifle was still in the back of my car. This was the same weapon that I had been issued at boot camp. I drove back to the processing area, located at the armory, and told one of the Marines on duty to "give me a receipt and the rifle is yours." Then, I headed off toward San Diego.

As I was driving down Highway 101 toward my mother's house, I suddenly realized that I was a civilian. I had wanted to stay in the Corps and had indicated this in letters to both of my parents, although I knew that my father was still hoping I would come home and help him with his laundry business. As a Marine reservist, however, I could not reenlist—the Marine Corps was reducing its personnel from a wartime peak of 485,000 to less than 100,000. Only regular Marines had a chance of being retained.

I arrived at my mother's house, took off my uniform, dug out some civilian clothes, and decided to relax. My mother was delighted that I had returned home safely. I saw my father and had dinner with him several times. I reestablished relations with my brother Sonny, who had been only nine years old when I left home. He immediately dragged out all of the souvenirs I had sent him—a Japanese rifle, a bayonet helmet, and a battle flag.

My sister Marion and brother-in-law Scotty drove down from their home in Oceanside. We spent several hours catching up on what had happened to all of us over the past years. It was all behind me, or at least I thought it was. The war was over, peace had been established, and I was home.

# 4

# Return to War

LIFE IN THE United States was beginning to return to a degree of normalcy by the time we arrived home. Gasoline rationing and the majority of other types of rationing had all but ended. Veterans were looking for work, and some reclaimed the jobs that women held during the war.

Happily, many of my closest friends came home to San Diego. Farris Kolbeck had met and married a young lady while he was stationed in the San Francisco Bay area. Art Alford, who had been ready to complete flight training when the war ended, was home. Only Bud Wilkinson and Don Alford were still in the Navy; they had enlisted a year after I went into the Marine Corps. Bob Sullivan would not be coming home. He had been killed in action somewhere in Europe, but I never heard the complete story of how and when he died. He had married and had a child before he went overseas, but his wife and child had moved away from San Diego. Bob Hasha also returned to Pacific Beach. He had been wounded while serving in the U.S. Army.

Although there was doubt about our future, one thing was certain. We all needed jobs as soon as the partying was over and our mustering out pay was gone. My father had asked me to come back to the dry-cleaning plant, and I agreed to give it another try. He wanted me to learn the management end of it. I still felt that I didn't possess a keen business sense, and, deep down inside, I was not interested in spending my life in one place.

My father's dry-cleaning business was not in the best shape. When his partner, Don Dix, went into the Army, my father had been bedridden. The plant still had plenty of work, but the business had deteriorated without my father's attention to detail. Even after Don returned and my father was able to work on a part-time basis, several months passed before things began to straighten out.

In the meantime, there were jobs available at the plant for any members of the Bay Park gang who wanted them. Soon, Bud and his brother Dave, Art, and I were all working there. We considered ourselves fortunate to find work while millions of returning veterans were still searching for jobs and long lines formed at employment services and businesses. The severity of unemployment was clearly demonstrated when Don placed an ad in the newspaper for a delivery man. The next day, at least twenty men were waiting outside the office for the chance to apply for the position.

The dry-cleaning plant continued to do a great deal of business with the Navy. In addition to other ships, we were servicing two submarine squadrons in San Diego Bay. The submarines were tied up alongside their tenders, the *Nereus* and *Sperry*. I decided to take the route that serviced the Navy because it was interesting and also kept me out of the plant for most of the day. Early each morning, I went to the dock at the foot of Broadway and caught a ride in a liberty boat to one of the tenders. After crossing over the ship's deck, I went down to the submarines, which were linked together by gangways. Once on board a sub, I wrote up the orders and placed the clothes inside a mattress cover, then went to the next submarine and repeated the process. When I was finished, I took the liberty boat back to the dock and returned to the plant with a load of dirty uniforms and laundry. The next morning, as I repeated the drill, I delivered what I had picked up the day before. Because I was working on a percentage basis, the harder I worked, the more money I made.

Sometimes, five or six submarines were tied up next to their tender. When an inboard boat was ready to depart, the boats on the outboard side had to move to let her out. This shuffling of boats was always preceded by a long blast from the horn of each moving submarine.

One morning, as I was writing up orders on the forward deck of one of the boats, I heard the horn blast and figured the boat was moving to let another sub out. I kept on writing orders and stuffing laundry into the mattress cover and didn't pay any attention to our position. Suddenly, someone yelled down from the conning tower, "What in the hell are *you* doing still aboard?"

I stood up, looked around, and realized that I was standing on the deck of a submarine halfway out around Point Loma—and headed out to sea! In the flurry of excitement, the chief of the boat and the executive officer came running to find out why I hadn't left the boat before she sailed. My answer was simple: I hadn't known she was going anywhere. The boat had to turn around and take me back to the tender. Someone must have been on the receiving end of one hell of an ass-chewing for failing to check the deck before getting under way, but I was just grateful that the submarines didn't practice their diving in the bay.

In my opinion, the submarine sailors were the finest in the U.S. Navy. Both the officers and the enlisted men were proud of the Submarine Service, and I was always made to feel welcome. The chief of the boat had his laundry and dry cleaning done free of charge (a long-standing tradition). He made sure that I always had a full cup of coffee—as soon as I came aboard, a hand holding a steaming cup rose up from a hatch. When I had time, there was always an open place at the mess table.

Most of the submarines and the officers and older crewmen had seen service in the Pacific during World War II. Some of the men told fascinating stories about their long-range wartime patrols. They were a highly decorated group; a Medal of Honor recipient was on one of the tenders, several of the submarine skippers wore the Navy Cross, and a number of chiefs and petty officers first class wore Silver Stars.

One weekend in October 1946, Bob Hasha and I decided to attend a football game in Imperial Valley between La Jolla High School and Calexico High School. Bob had relatives living in nearby El Centro, and he knew some of the local girls. We drove down on the afternoon of the game, and one of Bob's friends introduced me to a very pretty girl named Sharon Stiles, a senior at Central High School in El Centro. We attended the night game together and later drove across the border to Mexicali. The cities of Calexico and Mexicali are actually one large city divided by the international border, hence the names Calexico for the California side and Mexicali for the Mexico side. The town of Mexicali was filled with Americans that evening, and like Tijuana a few years earlier, no one checked ID cards for drinks. Everyone had a great time, and Sharon and I seemed to hit it off.

The local parties continued at home, mostly in the vicinity of Pacific Beach with La Jolla High girls. At one of these parties, I saw my old flame Phyllis for the first time since I had gone overseas in February 1944. We went out to my car for a little talk, and I congratulated her for having won the beauty contests and for having done so well in the Miss America contest. She sat in the car and only said something about there having been "a lot of water under the bridge" since we had last seen one another. Feeling sorry for her and sensing her embarrassment and awkwardness at that moment, I wished her well and we said good-bye. That was the last time I ever saw Phyllis. A few years later, I learned that she had married Dan Rowan of the Rowan and Martin comedy team, long before it would become a national icon with the hit television show *Laugh-In*.

Although I continued to date a few local girls, my relationship with Sharon was getting serious and I was making frequent trips to El Centro on the weekends. On Thanksgiving Day in 1947, we drove to Yuma, Arizona, and were married. Dave and Bud Wilkinson had already married, Farris Kolbeck and his wife Dina had a child, and Art Alford was about to get married. The only one of our gang still single was Art's brother Don. Wedding bells had definitely broken up the old gang, but we still saw one another frequently.

My father and Don Dix had taken on a third partner, John Robinson. To me, his attitude seemed to say, "I don't care if you are the son of one of the bosses." I was always respectful to him, but I was tired of the difficult time that he was giving me and, one day, told him exactly what I thought of him. That was it. My father realized that it would be only a matter of time—I simply was not interested in the business—and we again parted with no hard feelings.

The time was around mid-1948, and there was still something of a recession going on as far as jobs were concerned. Even with a shortage of jobs, President Harry S Truman and his hatchet man, Secretary of Defense James V. Forrestal, believed that there would never be another war, and they cut the military services to the bare bone. I had been out of a job for only a few days when a couple of friends mentioned that work was available in the lumber camps in Oregon. None of us knew a damned thing about lumbering, but we heard that the money was good for those who worked hard. I had bought a new Chevrolet coupe while working for my father, and away we went, chasing after a dream, and promising our wives bags of money once we got started.

We lasted about one month. First, the lumber mill started me out on what was called the "green chain." It was the most difficult job there was. I had to grab huge planks of fresh cut (green) lumber as they came down a conveyor belt and slide them onto their proper stacks, depending on their size. I simply was not big enough to handle that job. Ending up on the business end of a jackhammer, I drilled holes in large rock formations so that the powder monkey could set his charges of dynamite. Then, we scattered to safety and he let it blow. This type of road clearing was done to allow the lumber trucks into new areas to be cleared. The work was fun for a while. We ate well at the mill boss's house, and the air was fresh and clean, but we got homesick for our wives and drove back to San Diego with the money we had managed to save.

I landed a job with Montgomery Ward as a "swamper" on a furniture delivery truck. That meant that I was an assistant to the driver, who helped me carry large sofas and other bulky items into customers' houses and apartments. It seemed as though no one ever lived on the first floor. We hauled items up narrow staircases, around tight corners, and into odd-shaped rooms. I weighed 140 pounds, not a large man. The work was pretty tough, but I was getting by and was determined to make it on my own. My take-home pay wasn't much, but it bought a lot of Chef Boyardee canned spaghetti.

I tolerated that job for a few months. Then, my pal Farris told me that his father was looking for a mechanic's assistant at his truck and trailer repair shop. I knew that my mechanical skills weren't that great, but I was able to follow instructions well and I learned things quickly. The shop serviced and repaired the largest trucks and trailers and performed other jobs, such as extending the frames on eighteen-wheelers.

In March 1948, I read an article in the local newspaper about a unit of the Marine Corps Reserve at the Marine Corps Recruit Depot (MCRD). The 11th Tank Battalion's headquarters and A Company were located at the depot and B Company at Camp Pendleton. Initially, I had been interested in tanks and had almost gone to tank school, so I went over to the depot to find out about the Marine Corps Reserve. After a physical examination and the necessary paperwork, I enlisted for a two-year hitch and talked Bud Wilkinson into joining me. I was given back my rank of corporal and started attending drills on Wednesday evenings and an occasional weekend. Bud had been a sailor and had a little trouble adjusting to the "Marine Corps" way of doing things, but we had fun learning how to drive the M-4A3 Sherman tanks in the same sand dunes that I had run through during boot camp.

We did well for a few months, but then the entire gang became interested in the early stock car racing scene. We called our stock cars "jalopies." Within a few months, every guy owned one, and we were racing them on the dirt tracks and quarter-mile circuits around San Diego County. It was a lot of fun, but it took a lot of time and money; we had to work on the cars every evening in preparation for a Sunday race. I had the advantage of working for Kolbeck Auto Works, where there were all kinds of tools, but there wasn't much time for anything else and I started missing the Reserve drill nights. The Marine Corps notified me that I had been transferred to "inactive status" and asked that I return my complete uniform issue. It had assigned me the basic 1800 MOS (military occupational specialty) for tanks and amphibious tracked vehicles, but I had not received any tank gunnery training.

In early 1949, I read a newspaper ad stating that Standard Stations, Inc., a division of Standard Oil Company, was hiring attendants for their new stations. I applied for a position and was accepted. After a ten-day training course, I was assigned to one of the largest stations, located on Pacific Coast Highway and Rosecrans Street, near my old neighborhood of Old Town. It was a busy station, open twenty-four hours, and, as was the policy, the new man worked the graveyard shift, midnight to eight. I enjoyed the work, the wages were good, and I met all types of people. With the station so busy, time seemed to fly by. Sleeping during the daytime took a little while to get used to, but Sharon worked during the day (at a dry-cleaning shop), and the house was quiet.

After six months, I transferred to Standard's busiest service station, on the corner of Pacific Coast Highway and Ash Street. At the time, this was the busiest intersection in San Diego. Across the street was the Pacific Square Ballroom, where major bands and well-known entertainers performed. The station had a small parking lot, and I parked and sometimes serviced the entertainers' cars. In the course of only a few months, I met Tommy and Jimmy Dorsey, Harry James, Frankie Lane, Duke Ellington, Les Brown, and others. All of them, with one exception, were always friendly and courteous to me.

Also in 1949, my mother and father reconciled their differences—they had never divorced—after a ten-year separation. Our family was overjoyed with this news. Their separation had been particularly hard on my brother, who had been four years old at the time, and I never doubted that it had something to do with my lack of self-discipline as a teenager.

My discharge from the Marine Corps Reserve was effective 26 March 1950, and, on 25 June, the North Korean People's Army (NKPA) attacked across the thirty-eighth parallel and, facing only light opposition, quickly moved south. Within days, the South Korean capital of Seoul fell and the entire peninsula that constituted South Korea was threatened by the Communist forces. The majority of Americans could not have found Korea on a world map. President Truman had reduced the armed forces to a skeletal paper tiger, but, when he announced that he was sending American forces into a shoot-ing war in South Korea, people began to sit up and take notice.

The newspapers were soon full of stories about Marines from Camp Pendleton preparing to move out, and the word spread that reservists also were being called up for duty. When I read an article about the Reserve, including the 11th Tank Battalion, being activated, that did it—my former battalion was headed to war. On the spur of the moment, I called the bat-talion, identified myself, and told the Marine officer at the other end of the telephone that I had served briefly in the bat-talion. I asked him if there was any possibility of getting back into the unit.

The officer laughed and said, "Maffioli, you get down here, and you'll see how fast you can get back in!"

On 21 July, I reenlisted. The 11th Tank Battalion was acti-vated on 31 July, with the greater part of the outfit going directly into the 1st Tank Battalion at Camp Pendleton. I ended up with my former reserve company commander, Capt. Phil Morell, a veteran tank officer of World War II.

Camp Pendleton was the busiest that it had been since the end of World War II. The 1st Provisional Marine Brigade had sailed in mid-July for Korea, and now thousands of Marines were needed to fill the 1st Marine Division. Because of the severe personnel cuts, the division had fewer than 8,000 troops—down from an authorized strength of 17,000—when the Korean conflict began.

Trains and buses were arriving daily, and the base was fill-ing up rapidly. The processing began with most men needing dog tags, ID cards, inoculations, and quick medical checkups. There was little time for training, and Marines were rushed out of there so fast that many never got the tags or cards, including myself.

My nose was a little "out of joint" from the moment I arrived at 1st Tank Battalion. During the classification and assignment process, I ended up as a truck driver again, with the same MOS that I had during World War II. I had not completed tank training, and now there was no shortage of tank crewmen.

It was a case of déjà vu—driving truck convoys to San Diego and loading ships with men, equipment, and tanks at the

Thirty-second Street Naval Station piers. Sharon continued to live in San Diego, and I was commuting home from Camp Pendleton as often as possible. To complicate matters, Sharon was pregnant with our first child, and she was due to deliver soon. On 13 August, I took her to Mercy Hospital, where, the next morning, she gave birth to our daughter, Deborah Lynne. I couldn't get much time off to be with her because we would be leaving soon, but, thankfully, Sharon had the families—hers and mine—to watch over her.

On the evening of the 17th, I visited Sharon and told the nurses on the ward that I was shipping out on the following day for Korea. They fitted me with a green hospital gown and a face mask, and I was allowed to enter the nursery and hold my baby daughter—a thrill I remember to this day. That night, I boarded the USNS *General M. C. Meigs*, a huge troopship. Early the next day, 18 August 1950, our battalion sailed for Japan with the ultimate destination of Korea.

The *Meigs* had several thousand Marines on board. Although the trip was comparatively short, without the necessity of having to zigzag, there were still problems. Only recently, the ship had been taken out of mothballs in the Navy's hurry to reach its required transport capability, and there had been little time to work out all of the bugs before she was placed back into service. The unusually long chow lines were so slow that many men found themselves finishing one meal only to return to another line for their next meal. The food was not good, and the mess cooks were unable to cope with the large numbers of hungry men.

Needless to say, the berthing compartments were overcrowded, and the smell of men in close living conditions during a hot summer passage only got worse as the lines for the limited number of showers continued to grow. One day, a sewer line that ran along the ship's bulkhead burst inside a living compartment located three decks below the ship's main deck and sent a fine spray of stinking brown water across half of the area. This event resulted in a mass exodus from the compartment until the line could be fixed, and some poor guys spent days scraping and washing their equipment.

The Marines had some good times, too. Many of the reservists were veterans of World War II, and they often sat on deck and swapped stories. There were men on board who had fought as members of every one of the six Marine divisions. I was surprised to find at least three Marines with whom I had served in my former company, the 4th Motor Transport Battalion. Two of them were Corporals Earl Harshman and Theodore R. ("Ted") Wheeler, who had come from a Marine Reserve engineer battalion in Phoenix, Arizona. They were assigned to different battalions now, but Wheeler and I would meet again within four months under very different circumstances.

Of course, there was always a poker game or two in progress on the main deck; some had several thousand dollars in the pot. Those of us who avoided the card games got together to sing. The song "Good Night, Irene" was quite popular when we left San Diego, and not a day went by that we didn't hear a group or individual singing it. As usual, I had brought along my harmonica, which I had played since I was a kid. I was fairly good with it and there were a number of other Marines who carried mouth harps, so we got together to play once in a while. As I had done on the long sea voyages during World War II, I tried to sleep on a weather deck whenever this was allowed. Unfortunately, this time I didn't have the luxury of a cot because no vehicles were on board, but I was able to curl up on a hard deck and managed to sleep fairly well.

We had been told that we were headed for Yokohama, Japan, where we would off-load and board LSTs and other landing craft that would take us to Korea. Most of our battalion was on board the *Meigs*, but our vehicles, wheeled and tracked, had been loaded onto cargo ships. Just a few days before we were due to arrive in Yokohama, the word came down that our destination had been changed to the Japanese port of Kōbe, where we arrived on 1 September. Unfortunately, typhoon Jane arrived at the same time and caused incredible problems. The winds were tremendous, and the waters around Kōbe became extremely rough. We had trouble docking because the Japanese tugboats could barely make it through the sea swells, but we finally made it into port.

Directly behind our ship was a huge Japanese floating crane that began to tilt wildly in the wind and hit the stern of our ship.

An idiot panicked and started to yell that we were sinking. Some of the troops cut the ropes holding the cargo nets to the ship's railings; as the nets fell away, dozens of young "green" Marines started down the nets toward the dock. At about the same time, the hawsers holding the ship's bow to the dock parted, and our ship began to drift away from the pier. The Marines on the nets were left hanging, with no place to jump.

Lt. Col. Olin Beall, commanding officer of the 1st Motor Transport Battalion, who would later gain fame at the Chosin Reservoir for saving the lives of several hundred soldiers, stood on the dock and yelled, "Get right back up there on that ship. No one gave you the order to abandon that ship!"

As they crawled back up the nets, the rest of us were cracking up with laughter. A tugboat finally made it across the harbor and pushed our ship back into place alongside the pier. We were secured once again.

Just a day after we came into port, the mail arrived and everyone seemed to have plenty of letters to read, as well as many packages. I received a dozen letters from Sharon. She had written almost every day, and I was delighted to hear that our baby girl was healthy and doing well.

One day, a buddy from the 11th Tanks, Cpl. Lowell Burnette, and I volunteered for duty with a working party located alongside the ship. We were wearing dungarees, but we rolled up our cotton khakis, put them inside a couple of discarded shoe boxes, took them ashore with us, and hid them in a pile of empty crates. When we were secured from the detail, we changed into our khakis.

No liberty had been granted—we weren't sure there was going to be any—but we decided to risk it. Hailing a cab, we took off for town. We had only U.S. currency in our pockets, but our cabby didn't seem to care and took us to one of the better entertainment spots in town. Early the next morning, we returned to the dock, changed back into our dungarees, and walked on board the ship as though we had just been secured from the working party, with no one the wiser. Within six months, Burnette would be accepted for Officer Candidate School (OCS) in Quantico, Virginia. Years later, he would command the 1st Tank Battalion in Vietnam as a major and retire as a lieutenant colonel.

Finally, our tanks and support vehicles were off-loaded from the cargo vessels and then loaded onto the waiting LSTs. It was a unique experience for the tank crewmen. They had trained on the M-4A3 Sherman tank, with its 105-mm howitzer, until we had embarked from San Diego. There, the tank battalion was issued the new M-26 Pershing tank, which carried the new 90-mm gun. The biggest difference in the tanks was in the driving; shifting gears and steering were much easier. The tank drivers managed to get a little experience in shuffling their tanks around on the docks at San Diego and Kōbe, but their first gunnery training in the new tanks took place in actual combat.

I had been assigned to drive a 6 × 6 wrecker truck as part of the Maintenance Section, and my truck was loaded on board an LST (Q-042), one of many that had been given to the Japanese government at the end of World War II. She had a Japanese skipper at the helm. Someone said that he had been in the Japanese merchant marine; if so, he was a lucky man because few captains of Japanese merchant ships had survived the war.

We sailed from Kōbe on 10 September and caught the tail end of typhoon Kezia, which had whipped up the seas on the western side of Japan. Of all the ships to be on during a typhoon, a flat-bottomed LST was the worst. We were pitched and rolled so badly that hardly anyone on board cared to eat. Those who did took their food to their living compartments, where they tried to hold onto their trays and keep themselves braced from falling. It was so bad that one of the tanks, stored below in the well deck, broke loose from its lashings and started to bang against the bulkhead. To make matters a little worse, the tank smashed into a fifty-five-gallon drum of oil tied to the bulkhead, and the entire deck was covered with a film of slippery oil. Both ship and tank crewmen were trying desperately to dog the tank into place, but they had to time their moves until the tank slid into place and allowed them to move with any degree of safety. It was a dangerous job, but they finally managed to get the tank secured. My wrecker truck was parked behind the shifting tank, and it was badly dented.

On the morning of 15 September 1950, we were sitting off the western coast of South Korea near the port of Inchon. It was D-day, the first day of the Inchon landing, and we were waiting to get into Green Beach on Wolmi-do, a small island connected to Inchon by a concrete causeway.

That afternoon, our ship was ordered to land in a slot between two other LSTs, and our captain headed her in at a pretty good clip. There appeared to be plenty of room between the two flanking LSTs, but the ship rammed directly into the stern of the LST on our port side with quite a jolt. Whether the current was too strong or the captain just couldn't handle her, we never found out. Most of us were topside and saw what was about to happen, so we had enough time to find positions to brace ourselves against the impact. I don't know if the skipper understood any English, but cries of "you dumb shit!" could be heard echoing throughout the ship. He managed to back off, gave it another try, and finally got his ship into the slot.

We received orders to begin landing that evening, but when the ship's crew tried to open the steel bow doors, they discovered that the earlier ramming had jammed the doors shut. An emergency call went out for an acetylene cutting torch. After one was finally located, the welder spent the better part of the night cutting the doors free. It would be morning before we could land, so I volunteered to stand radio watch for a U.S. Navy chief who was in charge of radio communications for the ship. While he got some needed rest, I was able to follow the landing and listen to the radio traffic as Marine units made their way ashore. Around 0300, I requested permission to secure the radio net, as had most of the other LST watches, and I hit the rack.

The next morning, our bow doors were open and we were able to off-load our vehicles, men, and equipment. We hit the beach on 16 September, D + 1. This was my fourth amphibious campaign in the U.S. Marine Corps, and, for the fourth time, I had been denied a D-day landing!

# ===5===

# Inchon, Seoul, and Beyond

WE HAD NO sooner hit the beach on the tiny island of Wolmi-do when I was called to get my wrecker truck and move to a couple of stalled 6 x 6 trucks that had conked out for one reason or another. Finally, I had something to do!

This was my first assist, but as often as I had been warned about being careful with the winch—not to break the shear pin—I let the winch cable run all the way out, and the shear pin snapped. I had to use a regular tow cable to haul the two vehicles in for repair. When I told WO ("Gunner") Fred Brutsche, the OIC (officer in charge) of the motor transport maintenance platoon and also my boss, about the winch, he hit the overhead (ceiling) and told me to go and draw a toolbox—I was relieved of my wrecker-driving duties.

Although I really didn't mind tinkering with the trucks and Jeeps, I was definitely not a mechanic. I told Burnette, who worked with me, that I was going to get out of this job—I still had my 1800 basic tank crewman MOS, and I wanted to get into a tank crew. But, my plans for transfer would have to wait.

I explained to Gunner Brutsche that I wasn't mechanically inclined. He had already witnessed my fumbling around with the wrenches, and he readily agreed. I asked him for permission to speak with WO Richard Herlong, OIC of the drivers platoon for Service Company.

Brutsche said, "Sure, go ahead. If he's got someone who'll trade with you, I'll okay it."

It so happened that Offie Lane, a truck driver, didn't

particularly care for getting out on the road all the time, but he had some mechanical experience. Gunners Herlong and Brutsche agreed on the deal, and we swapped jobs—Lane took my tool-box, and I took his truck. (I ran into Offie some forty-two years later at a tankers' reunion, and he was still laughing at what happened to me and to his truck.)

We set up a CP and spent the first night ashore on Wolmi-do. The next day, D + 2, the 1st Tank Battalion moved its CP into the capital city of Inchon. The division CP had been moved from shipboard onto the outskirts of Inchon on D + 1. Wolmi-do and Inchon had fallen quickly with minimal casualties for the U.S. Marines, but the numbers of NKPA soldiers killed and captured were high.

Early on the morning of 17 September (D + 2), I had an early run to pick up some supplies when I was stopped by the MPs, who had thrown up a series of roadblocks. I soon found out the reason. Down the road came a convoy of at least twelve Jeeps loaded down with MPs. In the middle of the convoy, three Jeeps were carrying all kinds of brass and photographers. Then, I saw him. With his crushed cap, dark glasses, and corncob pipe—the famous U.S. Army Gen. Douglas ("Dugout Doug," as the troops referred to him) MacArthur was riding in the middle Jeep. Several admirals and generals, including Marine Lt. Gen. Lemuel C. Shepherd, were with him. The convoy stopped down the road a little way from me to meet someone, and the photographers hopped out and began snapping pictures. The Marines had always thought, especially during World War II, that MacArthur was pretty much a publicity hound. In my opinion, this little scene supported that view. Later on, when the facts came out about his planning of the Inchon landing, we had to give him credit; many military planners had said that it could not be done.

Meanwhile, our tanks were having a field day, with Capt. Max English's Company A getting a major portion of the action. His tank company had come over with the 1st Provisional Marine Brigade and had fought up from Pusan, with the company's brand-new M-26 Pershing tanks getting credit for the first Soviet T-34 tank kills. The company was now actively engaged with the 5th Marine Regiment (5th Marines) and counted several more enemy kills, as the NKPA continued to roll its T-34s down the road and Marines fought along the Inchon-Seoul highway toward Ascom City and Kimpo airfield. Attacking the T-34s soon became a contest among U.S. tanks, aircraft, and rocket launcher/recoilless rifle–equipped infantrymen. In several instances, all three groups claimed credit for certain tank kills. The fighter aircraft, of course, had a decided advantage because they were always ahead of the ground troops and were usually able to spot the enemy first.

Our trucks supplied the tank battalions with ammunition, fuel, and other essential items. The truck drivers vied for the runs because they wanted to get in on a "little piece of the action" from time to time. I participated in a few of these runs and had a few enemy rounds cranked off at me once in a while but never managed to get myself or my truck hit. Normally, I didn't give the situation too much thought unless I happened to be driving a gasoline tanker truck or a 6 x 6 loaded with fifty-five-gallon drums of fuel. Then, I wondered what a well-placed enemy round could do.

Ascom City had derived its name from Army Service Command, a huge area of warehouses, residences, and storage facilities built by the U.S. government during the occupation of Korea following World War II. The warehouses had been crammed with supplies, which the Allies had been forced to abandon when they retreated from the area. Bombs had destroyed much of the city, and the North Korean soldiers had looted what they could use when they first captured the area.

The 5th Marines had retaken Ascom City by D + 2 after a counterattack, during which Company A tanks and supporting Marine infantry had knocked out several T-34 tanks. Getting the lion's share of the credit for this action was 1st Lt. Bill Pomeroy's 1st Platoon.

Kimpo, including the airfield and surrounding villages, was declared secured on the morning of 18 September, D + 3. The 2d Battalion had captured the prized airfield just twenty-four hours after leaving Ascom City. Its casualties were considered light, compared with more than one hundred enemy dead left in the battalion's zone of action.

While the 5th Marines were taking care of Kimpo, Col.

Lewis B. ("Chesty") Puller's 1st Marines, supported by Capt. Bruce Williams's Company B tanks, continued the attack along the Inchon-Seoul highway. Company B had many reservists from San Diego's 11th Tank Battalion, my old outfit, and I knew more tankers in this company than any other. (Generally, Company A's tanks were attached to and supported the 5th Marines, Company B supported the 1st Marines, Company D supported the 7th Marines, and Company C was on call to support all three regiments.)

As the 1st Marines and Company B's tanks advanced to the village of Mahang-ri, they got into one hell of a firefight. Two tanks were temporarily disabled, but the crews escaped any real harm. Supported by tanks, artillery, naval gunfire, and Marine aircraft, the 1st Marines and Company B continued the march until they completed the capture of the town of Sosa on 18 September.

On the 20th, the 3d Battalion, 5th Marines (3/5), crossed the Han River on LVTs in a daylight assault. Just a few hours later, thanks to the quick work of the 1st Engineer Battalion, the tanks of the 2d Platoon, Company A, were able to cross the river on float rafts in support of 3/5. More of the division soon followed.

On 21 September, D + 6, the 7th Marine Regiment landed at Inchon to complete the division ashore. Accompanying it was Company D, its attached tank company commanded by Capt. Lester Chase. The division, with light casualties, continued to move inland on its advance toward Yongdungpo and killed hundreds of NKPA troops. Capt. Richard ("Roughhouse") Taylor's Company C tanks joined the fray and supported the 1st Marines. Company B's M-26 tanks were held up by minefields strewn with wooden box mines until Company C engineers cleared a path in the field. With casualties increasing on both sides, the regiment, supported by the usual shock power of tanks, artillery, and Marine close air support, finally was able to secure Yongdungpo on D + 7.

As the division moved forward, our battalion CP moved in behind it to support the tank companies. We moved from Inchon to Kimpo airfield, and I was getting plenty of runs back to Inchon and Ascom City for needed supplies. One day, another truck driver and I were at Ascom City and began poking around the bombed-out buildings as we looked for any usable gear. In one section of a warehouse where almost the entire concrete roof had collapsed, we found at least a dozen Jeep trailers that had escaped damage in a corner of the building. We attached a trailer to each truck and took two of them back to the motor pool. I saw some of my Company B buddies at the CP and told them about the trailers. We went back to the damaged building and picked up more of them— towing one and stacking the others on the bed of my truck.

The tank crewmen were pleased to have something in which to stow their personal gear, but it was comical to see a Marine M-26 tank towing a small trailer down the road. The trailers lasted only until the tank drivers, completely forgetting about them, backed down the first time. Their hitches broke off, and, more often than not, the trailers were crushed beyond use under the tanks. We truckers thought the trailers to be great additions, though, and used them carefully whenever we could.

One day while we were still at Kimpo, we had just begun to gather around the mail clerk for mail call, when an NKPA gunner hidden in a nearby village took the opportunity to fire a couple of rounds into our compound. Fortunately, his gun wasn't a large-caliber weapon, but the rounds came close enough to wound two or three of our men with exploding shrapnel. My platoon sergeant was hit badly enough to be evacuated. A patrol quickly went out to search the village but came up with nothing.

Our battalion CP continued to move with the action. A company of ROK Marines followed us to check each town and village for collaborators, individuals who had aided the North Korean soldiers in any way while they had occupied the area.

We had settled in at a small village just outside of Seoul, and the ROK Marines began rounding up suspects. They held a trial in the local mayor's house, which was across the road from our compound. The trial lasted all day, with witnesses streaming in and out of the house. Finally, late in the afternoon, the ROK Marines herded about a dozen people outside, lined them up, and started reading the verdicts to the public.

The accused ranged in age from a boy of about fourteen years to an elderly woman who must have been in her seven-

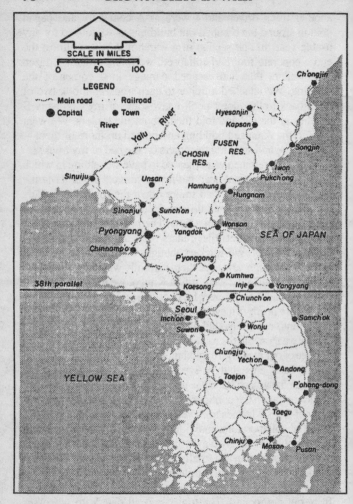

Peninsula of Korea. North Korea lies above the thirty-eighth parallel and South Korea below it. (Source: Lynn Montross and Nicholas A. Canzona, *U.S. Marine Operations in Korea,* 1950–1953, vol. 3, *The Chosin Reservoir Campaign* [Washington, D.C.: Historical Branch, G-3, Headquarters Marine Corps, 1957], inside back cover.)

ties. We didn't understand the Korean language, but, as each name and verdict was read aloud, we could tell the results of the court's decision by the way the accused dropped their heads. The young boy began to cry, and the old woman was protesting, but apparently there was no type of appeal.

The ROK Marines marched them off to the nearby hills and had them dig their own graves. Some of us started to go out there, but our company commander screamed that we were to stay put—it was not our affair. I borrowed a pair of binoculars and jumped up onto the top of my truck to watch the proceedings.

When four graves had been dug, the ROK Marines had the diggers stand in front of the graves, and, with a burst of rifle fire, they were executed. Four other prisoners filled in the graves, and then they, too, were shot, with the remaining prisoners ordered to fill in those graves. Finally, when there was only one man left standing, he was shot and a ROK Marine covered his grave.

This entire scene had taken place less than a thousand yards away. It was the first execution that I had witnessed and something that I would never forget. As for justice, it was their country, their system, and two things stood out in my mind. There had been plenty of witnesses, and the trial had not been overly hurried.

The battle for Seoul raged fiercely, with the U.S. 1st and 5th Marines, supported by Company B's tanks, the most heavily engaged. Chesty Puller's 1st Marines, however, took downtown Seoul, largely with help from the tanks of Company B's 2d Platoon. The capital city of Seoul was declared secured by 3 October.

On 1 October, the 3d Battalion, 5th Marines, was ordered to proceed northwest of Seoul, with the town of Suyuhyon as its principal objective. Supporting the battalion were a battery of artillery, a platoon of engineers, and the tanks of Bill Pomeroy's 1st Platoon, Company A. I had been chomping at the bit to get one of these runs, and I was selected to accompany them with my 6 × 6 loaded with fifty-five-gallon drums of tank fuel.

We hadn't yet cleared the outskirts of Seoul when Sgt.

"Tiny" Rhodes's retriever tank hit a mine and a track blew off. There was a delay while the track was repaired, then we headed off again. The combat engineers inspected several small bridges, and we had to bypass some of them, which caused further delays. The column finally stopped about ten miles out of Seoul. So far, there had been no opposition.

I helped to refuel the tanks. When my truck was empty, Captain English, Company A commander, who had come along with the column, notified me that I would have to return to Seoul for more fuel. It was getting dark. The captain gave me a "shotgun" rider, and we started back. There was nothing but darkness between us and the city, and I drove as fast as the empty 6 × 6 would travel. I completely forgot about those bypasses, as I rolled across the bridges with my rider hanging on for dear life. We managed to reach Seoul, load up, and race back. The entire trip took no more than a couple of hours.

By the time we rejoined the column, night defenses had been set up. The infantry was dug in and the bulldozer tank had scooped out hull defilades for the tanks. The three trucks from our battalion, two loaded with gasoline and one with ammunition, were parked well behind the tanks. The other truck drivers and I were told that we could bed down in a small hut next to Lieutenant Pomeroy's tank, A-11.

This was only my second extended run with the infantry and tanks. As I looked around, something unexplainable made me slightly uneasy, particularly about that flimsy little hut where I would sleep. I saw the driver of A-11 crawling under his vehicle, and I asked him if he was planning to sleep under the tank. He said he was, and I asked if it would be okay for me to climb into the driver's compartment of the tank and sleep there. He said, "Yeah, go ahead."

I climbed aboard and dropped down inside the tank. After battening down the hatch, I began to look around in front of our position through the tank periscope located in the hatch cover. In the limited amount of light, I could see a large earthen dike about one hundred yards forward of the tank. Immediately below us, in the foreground, were some rice paddies with the usual number of smaller dikes used for field separation and pathways. Now knowing what was in front of me, I got comfortable and fell asleep.

Just after 0200, the assistant driver dove through his hatch in the tank and yelled, "They're lining the dike out there," meaning that enemy troops were crossing the dike and coming straight toward us. Waking up in a hurry, I looked through the vision block and saw several North Korean soldiers just a few yards from our tank and coming at us fast. The assistant driver got his bow .30-caliber machine gun firing and hit a few of those closest to us. I started calling shots for him as I swung the periscope in a small arc.

I hadn't realized it, but Lieutenant Pomeroy had been stretched out on the tank's turret deck. He jumped up as soon as the firing started and warned us that he was going to move the turret a bit to swing the gun around; he loaded and cranked off about three rounds of 90-mm fire directly to our front. We could hear a few rounds from small arms pinging off the tank. Then, someone banged on the hatch directly over me and yelled, "Let me in!" I assumed it was the driver, but I yelled back that I was too busy at the moment, and he crawled back under his tank.

The firefight didn't last more than fifteen or twenty minutes. At dawn, we climbed out of the tank and started looking around. Several bodies were lying directly in front of us, and we noticed that the North Korean soldiers had been carrying Molotov cocktails (bottles filled with gasoline) to be used on our tanks. What a hotfoot that would have been!

The tank crews got the word to move out with the infantry. As the driver of A-11 crawled into his tank, he looked at me and said, "That's the last time anyone ever sleeps in my compartment!"

The fuel and ammo trucks were ordered to stay behind with the tank retriever while the infantry and armor moved toward Suyuhyon, not far away. The drivers and the retriever crew were looking around, and I noticed that the building where I was supposed to have slept was riddled with bullet holes. The other drivers said they had left the hut and taken cover under other vehicles when the shooting started.

Not long after the tanks left, a major came up to us and said that he was from G-2 (Intelligence Section). He had to go into the paddies and count the number of enemy bodies, but he didn't relish the idea of going out there alone. Several of us agreed to go out with him. We had been peering out at the paddies and could see more bodies, but we had not ventured out there yet.

We moved out slowly because someone had been moaning and wounded North Korean soldiers might still be close by. Another driver and I were moving along a small paddy when we spotted a North Korean officer in his dress uniform. He was lying on his side, and the back half of his head was gone. I knew that any kind of small-arms burst could have done it, but my first reaction was, "Gee, Pomeroy must have got him with the 90-mm!"

The other driver spotted the dead officer's binocular case and dove for it. At about the same time, I noticed the pistol holster on his belt, open and empty. I rolled him over carefully, mindful of booby traps, and he was lying on a beautiful Soviet-made Tokarev semi-automatic pistol, with the lanyard still attached to his belt. Now, it was mine!

As we moved along with the major, we found seventeen bodies and evidence that many more had been dragged off or had crawled away. The next day, a ROK patrol found fifty more bodies on the other side of the big dike. The South Koreans figured that it had been at least a company-sized attack. There had been no friendly casualties.

The advance column reached its objective with no further opposition and radioed the tank retriever to have us come up to its position. We spent that night at the objective. Volunteering for guard duty with the tanks, I stood watch with a Thompson submachine gun and then caught some shut-eye under a tank. The next morning, I was released to my company, and an Associated Press (AP) news correspondent went back to Seoul with me.

On the same day that we had left Seoul for Suyuhyon, the 7th Marines had headed north of Seoul for Uijongbu. They were supported by Company D's tanks; artillery of the 3d Battalion, 11th Marines; Company D's engineers; and one com-

pany of ROK Marines. With light casualties, the units secured
Uijongbu and occupied it by 3 October.

The Inchon-Seoul campaign had cost the 1st Marine Division more than four hundred dead, two thousand wounded, and
several Marines missing. The NKPA had paid heavily with
thirteen thousand casualties and more than six thousand soldiers captured. With the campaign over, the division units were
ordered back to staging areas at Inchon for shipboard loading
in preparation for another amphibious landing. We didn't
know its location, only that it would be into North Korea. Most
of the tank companies were back with the battalion in the tank
staging area, and I saw some of my old friends for the first time
in several weeks. After being with Company A's 1st Platoon at
Suyuhyon, I was more determined than ever to get into a tank
company and crew. I looked up B-22's crew—I knew both the
tank commander, Sgt. Bob Dolby, and his driver, Cpl. Andrew
("Chief") Aguirre, from San Diego. When I told Sergeant
Dolby that I'd like to get into a crew, he said that he had a
crewman whom he considered a bit shaky. He would talk to his
platoon leader and see what he could do from that end. I said
that I would talk with Gunner Herlong and work the plan from
my end.

Most of the tankers were cleaning and repairing their
vehicles before boarding the Navy's ships. When parts and
equipment were needed, tankers were notorious scroungers.
They reasoned that if it could be located, it could be had. One
day, a brand-new Army Jeep found its way into our compound.
Someone, either the headquarters or service company commander, told me to get some paint and a stencil brush and start
putting Marine Corps tactical markings on the Jeep. I was
busy, working away with my paintbrush, when I heard a
clearing of the throat, "Ahem, er, uh, Maffioli, you can stop
marking that Jeep. We have found the owner." Looking up, I
saw our commander and one very pissed-off Army colonel,
who was glaring at me and tapping his leg with a swagger
stick. I stowed the painting gear, and the colonel roared out of
our compound with his recaptured Jeep.

Finally, around 15 October, we boarded ships. This time,
luck was with me, and I was on board a fine vessel, the USS

*Pickaway* (APA 222). She had cooled troop compartments and was not overcrowded, and her crew fed us well. I immediately volunteered for mess duty, a trick I had learned during World War II on our long voyages. Those of us assigned to mess duty got plenty to eat, including any leftover desserts, and weren't bothered with guard duty or training while on mess detail. Also, our time off was our own.

The word soon spread that we were headed for the port city of Wonsan on the eastern coast of North Korea. The *Pickaway* would sail around the southern tip of Korea and then head north toward our new objective. We had been given a landing date, but then the word came that the ROK Army had advanced quickly up the eastern coast by land and captured Wonsan on 10 October. When we reached our objective area, the ship turned around and started south. The Wonsan harbor had been heavily mined, and our ships could not approach. For ten days, we sailed back and forth, and the nickname "Operation Yo-Yo" was given to the whole affair. During this time, the U.S. Navy and ROK Navy each lost several minesweepers detailed to clear the minefields.

On 25 October, when we were able to make some "administrative" (unopposed) landings, we found Bob Hope, Marilyn Maxwell, and the rest of a USO troupe waiting for us. They had flown in from Japan.

The next day, the 1st Battalion, 1st Marines, was ordered into the town of Kojo, some forty miles south of Wonsan, to help guard a large ROK Army supply dump located near the town. A narrow-gauge railroad with one locomotive and several cars had been captured intact at Wonsan; the train was used in transporting the infantry to Kojo. An artillery battery, engineers, and a medical detachment followed by truck convoy. No tanks were with the column, but the group reached Kojo without opposition.

Kojo was a small seaport town practically untouched by the war. The ROK Army battalion that had been guarding the supplies boarded the same train for the ride back to Wonsan. Oddly enough, it took most of the supplies, or what its troops hadn't used while they were in Kojo.

The Marines spent a quiet night, but enemy contact was

made the next day. That night, hell broke loose. All three infantry companies were hit hard, and the supporting troops had their hands full, too. A regular NKPA unit had been able to sneak up to within hand-grenade distance before being discovered and overran one Marine company. Some Marines died in their sleeping bags.

Ten tanks from Captain Taylor's Company C were rushed onto an LST, but the ship got hung up on a sandbar and had to be pulled off. By the time the ship was able to get under way, the emergency was over, and the LST headed back to Wonsan.

U.S. Marine casualties included about 24 men killed (KIAs), 50 wounded (WIAs), and a few missing in action (MIAs); however, the Marines had accounted for more than 250 enemy killed and had captured about 100 North Koreans.

The 1st Battalion, 1st Marines, returned to Wonsan a couple of days later. I happened to be on the beach when the LST came in with the North Korean prisoners of war (POWs) and some of the Marine bodies still in their sleeping bags. The word was that some Marines had been bayoneted.

About thirty road miles west of Wonsan was the town of Majon-ni, the site of a major road junction, with roads leading south to Seoul, west to Pyongyang, and east to Wonsan. The 3d Battalion, 1st Marine Regimental Combat Team (RCT), went to Majon-ni by motorized convoy on 18 October, with a mission to deny enemy forces the use of the roads. They were reinforced by the usual complement of artillery, engineers, and naval medical personnel. Because of the dangerous terrain at a narrow mountain pass through which they had to travel, however, no tanks went with them. The possibility of ambush by enemy-induced landslides was far too great. Several ambushes and night attacks during the next few days proved that considerable numbers of NKPA regulars were still in the area.

The 1st Tank Battalion moved its command post on 2 November to a site near the town of Munchon, fifteen miles north of Wonsan. Our company was located right on the beach. Company A's tanks were with us, and all was quiet for the first few nights. We drivers caught our share of guard duty and night watches, but we felt a little more secure when our unit set up some .30-caliber light machine guns on the beach. On the night of 8 November, we could hear motors of small craft on the water. The guys manning the machine guns opened up, which quickly got the rest of us moving. We were shooting toward the sounds of the boat engines with both rifles and carbines and heard a couple of explosions. Things quieted down after a while. Keeping a close watch on the beach, we saw no enemy troops or their boats coming ashore, but we knew that they had been out there on the water. Our gunners were sure that they had hit some of the enemy's small craft. A patrol was sent out but made no further contact.

With the Wonsan, Majon-ni, and Munchon areas pretty much under control, the division received orders to proceed northward all the way to the Manchurian border. The 7th Marines had proceeded north to the Hamhung area on 30 and 31 October, and the 5th Regimental Combat Team was moving up behind them. If deployment continued as planned, it would stretch out the division more than three hundred miles north and south, with a fifty-mile width. The troops were wondering what the hell was going on by spreading out a Marine division this far. We would be pulling occupational duty instead of making amphibious landings.

The infantry had been issued long, cold-weather parkas with hoods; gloves that had only the trigger finger separated; and boots with removable mesh innersoles, called shoe-packs. It had already turned cool as far south as Wonsan, and we figured that we were in for some severe weather.

Our tank battalion, one of the last units to leave the Wonsan area, moved its command post on the 16 November. We had to travel over ninety miles of rough road and through some mountain passes. I was hauling a very heavy trailer on the end of my 6 × 6, and it was slow going. We finally arrived at the small town of Soyang-ni, about eight miles northwest of Hamhung, where we set up in an old schoolhouse. As expected, the weather had turned extremely cold. Everything froze at night and had to be thawed out in the morning. The men on mess duty lit a can of fuel oil underneath each water trailer so that the cooks could prepare our meals. Compared with what was to come, however, we would later consider these tough living conditions to have been moderate.

By this time, the 7th Marines had advanced to Hagaru, at 4,000 feet altitude, which sat at the foot of the Chosin Reservoir. RCT-5 (Regimental Combat Team, 5th Marines) was still some ten miles south at the small village of Koto-ri. Hagaru and Koto-ri were fifty-five and forty-five miles, respectively, from Hamhung. A treacherous mountain road, known as Funchilin Pass, about ten miles long, rose 2,500 feet in that area, and its narrow curves and extremely sharp bends would not allow passage of the large M-26 tanks. The 1st Engineer Battalion, however, was hard at work with bulldozers and other heavy equipment to widen the curves. Meanwhile, our tank battalion commander, Lt. Col. Harry Milne, ordered a provisional platoon of M-4A3 Sherman tanks and four bulldozer tanks to make their way through the pass and up to Hagaru to support the infantry as a gun platoon.

The other gun companies, located at Majon-dong and Soyang-ni, were tasked with guarding road junctions along the main supply route (MSR). From our command post, H & S troops conducted motorized patrols east and west along the smaller roads. They had an occasional run-in with retreating NKPA forces, although no heavy firefights occurred. I volunteered to take a couple of these patrols out in my 6 × 6, with at least one .30-caliber light machine gun mounted on a tripod in case trouble developed. It was difficult trying to tell who was who in these small villages. Most of the retreating NKPA soldiers had changed into civilian clothing, with the hope of blending in with the indigenous villagers, but their closely cropped hair and their age usually gave them away.

We caught our share of guard duty, as usual. Most of my watches were in a graveyard located up the hill from our CP. Large white gravestones stared at me all night as I stood watch with a light machine gun. Other Marines swore that they had seen these grave markers move toward them. Some of them had cranked off a few rounds, which always stirred up hell with the guard commander and raised up the rest of the Marines in our compound. I resisted the temptation to fire the machine gun, but I must admit that, during one pitch-dark night on the mid-watch, I let a "tombstone trooper" have a round from my pistol when it seemed to take a step toward me.

I felt pretty silly in the morning when I saw my "enemy" still standing in front of me.

Meanwhile, the 1st Marine Division's two motor transport battalions were being stretched to the limit as they tried desperately to keep Marines and supplies rolling from Hungnam to Yudam-ni, north of Hagaru, a total distance of eighty miles. As a result, motor transport assets from other units were being called on frequently for support. The Service Company Motor Transport Section of the 1st Tank Battalion was soon called on to do its part.

# =6=

# Task Force Drysdale

THE BRITISH 41 Independent Commando, Royal Marines, numbering 235 officers and enlisted men, landed at Hungnam on 20 November. Fighting in Korea since early September, they had conducted diversionary raids on the western coast in preparation for the Inchon landing, participated in that landing, and gone as far as Kimpo before withdrawing. Since then, during raids conducted on the eastern coast of North Korea, they had blown up railroad tunnels, bridges, and sections of railroad track.

Highly trained in reconnaissance tactics and extremely motivated, the unit was commanded by Lt. Col. Douglas B. Drysdale, Royal Marines, a decorated veteran of World War II. As their counterparts were soon to learn, the term *commando* referred to the unit, as well as to an individual trooper, and its members called it "four-one," not "forty-first." The title *independent* denoted a separate unit; it was not part of any commando brigade. Although the unit was much smaller than that of the World War II commando units, it contained its own assault engineers, communicators (signalers, as they called themselves), and a heavy weapons section, in addition to the regular infantry and reconnaissance troops.

All of the members were trained in reconnaissance and raiding procedures, and, like their commander, many were combat veterans of World War II and the postwar Malaya terrorist campaigns. We tended to call all of them Marines, but several were Royal Navy volunteers from the British Pacific Fleet who had been trained as commandos.

The 41 Commando had been attached to the 1st Marine Division for the purpose of working with the latter's reconnaissance company in scouting, patrolling, and flank protection. By the time transportation could be arranged, however, the division commander, Maj. Gen. Oliver P. Smith, decided that the 41 Commando was urgently needed at Hagaru, where only one infantry battalion (3/1), supported by two batteries of artillery, some tanks, and assorted engineers and service troops, was defending the town against ever-increasing enemy attacks.

Since 1 November, various units had reported clashes with Chinese Communist troops and had captured several of them. Interrogation disclosed that they were from regular Chinese Communist Forces (CCF) units, but General MacArthur and his G-2 staff officers still refused to believe that Red China would enter the conflict with any great numbers of troops. By now, however, it was evident that entire divisions of CCF soldiers were attacking on several fronts.

(As was later learned, four Chinese field armies, with some fifteen divisions, were in the area of the Chosin Reservoir. While few were at full strength, a CCF division usually numbered about ten thousand men—so much for MacArthur's intelligence capabilities.)

Because of its sizable motor transport section, my battalion was given the commitment to transport the commandos to Hagaru. Early on the morning of 28 November, a convoy of twenty-two 6 × 6s and assorted Jeeps and trailers left our CP for the fifteen-mile trip to pick up our Royal Marine allies at Hungnam. I had requested and received this assignment to the convoy. All drivers had been issued complete sets of cold-weather clothing only the day before.

Leading our trucks with a Jeep was M.Sgt. Mac Corwin, our service company truckmaster and the NCOIC (noncommissioned officer in charge) of the drivers' platoon. Accompanying him was Sgt. Charles W. Dickerson, a section leader who had volunteered to come along as a spare driver.

The Royal Marines were a friendly, cheery bunch, with their

heavy accents and, in the case of the Welshmen, almost a foreign language. They already had been issued the American cold-weather gear and were carrying U.S. arms, mostly M1 rifles. They had trained in Japan with these and U.S. machine guns and other crew-served weapons. Many of these weapons were still in crates, ready to be loaded on our trucks.

Instead of the American steel "pot" helmets they had been issued, they preferred to wear their dark green berets, their "berries" as they called them, each with the large gold globe and laurel emblem on the front. The commandos were proud of their berets and justifiably so. They had earned them only after successfully completing a lengthy and demanding training course.

The loading and boarding started. Because I had been near the rear of the convoy when we arrived, I carried cargo, as well as troops. The commandos loaded their galley gear on my truck—assorted cookstoves, burners, and, of course, their precious tea. Five or six commandos assigned to their mess jumped on the back, and their senior man, a young Royal Marine corporal named Kenneth J. T. ("Ken") Williams, hopped up in the cab with me. Also a World War II veteran, he had injured a knee during a coastal raid in North Korea and had been assigned to lead the mess until his injured knee healed. A Welshman by birth, he inescapably had been tagged with the nickname "Taffy," which, for some strange reason, most British troops called the Welsh. Supposedly, it had something to do with their love of candy.

We finally got rolling, with Colonel Drysdale in the lead, followed by Mac Corwin. The trip from Hamhung to Hagaru was about sixty-four miles long, mostly on fairly good, level road. As far as the terrain was concerned, the worst part of the journey undoubtedly would be the narrow, twisting Funchilin Pass, with, as someone later described, "a cliff on one side and a chasm on the other."

The ride went smoothly for the first forty miles. We stopped at Chinhung-ni, near the foot of the pass, for a break, while the convoy leader checked the road conditions ahead. The U.S. Marines immediately started looking around for coffee, but the British called for their tea. Someone took a couple of burners from the back of my truck and fired them up so that the Royal Marines could enjoy "a cuppa." The weather was turning bitterly cold, and some warming tents belonging to the 1st Battalion, 1st Marines, which was the defensive force in the area, felt wonderful, if only for a few minutes.

Being on the road together for the better part of the day, Corporal Williams and I got to know one another well. We exchanged stories of our families and, during occasional stops, looked at the photographs that we each carried in our wallets. He was married, and both he and his wife hailed from Neath, Wales. He had joined the British Army at age fifteen during World War II and later switched to the Royal Marines, where he served sea duty tours on Royal Navy ships. He had been transferred in August 1950 to join 41 Commando.

We finally got back on the MSR and started to move up the pass. It was still in bad condition. We were held up several times as the engineers continued their efforts to widen the curves and sharp bends along the way. The road was packed with snow and ice. Because we were not using tire chains, it was slow going, and we had to rely on lower gears and six-wheel drive.

We arrived at Koto-ri late in the afternoon, with ten miles to go. Colonel Drysdale was informed that the MSR between Koto-ri and Hagaru had been closed, off and on, by enemy attacks. Darkness was quickly approaching, and the convoy received word from division headquarters to wait until dawn before proceeding. We found Koto-ri absolutely jammed with vehicles from other convoys and with troops and equipment waiting to head north. Still more vehicles arrived after us.

The Marines of Company G, 3d Battalion, 1st Marines (G/3/1), had come up from below the pass where the regiment had been previously located. Their strength was 205 officers and men, and they, too, were headed to Hagaru to join up with their battalion. Company B, 31st Regiment, U.S. Army 7th Infantry Division (B/31/7), numbering 190 officers and men, was also headed north with its own transportation; it had been ordered to move east of the Chosin Reservoir and join up with the rest of the regiment.

The commandos pitched shelter halves (tents), but most of

the drivers decided to sleep in their trucks. The drivers with the foresight to bring along their sleeping bags spent a much more comfortable night than the rest of us. Many of the commandos and drivers also stood perimeter watch that night, but it turned out to be fairly quiet.

Just after dawn, the camp was aroused by an alarm signaling an attack. The drivers were put on a defensive line with the others, but nothing came of it. Little did we know that the other regiments had been under heavy attack that very night and were battling for their lives at such places as Yudam-ni, Toktong Pass, and Hagaru. The lack of reliable information, or "straight scoop," at the lower levels of command was always a problem and resulted in all types of rumors. Some commanders believed that the "snuffies" (the men in the lower ranks) did not need to know the big picture.

Chow was served that morning, actually a hot meal for the Royal Marines, and someone built a bonfire to help us get warm. The commandos, as well as other infantrymen, were loading up with hand grenades and throwing the empty containers on the fire. Made of a heavy cardboard-type material, they burned slowly and hot, thus adding to the comfort margin of the men who stood around the fire. Then, some idiot, and he was never identified, tossed a container in the fire before removing the grenade.

No one knows how long it took for the grenade to "cook off." I had just walked away from the fire when I heard a loud boom, and I immediately looked back to see a large dark cloud of black soot and smoke over the fire. In a way, it was funny— several black-faced U.S. and British Marines standing around, wondering what had happened—but there was no comedy in the results. Several men, including one truck driver from my outfit, were wounded by the exploding fragments. Our driver was taken to the aid station, and Sergeant Dickerson was assigned to drive his truck.

Added to the troops and equipment waiting to move north were some sixty members of the 1st Marine Division's Headquarters Battalion headed for Hagaru, where the division CP was now located. So, on that cold, dreary morning of 29 November, about eight hundred men and more than 140

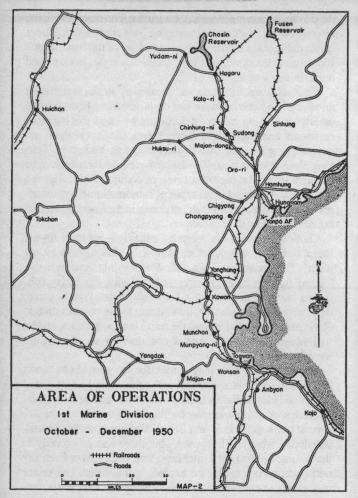

Area of operations, 1st Marine Division in North Korea, October–December 1950. (Source: Lynn Montross and Nicholas A. Canzona, *U.S. Marine Operations in Korea, 1950–1953,* vol. 3, *The Chosin Reservoir Campaign* [Washington, D.C.: Historical Branch, G-3, Headquarters Marine Corps, 1957], inside back cover.)

vehicles were waiting to move out to the north. Because of the size of the column, Col. Chesty Puller designated the convoy "Task Force Drysdale," under the command of the senior Royal Marine.

The infantry moved out first on foot, while the vehicles and other troops waited at Koto-ri. The British Marines took the hill just east of the village, and plans were made for Company G (G/3/1) to pass through the British lines and attack a hill farther out from the village, with B/31/7 in reserve. The Marines of G/3/1 ran into well-entrenched CCF troops near their objective and neutralized them. Along with the commandos, they continued to move ahead for two miles north of Koto-ri, where they met heavier resistance from enemy machine guns and mortars fired from higher ground. They were then ordered to withdraw down to the road and wait for further orders.

The word came down that three platoons of tanks from Company D would be available to lead the convoy, and they would arrive sometime around noon. Company D, now commanded by Capt. Bruce W. Clarke, was coming up from the town of Majon-dong. Clarke had come on active duty from the 11th Tank Battalion at San Diego and, at one time, had been my commanding officer. Another message reported that Company B tanks, coming from their positions south of Majon-dong, were also headed for Koto-ri.

At 1400, our convoy moved out from Koto-ri with Company D tanks leading, followed by G/3/1 on its trucks, with 41 Independent Commando on our tank battalion trucks, B/31/7 riding on Army trucks, and about seventeen trucks and Jeeps from Headquarters Battalion. With the three platoons of tanks leading and Company B tanks coming on to bring up the rear, we now had more than 170 vehicles and 950 men in the motorized column. It would take several hours before the last vehicles in the column could leave Koto-ri.

The going was very slow. Periodically, the convoy was fired on from the hills. The vehicles had to stop so that the troops could dismount and return fire until things quieted down. We could clearly see the enemy soldiers up in the hills as they ran between pine trees.

Because of the great length of the column, coupled with the

accordion effect from the stop-and-go movement, it was already dark by the time the column pulled off the MSR and onto a frozen streambed. While we waited for the tanks to be refueled, Captain Clarke told Colonel Drysdale that he thought the tanks could continue, but he had doubts about the "thin-skinned" (wheeled) vehicles. Drysdale radioed ahead to Hagaru with this information, and General Smith informed him that the convoy must get through at all costs. The troops were badly needed at the division CP in Hagaru.

Unfortunately, when the column pulled out onto the road again, it was pitch dark. Vehicles from different units were mixed together, and unit integrity was lost as some infantry troops and service and support troops merged. Only the lead vehicles, Company D tanks and G/3/1, somehow managed to keep their vehicles and men together.

Continuing to move north, we traveled without lights and remained close to the vehicle ahead to watch for its blacked-out brake lights. I was following Pfc. Theron L. ("Leon") Hilburn, a San Diego buddy, and he was directly behind Cpl. Clifford R. ("Roy") Hawkins from our company. We had been receiving small-arms fire from both sides of the road. Soon, I was driving with the door open, my left foot on the running board, and my right foot on the gas pedal—ready to jump if necessary. I braced the door with my left hand, while I steered with my right. On the other side of the cab, Corporal Williams was riding in much the same manner.

Suddenly, from both sides of the road, came a steady stream of tracers from enemy machine guns. Bullets hit Hawkins's truck and practically shot the engine right out of it. The vehicle stopped dead. Before he could try to get it off to the side of the road, all hell broke loose. Hilburn ground his truck to a halt and, diving for a ditch, yelled back to me that the road was blocked. By this time, Williams and I had done the same thing. Small-arms, machine-gun, and mortar fire started sweeping the road. Amid complete chaos, troops piled off of vehicles and yelled for their buddies and units.

The ditch on the right (east) side of the roadway was fairly deep and provided excellent cover and concealment. It sloped up to a railroad bed with a set of narrow-gauge tracks. The

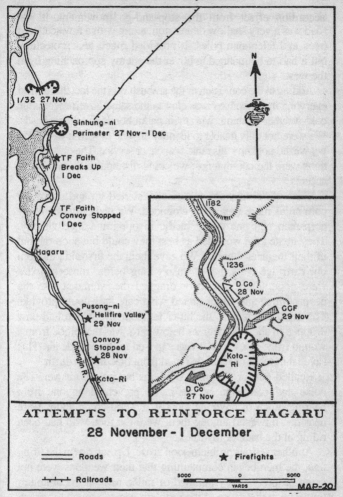

## ATTEMPTS TO REINFORCE HAGARU
### 28 November - 1 December

Roads ★ Firefights

Railroads

MAP-20

The battle around Hagaru, North Korea, 1950. (Source: Lynn Montross and Nicholas A. Canzona, *U.S. Marine Operations in Korea, 1950–1953,* vol. 3, *The Chosin Reservoir Campaign* [Washington, D.C.: Historical Branch, G-3, Headquarters Marine Corps, 1957], 226.)

slope offered good firing positions. On the left side of the road was a very shallow depression, along with a few scattered trees and telephone poles. It provided much less protection, but it had to be manned to cover the enemy approaching from the west.

Adding to the confusion of the ambush was the fact that almost everyone in the convoy was clad in the same government-issue cold-weather clothing, with their parka hoods over their heads. We were not only unable to identify anyone to whom we spoke, but we did not know his rank, branch, or service. The only exceptions were the commandos; we could distinguish them by their accents.

Cries of "corpsman" or "medic" started up and down the column as more men were wounded. We had only one Navy corpsman and one Army medic in our immediate vicinity. They treated the wounded as best they could but soon ran out of their medical supplies. We gave them the first-aid kits from our cartridge belts, but it wasn't long before those supplies were gone. They carried or dragged the wounded into the deepest ditch and administered what care they could provide. The one advantage to the bitter temperature, which had now dropped to about 20 degrees below zero, was that blood from a wound froze as soon as it was exposed to the outside air. This saved a number of wounded men from bleeding to death.

I called out for Corporal Williams but got no answer. The noise and confusion of the battle prevented anyone from hearing much of anything clearly. Several commandos were near me, however; among them were the men who had been riding in the back of my truck.

Another serious problem soon arose. Up and down the firing line, the men began complaining that their weapons were not firing properly—they jammed or failed to feed the ammunition. The major cause of the problem was too much lubricant. Trained to keep a light coating of oil on our weapons, we had no idea that we would be fighting in such extreme cold and did not realize the effects of subzero temperatures on our weapons. The rifles of several men failed to eject spent shells. I took out my carbine bayonet and was able to pry out the cartridges from some of them. I had to take off at least one glove to do this, and the cold became too much to bear.

The only members of my company whom I could locate were Hilburn, Hawkins, Cpl. Ernest E. ("Ernie") Hayton (another buddy from San Diego), and Cpl. William ("Bill") Harrison. I had no idea as to how many of our trucks were traveling ahead or behind me because of the mix-up after we had stopped by the streambed.

Just a few hundred yards before we had been ambushed, an MP had signaled me to pull over and stop. He said that he was putting three prisoners on the back of my truck and he would be riding with them. If we got into trouble and had to get off and fight, he added, the three POWs would be the first to go. When we were stopped by enemy fire, the POWs tried to run, but they were shot and killed.

As we started setting up hasty defenses, I found that large numbers of B/31/7 soldiers were around us, as well as several MPs from our division's Military Police Company. It was still pitch dark, and the only illumination was coming from the enemy's machine-gun tracers. We didn't have a single machine gun with us. A few officers and NCOs (noncommissioned officers) were trying desperately to get our defense organized, but the lack of unit integrity hampered their efforts. Finally, Marine W.O. Lloyd Dirst, assigned to the MP company, came marching up the road as he yelled that he wanted "some Marines, some *real* Marines," to get out of the ditches and start firing. It was obvious that he had seen some of the soldiers, huddled in the ditch, who were not firing back at the enemy. For his efforts, Dirst was shot in the head while he tried so bravely to rally the troops. He was pulled into the large ditch and evacuated several days later, but he never completely recovered from his wounds. He was a true Marine hero and was later awarded the Navy Cross for his action.

Not long after we had hopped off the trucks, a British Marine next to me said that he needed a weapon; he had lost his in the confusion of getting off the vehicles. We were looking for one among the wounded when someone said, "That captain down in that hole has two of 'em. Get one from him." It was so dark that we couldn't see the bottom of the ditch, but an

American Army officer had taken refuge in a hole, rather than lead his men. The commando yelled down that he needed a weapon and a frightened voice replied, "You can't have one of these."

The Royal Marine grabbed my carbine, pointed it down toward the hole, and said, "Captain, I've got a bloody weapon pointed down at you. If you don't hand me up one of yours, I'm bloody well opening fire."

A shaky hand reached up slowly with a rifle. The commando then returned my carbine, and we got back to the business of fighting the enemy.

The Chinese Communists continued to pour across the streambed on the west side of the road and over the level ground just east of the railroad tracks. By this time, our men had both sides of the road well covered. We did not anticipate that the enemy would approach us from the south because the men in the vehicles behind us were continuing their own fight. To the north, several men lay on or underneath the lead truck to cover that approach. As Chinese infantrymen came at us, we continued to mow down their ranks, although we had only small arms—rifles, carbines, and pistols—and a few hand grenades that were soon used up. Suddenly, not far from my vehicle, a truck was hit by an enemy mortar round and began to burn. Casting an eerie glow over the scene, the flames silhouetted anyone foolish enough to stick his head above the level of the ditch. Someone said that the burning truck was carrying ammunition. Although it never blew up, it burned for several hours.

The Chinese had set up their mortar on the west side of the road, out in a streambed, not more than 150 yards away. We actually saw the flashes from the tubes and heard the sound of "duke, duke, duke." Then, we waited for the incoming high-explosive round to detonate. The Chinese began dropping their mortar rounds right into the large ditch, where they landed among the dead and wounded and killed more men. As I lay in the ditch and reloaded my carbine, my foot struck something hard and I reached down to find a pack radio that someone had been carrying. I attempted to call out on it but received no answer. Not being overly familiar with that type of radio, I'm not sure that I even had it turned on.

The men firing at the flashes couldn't seem to stop the mortar from firing. We figured that the enemy soldiers were replacing the mortar crews as fast as we were killing them. Directly behind my truck was an Army weapons carrier with a 75-mm recoilless rifle mounted right behind the cab, and someone yelled out for the crew. Three or four soldiers braved the enemy fire still sweeping the roadway and climbed aboard the vehicle. Waiting for illumination from the next mortar flash, they bore-sighted the gun tube and prepared to fire. They managed to crank off two rounds before they were all hit, either killed or wounded, by enemy small-arms fire, but that mortar did not fire again that night.

In the meantime, some Army NCOs ran over to the hole where their captain was hiding and asked for directions and orders. The captain mumbled something about "good defenses," but I couldn't hear him very well. He did not come out from the safety of his hole.

In the distance behind us, we could hear the rumble and roar of tanks as Company B was trying to move forward, but they ran into the same problems as had the rest of us—a jammed roadway and a heavy volume of enemy fire. Our hopes faded as the tanks turned around. When the sounds of their engines faded in the darkness, we realized that they were headed back to the RCT-1 command post. At this point, I could not help but think, as I had done several times during the night, that if I had been able to transfer to Company B tanks, I would not be in this terrible mess. More than likely, I would have been riding in tank B-22 with Sergeant Dolby and my buddy, Chief Aguirre. But, as often happens in war, fate was about to take a strange turn of events.

As the night wore on, our men began to run low on ammunition and the situation worsened. I had a stash of more than three hundred rounds of carbine ammunition under the seat of my truck and had managed to crawl up onto the road and retrieve it. I passed it out to those men armed with carbines, mostly truck drivers and senior NCOs; the infantrymen, including the commandos, were armed with M1 rifles. Keeping plenty of rounds for myself, I spent a good deal of time reloading magazines. I quickly learned that prolonged bursts of automatic rifle fire were inaccurate and a waste of precious ammunition.

The Chinese continued to approach from three sides. They let us know, with their bugles, whistles, and even a cymbal-type musical instrument used as signals to direct their troops during the assault, that we were all but surrounded. Of course, we had no idea what the signals meant, but the noise added to our feeling of absolute helplessness and the knowledge that we would soon be surrounded on all sides. At one point during the night, a Chinese bugler evidently blew a cease-fire because the enemy immediately stopped firing. There was a strange lull, and we couldn't figure out what was happening. Later, we learned that the Chinese were trying to determine if we were ready to surrender. We began to see figures popping up before us in a field as they came out from their cover and places of concealment. Directly in front of me, not more than fifty yards from the railroad bed, appeared three figures. I slipped the selector switch on my M2 carbine to automatic and fired a short burst, starting with the figure on the left. All three went down screaming, moaned for a while, and then fell silent. All around me, others were having similar experiences. The Chinese might have "called" for a cease-fire, but we certainly didn't understand it and nobody told us to stop firing.

Someone came running up the road from behind us and yelled for the drivers of the vehicles to get in them and start turning them around. I recognized this individual from one of our early stops a short way out of Koto-ri, when his Jeep was parked directly behind my truck. As we stood out there watching the CCF troops dart back and forth among the trees, I had asked him if he was an officer; he had no rank insignia showing. He had said that he was the assistant G-4 (logistics officer) of the 1st Marine Division and identified himself as Lt. Col. Arthur Chidester.

Several of us jumped into our trucks, and two vehicles managed to get turned around, but the hopeless traffic jam prevented us from going anywhere. Shortly after we saw him, Colonel Chidester was wounded and captured. He was never seen or heard from again.

Later, we were stopped for a while when a Jeep came roaring down from the north. In it was Royal Marine Maj. Dennis Aldridge, second in command of 41 Commando. When he had reached Hagaru with part of his unit, he wondered what had happened to the rest of the commandos. He had driven all the way back through five miles of enemy-held territory. We couldn't figure out how he had gotten this far without being blown off the road.

Aldridge asked what was going on, took a look around, and soon realized our predicament. Just about the time I was explaining about the situation behind us, two Chinese soldiers broke from cover and began running straight toward the lead truck, which was very close to us. Pulling out his .45 Colt automatic, Aldridge said something like "there go a couple of blokes now" and brought them both down as I was taking aim with my carbine. Seeing there was nothing he could do and feeling that he belonged back with his unit, he hopped back into the Jeep and drove the five miles back to Hagaru! I could only reason that, because nothing in that five-mile gap had stopped Aldridge, the CCF troops had moved down to where the action was.

Knowing that some of the commandos had made it to Hagaru, we thought that perhaps G/3/1 had gotten through, as well, because it had been in front of the 41 Commando convoy. Rumors were beginning to spread, and the men were starting to speculate about this and that unit. Did it get through? Was any help coming for us?

What we did not know, and had no way of knowing, was that Company D tanks, G/3/1, and about 40 percent of the commandos had managed to reach Hagaru. Although they had heavy casualties and lost one tank, these units constituted nearly one-third of the entire task force. To the rear, another third had managed to turn and fight its way back to Koto-ri. The middle third was us—some sixty commandos; nearly all of B/31/7; many personnel from Headquarters Battalion, including at least twenty MPs; and, of course, the vehicle drivers.

Making the situation even more serious was the fact that the Chinese had split our middle section of the convoy into three smaller segments, with each group fighting its own battle and separated by several hundred yards. This tactic prevented the groups from consolidating and communicating.

As ammunition continued to dwindle, some men who had run out groped around among the dead and seriously wounded for whatever they could find. We knew that there was ammunition in some of the trucks, but, because of the earlier convoy mix-up, no one knew where these trucks were located. It was practically suicide to stand up on the roadway, especially with the light from the burning truck. Several men were hit while looking for ammunition among the abandoned vehicles.

Casualties grew as additional enemy mortar rounds walked up and down the road and the ditch. Hayton and Hawkins were both peppered with shrapnel, and I had a fragment in the side of my left knee, but we all remained on the firing line. Harrison had been hit pretty badly in the leg and hand, and he was now in the large ditch with the other wounded. From our driver section, only Hilburn had escaped injury, although I still did not know where Dickerson was.

Down the road, two soldiers had managed to turn around a Jeep and head back to Koto-ri for help. Frank Noel, an AP photographer who had been traveling with our convoy, went with them. They didn't get very far before they were captured by the Chinese. A short time later, they were told to return to our perimeter and tell us that, unless we surrendered, an all-out attack would be launched and we would all die. With the number of casualties and the ammunition situation, we didn't know how we were going to get out of the trap. Dawn would break in about an hour, however, and there was always the hope of Marine close air support.

With Colonel Chidester missing, the senior officer present was Maj. John N. McLaughlin, an assistant G-3 officer assigned to the 1st Marine Division but attached to the U.S. Army's X Corps as a liaison officer to the division. When he received the message sent by the Chinese, he gathered us around him and left the decision to us. By this time, there were about forty or fifty in our group who were still standing.

Several of us told McLaughlin that we would not surrender to the North Koreans. We knew their past track record with

American prisoners, and we still weren't positive about who was out there shooting at us, the North Koreans or the Chinese. McLaughlin walked down the road to the enemy CP to negotiate and learned that our enemy consisted of CCF troops. There were no North Korean units with them. The major agreed to the surrender on the condition that our most seriously wounded be returned to Koto-ri. He tried to stall for time, in the hope of air support at dawn, but the Chinese were also aware of this possibility and gave him only a few minutes to make his decision.

While McLaughlin was gone, the rest of us went around shaking hands and saying good-bye to those whom we knew. Many of us thought this was really it, and we resolved to take as many of the enemy with us as we could.

Major McLaughlin returned with the information about the Chinese units and told us of the plan for the wounded. We decided that, if those poor bastards could have a chance for survival, we would take our chances with the terms of surrender. After we agreed to the terms, the Chinese soldiers ceased all firing. The battle of what was later to be known as Hell Fire Valley was over, and Task Force Drysdale had ceased to exist. Early on the morning of 30 November 1950, the survivors of that battle were about to become prisoners of war.

# === 7 ===

# Capture

DAWN HAD COME—too late to help us—and all along the frozen road, men were starting to assemble as they stumbled around dazed and numb, in a state of shock, and wondered how this could have happened. Foremost in our minds were the questions: "What happens to us now?" "Should we have trusted the Chinese?" "Will they really evacuate our wounded?" And, certainly, "Will we be marched away to some remote area, only to be shot and left to rot?"

We had little knowledge of how the Chinese Communists treated their prisoners of war. They had not been involved in the war long enough for us to have captured many and to learn enough about them through our interrogation process. We had no doubts about the NKPA. The stories of their despicable brutality and their penchant for summary executions were well known. Many of these stories had been confirmed.

I was busy smashing the stock of my carbine against the bumper of a truck when I felt a sudden tap on my right shoulder. I turned and was face to face with a Chinese soldier, not more than 5 feet 2 inches tall, standing with his right hand outstretched toward me. Over his left shoulder was slung a brand-new Thompson submachine gun. I thought that he wanted my carbine, but he grabbed my hand and began to shake it vigorously. I would learn later that he was congratulating me for having surrendered. He had a wide grin on his face, and he seemed happier than a pig. After all, he had won the battle.

From our position at the north end of the Chinese ambush site, we could see a line of our vehicles stretching to the south for several hundred yards. Littering the roadway and skewered at all angles, some were wrecked and others only stalled, but all of them had been riddled by small-arms fire and chunks of shrapnel.

Oddly enough, the Chinese seemed much more interested in looting our trucks than in rounding up American and British prisoners. On several vehicles, all I could see were the heels of the looters' boots sticking up in the air, as they burrowed like rats through the cargo and searched for anything of value.

One of the 6 × 6s had been carrying mail, including Christmas packages meant for one of the Marine regiments. Bright pieces of wrapping paper fluttered in the cold wind as the Chinese infantrymen ripped open package after package and found wristwatches, pen and pencil sets, food, and other gifts that would never reach their intended recipients. Many Marines had written home to ask for heavy ski-type socks because the standard-issue boot sock was not heavy enough for the shoe pack. The Chinese looters had found several packages of these types of socks and were waving them around in the air, wildly, like so many trophies.

Another truck had been carrying PX (post exchange) supplies, including different kinds of candy and gum, commonly referred to by Marines as "pogey bait." The Chinese troops dove in greedily. It was obvious that many were getting their first taste of such things as chocolate Tootsie Rolls, Baby Ruths, and Dentyne chewing gum.

I began looking around for Harrison and finally found him lying in the ditch among the seriously wounded. I told him that we had surrendered and would probably be leaving shortly. He said that he was hit too badly to walk and would stay there and take his chances. I mumbled something like, "Good luck, see ya later," and walked back to join the others.

Passing the line of shot-up trucks and Jeeps, I came alongside the 6 x 6 that had burned for so long during the night. The tires had all burned; the vehicle was resting on its rims. Anything on it or in it that could burn had surely done so. In the truck's cab on the passenger side was one of the most gruesome sights that I would ever see. A trooper had been sitting inside the cab while the truck burned. The fire had been so hot and had burned for so long that his flesh had disintegrated and his clothing was burned away from what remained of his skeletal body. Yet, still on his head, which had been reduced to not much more than a skull, was his steel helmet. He was sitting upright, tilted back against the rear of the cab—a truly horrible scene. I could only hope that he had been killed, where he sat, early in the firefight.

A Chinese officer must have finally passed the word to knock off the pillaging. More CCF troops began to gather around us, and they lined us up for an accurate head count. As the morning light increased, we began to take stock of the carnage around us. We had dozens of dead and wounded in the big ditch, and some lay dead on the road and in the vehicles. But, on three sides of where we had taken up our defensive positions and particularly to the east of the road were the bodies of more than a hundred dead Chinese infantrymen.

By now, the road was swarming with Chinese troops. Hearing a plane coming down the valley, we looked skyward to see a single Marine F4U Corsair coming in low. When the pilot got to our position, he began circling slowly as he looked over the situation. Some of us held our hands over our heads to show him that we had been captured, but he was so low that he probably realized that. We could see the pilot clearly in his cockpit. The Chinese made no attempt to fire at the circling Corsair.

With the roundup of prisoners, Dickerson finally appeared. He had spent the entire night hiding under some gear in the back of a truck. He had fired at those approaching from that angle of the truck and tossed back hand grenades lobbed into the truck. Although peppered with shrapnel, he had not been seriously wounded. Hayton had been with him for a while and got the same treatment.

We could now account for six of our drivers from Service Company, 1st Tank Battalion—Harrison wounded in the ditch and five of us still standing. There was no way to know where the other sixteen vehicles had been in the convoy because of the mix-up and the pitch-dark night. We could only hope and pray that they had made it through to Hagaru or had been far enough back in the convoy to turn around and get back to Koto-ri.

A real surprise for me was to see my old World War II buddy, Cpl. Theodore R. ("Ted") Wheeler, from the Phoenix, Arizona, Reserves. I knew that he was in Korea because we had been on board the same ship coming over, but I had no idea where he had been assigned. He was driving a truck in the convoy for Service Battalion, somewhere behind us, when the ambush was set. He and I were to share some interesting experiences during the coming months.

I was still looking around for my new British friend, Ken Williams, but he was not among us. In fact, I had not seen him among the dead or wounded while I had been looking for Harrison. Incredibly, it would be forty years to the day before Ken and I would meet again and I would hear the story of his amazing ordeal of survival.

In November 1990, more than 1,500 veterans of the Chosin Reservoir campaign were reunited in Las Vegas, Nevada. Attending from Great Britain were twenty-five veterans of the 41 Independent Commando, among them former Royal Marine Kenneth Williams. After much hugging and not a few tears, we got down to discussing what had happened that night forty years before.

Immediately after jumping from my truck, Williams had moved forward to try to locate his comrades. Some officer grabbed him and put him in charge of ten men. He told them to defend the right side of the road and sent a U.S. Marine sergeant with another ten men to defend the left side of the road. Williams and his men fought all night, as had the rest of us; by 0400, there were only four of the original ten left. Ken took up a firing position under a truck, and he had a couple of hand grenades with him. By the light of the burning truck (he could not have been very far forward of my position), he saw one of two enemy soldiers toss a grenade under the truck and he felt his right leg hit. He tossed one of his own grenades to a soldier who was behind him, and that soldier, in turn, lobbed it over the truck and killed both of the Chinese. The soldier was then killed in a burst of automatic fire.

A Chinese officer took up a position in the big ditch, right next to Williams's truck, and started commanding his troops with whistle blasts. Ken waited until the other CCF troops had moved away from the immediate vicinity before taking a bead on the officer, who either didn't know Ken was there or thought he was dead. Ken killed the officer and two more Chinese troops who came running up minutes later to find out why the whistle commands had stopped. Taking advantage of the situation, Ken crawled out from under the truck and, grabbing onto vehicles for support, started hobbling down the road. He heard groans coming from one of the trucks and found a badly wounded U.S. Marine huddled inside. Ken pulled the Marine out of the truck, started treating his wounds, and gave him a shot of the precious morphine from a medical kit.

Ken then realized that he, himself, needed medical attention. He found part of the grenade's fuse sticking out of his knee and pulled it out with a knife. Then, he poured some brandy from his medical kit on the wound and drank the rest.

Ken and another wounded Marine got into a Jeep and managed to get it started, although Ken had never driven a vehicle. With the use of only one arm, one leg, and one foot between the two of them, they drove down the road for a half mile before being stopped by a Chinese soldier brandishing a Thompson submachine gun. They could stop the Jeep only by running it into a bank of dirt.

They were taken to a farm and placed in a barnlike structure with four Americans. Abandoned by the Chinese when our larger group was marched away to the log cabins, Williams and his group lay there in a straw bed for days, with only some small tins of hard biscuits for their fare. One by one, the men started dying. On the eighth day, when the U.S. Marines came down the road from Hagaru during the withdrawal from the Chosin Reservoir, they found only Ken and one other man alive. He and Pfc. Marvin E. Pugh, USMC, were the last survivors of Task Force Drysdale to be rescued.

\* \* \*

As we waited on the road, it was apparent to me that many of the military police and service troops who had fought in the battle that night were Marine World War II veterans. To their credit, they had performed admirably and had accounted for themselves well when the going got tough. The Marine Corps' age-old insistence on its training demands and the principle that every Marine be trained as a rifleman first had paid off.

When the roundup of prisoners was completed, 123 of us could stand up to be counted—some 35 U.S. Marines and 20 Royal Marines, with the balance being U.S. Army personnel, mainly from B/31/7.

It would be several weeks before those units involved in Task Force Drysdale could account for their personnel and arrive at an approximate casualty figure. Because of the confusion commonly referred to as the "fog of battle" and the scattering of our units, a true account would never be known. Although only approximations, the following figures are as close as one can get for accountability. Of the 900 men involved, more than 300 were casualties: 40 dead, 160 wounded, and 125 missing in action. Almost all of the MIAs eventually became prisoners of war.

The casualties of the 1st Tank Battalion had been moderate because the majority of its personnel had been traveling in armored vehicles. Company D, leading the fated convoy, had made it to Hagaru with the loss of one tank, 10 wounded, and 1 MIA. Company B, assigned to bring up the rear, had 2 dead, including a first sergeant, and 12 wounded. Service Company, in addition to the 5 drivers listed as MIAs, had 6 other wounded, including Corporal Harrison. Master Sergeant Corwin, who was leading our section of the convoy, was killed when, according to a witness, two Chinese soldiers popped up from the big ditch and riddled his Jeep with their Thompson submachine guns.

During the early morning hours of the ambush and subsequent firefight in Hell Fire Valley, probably during the first bugle-call cease-fire, two or three of the groups located to the south of our position were able to link up with each other. Among them were Capt. Michael Capraro, 1st Marine Division public information officer, and 1st Lt. John ("Jack") Buck, aide to Brig. Gen. Edward A. ("Eddie") Craig, assistant division commander. They had been in the group closest to us.

To the south of them was Maj. Henry ("Pop") Seeley, the division motor transport officer, along with several more Marines. Led by Major Seeley, Captain Capraro, and Lieutenant Buck, this group of Marines, commandos, and soldiers fought their way southwest across the river. Several hours later, they reached the safety of the 1st Regimental Combat Team CP at Koto-ri. Still later in the day, more soldiers from B/31/7 straggled back to this CP.

Considering the circumstances, most of the units in Task Force Drysdale had acquitted themselves well. Less than twenty-four hours later, a task force comprised of three U.S. Army battalions met a similar fate on the eastern shore of the Chosin Reservoir while trying to reach Hagaru. Of the 2,500 soldiers involved in this action, fewer than half reached safety, with most of the wounded suffering from the effects of severe frostbite. Fewer than 250 of approximately 1,200 MIAs ended up in POW camps; the remainder were unaccounted for.

The Chosin Reservoir campaign continued for another twelve days. Many military history books would record it as one of the most bitter defeats in the history of the United Nations (UN). The 1st Marine Division suffered more than 700 dead, 200 missing, and more than 3,500 wounded. In addition, there were more than 7,000 nonbattle casualties, mostly the result of cold-related injuries. The authors of these books, however, tend to exaggerate the Allied losses in this campaign by disregarding the fact that the four CCF field armies opposing the 1st Marine Division totaled almost 120,000 men. The Chinese and North Koreans both suffered near-annihilation, with a casualty count in the tens of thousands, enormous totals that would remain unknown, even to the Chinese Communist leaders themselves. (In 1952, the 1st Marine Division would receive a Presidential Unit Citation for its part in the campaign; see appendix A.)

When the Chinese finally gathered together all of us who could walk, we were marched off the roadway, under armed guard, to some small huts in a valley only a few hundred yards

away. Those of us who had not been wounded and those with
lesser wounds helped the more seriously wounded men. It was
obvious that many had opted to come along with us, rather than
lie in the ditch and freeze to death in temperatures hovering
around 20 degrees below zero. The Chinese allowed some of
the more seriously wounded to be taken to some nearby
houses, although no evacuation had started yet.

We hadn't been in the huts very long when the guards
herded us outside again, and we began marching up a long,
narrow valley that led into the hills. During this move, I suddenly realized that, underneath my parka, I was still wearing
the Soviet-made Tokarev semi-automatic pistol in a holster on
my cartridge belt; we had not been searched. Fearing what
might happen if I were caught with the gun and trying to avoid
any unnecessary attention, I reached under my parka and field-
stripped the pistol as we walked along. Piece by piece, I tossed
or dropped the gun parts into the snow. Later, I removed the
holster and tossed it, too.

As we climbed up the valley, we witnessed an incredible
event. The Chinese had found a 75-mm recoilless rifle positioned on a tripod in the rear of a weapons carrier that had fired
on them during the night. Pulling the rifle off the truck, the Chinese set it up on the ground and began to examine it closely.
Obviously, they were not familiar with this weapon. They
managed to open the breech, and one of them slammed in a
round. With four or five of them crowded directly behind the
gun, they fired it! The back-blast knocked them all on their collective asses and injured several of them. The snickering of
Marines, who found some small degree of satisfaction in the
stupidity and bad luck of these Chinese, could be heard up and
down our column.

At the top of the valley, well hidden in the pine trees to conceal them from the possibility of observation from the air, were
two large log cabins, apparently of recent construction, and we
were ushered inside. We would have a good deal more room in
them than in the tiny farm huts.

When we got settled in, a Chinese officer, speaking excellent English, came by and introduced himself as Lieutenant
Fung. He began by congratulating us for surrendering and then

stated that we would not be harmed in any way. He added that all of the wounded would be treated and we would be taken to "a comfortable prison camp in the North," where we would be "reeducated" and then "placed on a neutral ship bound for the United States."

There seemed to be no end to the good news that this officer had for us—treatment for our wounds, a comfortable camp, good schooling, and then a nice boat ride home. Hell, according to him, this POW life wasn't going to be so bad, after all. Actually, few, if any, of us believed that things would be as easy as Fung described, but little did we realize that, during the coming months, lies, deceit, and broken promises by our Chinese Communist hosts would be the order of the day.

A short time later, some Chinese medics came into our cabin and began to examine the wounded. They made ineffective attempts to help the more serious cases, but they were hampered by a lack of basic medical supplies. Their aid consisted of little more than bandaging or bandage changing.

In a few hours, some of the Chinese soldiers came trudging up the valley with cases of rations salvaged from our trucks. It was the last American food we would taste for quite some time. The POWs were separated into groups of four, with each group receiving one can of peas, corn, or tomatoes and one small can of dessert. It only amounted to a few bites per man, while the rest of the food was eagerly consumed by our hungry guards.

The shock was beginning to wear off, and we began to talk about what might be in store for us. We discussed escape but ruled it out because at least five miles lay between us and the nearest friendly lines in either direction. Also, it was broad daylight, and the area was teeming with CCF troops. Someone brought up the possibility of early release—maybe they didn't have the facilities needed to keep us all as prisoners. After a few hours, men began to drift off to sleep. Almost thirty-six hours had passed since any of us had slept.

Shortly before dawn, we were awakened by our guards, and Lieutenant Fung ordered all truck and tank drivers to fall out— we were to move some of the vehicles into hiding for later use

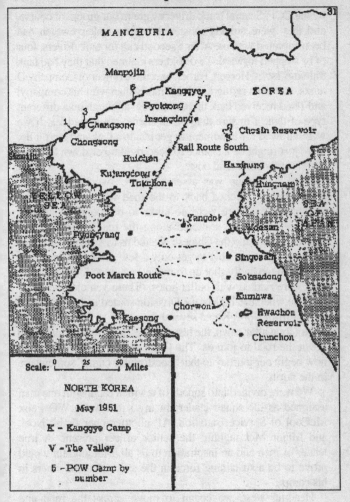

The route of U.S. prisoners of war from Kanggye to Chunchon, North Korea, 1951. (Source: James Angus MacDonald, Jr., *Problems of U.S. Marine Corps Prisoners of War in Korea* [Washington, D.C.: History and Museums Division, Headquarters Marine Corps, 1988], 81.)

by the CCF. Several truck drivers were in our group, of course, and they were quickly mustered, but no tank crewmen had been captured with us. After a second call for tank drivers, four of us stepped forward. Two soldiers claimed that they had tank training; 1st Lt. Herbert Turner, executive officer of Company D tanks, had been riding in a Jeep, rather than with his company; and I had received tank driver training, although on a different type of tank. I'm sure that we all shared the same idea. If we were allowed for a moment to get inside a tank and start it up, there just might be a chance to head right up or down the road to a friendly command post.

Once our group was assembled, we "would-be" drivers were quickly marched back to the road where we had been ambushed, but there were no tanks to be found. Dozens of other vehicles were scattered along the roadway and in the roadside ditch, and the Chinese wanted us to move them out of the way. We were able to get only a few of them started, but they were too badly shot up to move; radiators, fuel tanks, and tires were riddled with bullet holes. (These vehicles were still in place when the 1st Marine Division started its historic withdrawal from North Korea several days later.)

Not long after dawn, the rest of the prisoners came marching down the road to join us. The Chinese told us that we would now begin our journey to that "comfortable camp" somewhere in the north.

We were divided into squads of ten men each, with one man assigned as the squad leader. In my squad were WO Felix McCool of Service Battalion, AP photographer Frank Noel, and Major McLaughlin, the senior officer present. A true leader of men and an inspiration to us all, McLaughlin would prove to be a sustaining force in the survival of prisoners in his camp.

Heading west, we began to move across the road and climbed a ridgeline, where we grabbed a last look at the scene of destruction below us. The wounded had been moved, by whom or to where, we did not know, but the dead were still lying in the ditch. As we continued down the other side of the ridgeline, we stopped on a frozen riverbed for several hours, while the Chinese leaders waited for word to move out. The troops wearing field shoes, rather than the protective shoe pack, suffered from standing for such a long time on the ice. This was to have a more serious effect later on.

Finally, the word came down to begin moving again, and we began the long walk. The weather had turned bad, and the Chinese were no longer concerned with the possibility of our aircraft coming in.

Because of the continuous air activity over the entire area during good weather, we walked only at night or on days when it was snowing or foggy. We started at dusk and covered ten to twenty miles, depending on the terrain and road conditions. At dawn, we stopped at the closest village, no matter how small, and were herded into whatever shelter was there. If houses were available, each family was forced into a single room, while the remaining rooms were filled with prisoners. Often, there were so many men in one small space that we had room only to sit or, on several occasions, to stand up all day or night. When a village did not have enough houses to accommodate us, such structures as oxen sheds, some with only two walls and a thatched roof, were used.

Just before each day's march, we were told that we had only a short march ahead, that heated housing would be available at the end of the march, and that food would be plentiful. Also, there was always the promise of a hospital for the wounded and ailing at the next stop. None of these comforts ever materialized—the promises were lies, just empty words to keep us moving.

Some of our wounded were in more serious condition than we had originally thought, and we tried to carry them on stretchers that our guards had brought along. Because of our meager rations and the irregular terrain, this became increasingly difficult. The Chinese removed several of these men from our group, and we never saw them again.

For the first three or four days, we subsisted on small red potatoes, usually boiled into a soggy mess with no discernible taste and no salt to improve it. Few of the men had their mess kits with them. The rest, unless they had their canteen cups, were forced to eat out of their hands or, in the case of some Army personnel, their soft covers (hats). A lucky few had managed to hang on to a few small cans of rations or candy bars when they were captured, but these items were soon gone.

Although the food was strictly rationed and very meager, we had all the water we wanted, boiled and usually served piping hot. Our guards had forbidden us to drink from streams or to eat snow, which undoubtedly prevented much sickness.

The weather became increasingly colder. During the long marches, our feet sweated excessively, and when we stopped for a break or to sleep, they began to freeze. The men wearing shoe packs had been instructed, when they received their shoes, to remove the mesh innersoles when they removed their boots for any length of time and to dry the soles against their bodies before replacing them in the shoes. Those who did this fared much better than the rest. The men wearing only field shoes or regular combat boots suffered the most. One morning, after a very long night march, we were stuffed into Korean houses. A soldier next to me removed his field shoes, looked down at his blackened gangrenous feet, and said, "Ain't that a hell of a note." He died a few hours later.

At the end of each march, many of us paired off and removed our parkas. Covering our feet and lower bodies with one parka and our upper bodies with the other, we huddled closely together. This buddy system seemed to help in our pathetic attempts to stay warm. Very few of us had blankets, and I recall that one soldier had managed to grab his sleeping bag before he was marched away.

As we continued on our journey, we grew weaker and weaker from malnutrition, although our ration of food had changed to sorghum seed and corn, with an occasional ration of soybeans. We had no rice during the entire march, but it was evident that our guards were subsisting on pretty much the same fare as the rest of us.

During the day marches, we often passed by large groups of CCF troops headed toward the battle area. They had little motor transport. We saw some oxen and horse-drawn carts, but the main form of resupply transportation was on the backs of the Chinese and North Korean soldiers. We were amazed at the heavy loads those small men could carry. It was nothing to see one man with the tube of an 81-mm mortar strapped across his back and another soldier carrying the heavy base plate; they could cover many miles a day at a fast pace.

Another common sight was a particular Chinese soldier, obviously connected with cooking duties, carrying two huge iron kettles that were balanced on the ends of a long pole centered across one of his shoulders. He loped along in a strange jog that we called "Shanghai shuffle," with the pots bouncing at the ends of the pole, always in perfect unison and balance. He could maintain this odd pace for miles and hardly slowed down for the countless Korean hills.

Our guards seemed to come from the geographic areas through which we passed, and they changed every few days. Chinese combat troops had guarded us on our journey during the first few days, then turned us over to a new group of guards. Close to our tenth day on the move, we were turned over to a group of North Koreans, which was a shock to us all. The North Korean guards were mean-looking, punk kids in their teens, not yet old enough for conscript, apparently in some type of home guard unit. They were physically stocky, sturdy types, not very tall, and carried a variety of weapons, mostly foreign, such as the German Mauser rifle. One of them was so short that, as he stood with his rifle at his side, the tip of the bayonet was several inches above his head.

The North Koreans were as brutal as we had feared. They marched us for longer periods without breaks, fed us only twice, and did not provide any drinking water. We had to find water in unfrozen streams or look for clean snow.

One day during bad weather, we passed through a small village and the local civilians came out from their huts and began throwing rocks at us, hitting us with sticks, and spitting on us. The guards thought this was funny and did nothing to stop it for a while. The Chinese guards had never let this happen. They had not let any civilians or NKPA troops near us.

For some unknown reason, the short kid with the long rifle took a disliking to me. One night, we were marching along a narrow mountain road, with a cliff on the right side and a sheer drop-off on the opposite side. There was no way to tell how deep the canyon was, but I had an idea that it was a pretty good drop to the canyon floor. "Shorty," carrying his rifle slung over his shoulder, came alongside me. With his elbow, he began pushing his rifle butt into my ribs. He kept up this routine, which, to him, was humorous, until he tired of it. When I tried to change position in the column, he sought me out and started all over again. Then, he began urinating on my trouser leg as we walked along. He was giggling and acting as though his actions really gave him a thrill. I was on the left side of the column, the canyon side, and I thought quite seriously about giving him a quick shove over the side. Two possibilities kept me from killing him: if it was a long fall, he would scream; or, at dawn, the other guards would discover that he was missing and suspect foul play. In either case, we would all suffer. I was finally able to run forward and, in the pitch dark, managed to elude him.

At the end of the fourth full day with the North Koreans, we were damned happy to see Chinese guards waiting to take over again. Major McLaughlin immediately complained to the Chinese about our maltreatment, and we thought that nothing would come of it. To our surprise, the Chinese officer started yelling at our juvenile North Korean guards and even slapped around a few of them. We laughed while they fumed, but there was nothing they could do about it. Most of us had the feeling that the North Koreans had been warned about how to treat us, or we would have had a much rougher time than we did.

The terrain of North Korea became more rugged as we traveled northwest along icy mountain trails and frozen streambeds. Since the first day of our capture, escape had been virtually impossible because of the lack of food, the extreme temperatures, and the number of guards. Also, we would need shelter sooner or later, and, we learned later, there was hardly a house, hut, or shelter that had not been taken over for use by the tens of thousands of occupying Chinese troops in North Korea.

Sometime during our second week on the move, we reached a village after an all-night march, and our guards announced that we would have a rest for several days. The word came none too soon. All along the way, we had been losing men from wounds, sickness, and the freezing temperatures. Many survivors of the trek were in poor condition and had severe stomach problems caused by the sudden and severe change of diet. Some were badly constipated and suffered terrible stomach cramps.

Most of us slept for a full day during this rest stop. It was our first opportunity to check our feet, dry out our socks and inner-soles, and try to patch the holes in our socks. The shoe packs kept out the cold, but they were never intended for long marches because they didn't fit that well. I had blisters on the top of both big toes that I'm sure went all the way to the bone, but many other men were much worse off. Their blackened toes were evidence of severe frostbite, and most would face amputation of their toes, if they survived.

On the second day of the rest stop, we were warming up inside a small house when I took off my parka. I was still wearing four layers of clothing, with my field jacket as the outermost garment. I went outside to make a "head" call and was immediately attacked by several guards and the owner of the house with cuffs across my head and several well-placed kicks to my body. I didn't understand what the hell was wrong with these people, but I managed to break away and make my head call. When I got back inside, I told some of the other POWs about the incident.

One of them said, "Well, if you take that South Korean flag off the back of your field jacket, they just might leave you alone."

I removed my jacket, and on the back was a drawing of the South Korean flag that I had done with a white marking pen while I was on board the transport ship. Several of us had done this. Although the drawing was not in color, it was obviously a South Korean flag. I removed the drawing by scraping it off with a penknife—one more lesson learned.

During another trip to the head, which the soldiers referred to as a latrine, I saw a sight that bewildered me completely and convinced me that all of the "crazies" in the world were not in asylums. There was no such thing as toilet paper available to any of us, and those men who had kept the small packets of toilet paper from our ration boxes had long since used them.

The men used sticks, rocks, or whatever else they could find to wipe themselves clean. Some of the Army soldiers were carrying military script used on occupation duty in lieu of U.S. currency, and they began using this money as toilet paper. I'll be damned if I didn't watch two or three men, who just couldn't stand to see money wasted in this fashion, pick up the "used" money and try to clean it by shaking it. I couldn't help but wonder where in the hell they thought they were going to spend this money!

The officers were separated from us during this rest stop, and we would not see them again until we reached the prison camp.

When it was time to leave, we were told to gather on the road and were given the usual promise that we had only "a few miles to go" and that all of the ailing men then would be hospitalized. We were still in extremely mountainous country, and some of these mountains had no shortcuts around them. On several occasions, we took a half day to climb to the summit but only a few hours to slide down the other side. The climbing was rough. We slipped while trying to get good footholds and had to grab onto brush to pull ourselves up. The weather was terrible. We encountered snowstorms, with icy wind blasting our faces as we trudged along, and always needed a rest break, but we froze as soon as we stopped.

As the result of my hunger, stomach cramps, and sore feet, I felt at times as though I couldn't take another step. It finally happened one night—I was walking along when I fell flat on my face, and I thought that I would never get up. A Chinese guard prodded me and yelled to get up. I told him to go ahead and shoot—I was finished. A Chinese lieutenant came over to me when he heard what I said. He told me, "We no shoot you—we leave you to the North Korean civilians."

Well, if any incentive could get me going, that was it. I struggled to get back on my feet. About that time, Ernie Hayton came up behind me. He grabbed me by the waist with one arm and dragged me for several hundred yards, until I could get some strength back and make it on my own. This was the first of two occasions when my buddy Ernie saved my life.

Finally, on 21 December, after a torturous forced march

lasting fifteen days, during which we walked 150 miles to a destination that was only 60 air miles from Hagaru, our column reached a POW camp located about 8 miles northwest of the city of Kanggye. The camp, less than 10 miles from the Yalu River, the physical border between North Korea and Manchuria, also would become known as Kanggye.

It had been a death march. We arrived with at least twenty fewer prisoners than we had started with, not counting the officers who left us at the rest stop. About ten of these deaths were known to the other POWs and were recorded. Four of the men were U.S. Marines, who had died of gangrenous wounds and frostbite. Because there were no hospitals or any other types of care facilities in the rugged country through which we had passed, we could only assume that the rest of the missing men had perished, too.

# === 8 ===

# Our Welcome to Kanggye

"TOTAL EXHAUSTION" ARE the only words I can use to describe our condition, both physically and mentally, on our arrival at the Kanggye POW camp. Added to our wounds were stomach problems associated with the dramatic change in our diet, foot problems, and the terrible cold. We wondered how we had managed to make it that far.

The Chinese camp guards allowed us a couple of days to rest. During this time, we received haircuts and were allowed to shave with a few razor blades that were passed around. Next was the issuing of Chinese uniforms, a move that caught us by surprise. Although we were not pleased with the idea of wearing the enemy's uniform, the majority of us had a change of heart as soon as we tried it on. The cotton-padded, quilted coat and trousers were much warmer than any single item of clothing that we had; we had depended on layers of clothing to keep ourselves warm. The Chinese also gave us hats, the kind with flaps that could be buttoned under the chin or folded up over the top of the hat. We did not receive any type of overcoat. Fortunately, most of us had managed to hang on to our alpaca-lined parkas.

Until this time, few of us, except the officers, had been subjected to any type of interrogation, but now it began. Each man, one at a time, was called to a room located in the Chinese officers' quarters and came face to face with two officers, one of whom spoke English fairly well. When my turn came, they told me to sit down on the floor (there were no chairs) and gave me a cigarette. I was asked my full name, rank, serial number, and unit, which I gave to them. Although some people might wonder why I went beyond providing only the standard information required of POWs by telling them the name of my unit, I cannot recall ever having had any training on the subject, even in boot camp, beyond the Hollywood version portrayed in war movies. I don't know that any of my fellow POWs refused to give their unit designations to the Chinese.

At any rate, the interrogators had no interest in the name of my military organization. They asked only one question that I thought was a test: "How many men are in a tank crew?" They didn't ask what type of tank, and I answered that I didn't know how many men made up a crew because I was only a truck driver and had never been inside a tank. This was not the truth, but the Chinese dropped that particular line of questioning and went on to their real interest—personal information about me and my family.

The interrogators went into great detail on this subject. They were not satisfied with information about my being married and having a child but wanted to know how much money I had made when I was a civilian, how much money my father had made, what he did for a living, and where he worked. The Chinese seemed to disbelieve our statements about owning our own automobiles or that each of our parents owned a car. They argued with us, as though they were the victims of their own propaganda. They believed that there was no middle class of citizens in the United States. We were either rich or poor—a capitalist or a peasant.

It didn't take very long for any of us to realize that the less we said, the better off we would be. A prisoner could minimize his length of time under questioning simply by not offering any more information than was asked or by not answering all of their questions. This was later proved when certain prisoners were called back for further interrogations. They were the ones who had gone into specific details when asked about their family lives and social backgrounds. Interestingly, the last question I was asked by my Chinese captors was to what political party I belonged. I lied and said that I belonged to none—I had never registered to vote. I was dismissed from the interrogation room and never called back.

When the initial interrogations were over, the pace began to pick up. We were formed into new squads. The Chinese separated the dark-skinned POWs from all others and formed them into separate squads that included blacks, Filipinos, and men of Mexican and Puerto Rican descent. When we protested, the Chinese made such statements as: "We do not consider the Negro as an American citizen."

There was some indication that these men were separated from the others for purposes of exploitation. The Chinese were careful to concentrate on the theme of oppression of the blacks and other minorities because they believed these men to be more susceptible to conversion. Their theory, of course, proved to be false.

The newly formed squads averaged ten men each. The size of the squad determined the availability and size of our quarters. One man was appointed squad leader. For some unknown reason, I was selected as a squad leader for nine other prisoners, including a U.S. Army sergeant first class. Rank evidently made little difference to the Chinese, and they appointed whomever they pleased as squad leaders. They made it extremely clear that they would tolerate no problems from within the squads, and the Army sergeant did not protest the fact that a Marine corporal was his leader. Two of my buddies, Hayton and Hawkins, were in my squad, but Dickerson and Hilburn were assigned to an adjacent squad.

My squad was quartered in the home of a Korean family. The Chinese continued to billet us among the local civilians, as they had during the initial forced march. All members of the Korean family were forced to move into one room of the house, and the prisoners were jammed into the other rooms. Because most of the huts consisted of only two rooms and a kitchen area, ten POWs were usually housed in one room. There were no back doors to these huts, and one armed guard, posted on the porch, was usually sufficient for each hut.

The rooms were invariably small, no larger than eight by ten feet. During sleeping hours, five of us lay on each side, staggered, which allowed us a little room to stretch our legs. It was extremely cold at night, so cold, in fact, that the inside walls of the house were covered with a light coating of frost. We used the same system for keeping warm as we had on our march—doubling up—with one man's parka covering the feet and lower extremities and the other parka providing warmth to the upper bodies.

A thin-framed, paper-covered door led to the room where the Korean family stayed, and strict regulations governed our conduct toward the civilians. There was no communication allowed between the prisoners and the family. We had no problem with this because we could see the hatred in their eyes, even in those of the little children, when they stared at us. The Chinese lost no time in explaining to us that there was hardly a single household within the village that had not lost at least one family member to the war. The effect of this situation was obvious. There were no young, able-bodied men and very few young women to be seen—they all had been conscripted to help in the war effort. All who remained were the elderly and the children and their mothers.

Outside, and away from each house, was a head/latrine consisting of four tall poles stuck in the ground with a thatched roof overhead. This facility was no more than forty or fifty square feet; inside, logs had been placed two feet apart. We were supposed to balance ourselves on a log, in a squatting position, and make our deposit between the logs. During the winter months, the freezing temperatures reduced the possibility of odor, but summertime was a different story. There was never any waiting line to use the head. Because it had no walls, we could see if it was occupied, but there was always room for at least a dozen people. At first, I had a strange feeling when I was squatted down on a log and doing my thing and then saw Mama-san (the lady of the house) come in, squat down beside me, raise her skirts, and do her own thing. The children were the same way, only they always managed a giggle or a laugh when they saw us squatted down in a most unmilitary-like manner.

As soon as we had gotten settled in our close quarters, a Chinese medic came calling, along with one of the English-speaking lieutenants who referred to themselves as "political officers" or "instructors." The medic asked if there were any wounded or sick, and, of course, we had plenty of them. He carried a limited amount of medical equipment and medicine with him, and it was apparent that the "good medical treatment and the hospital for the sick" promised by our Chinese captors would not be realized. But, then, the "comfortable prison camp" damned sure hadn't materialized, either.

I made the mistake of showing this Chinese "doc" my deeply blistered big toes, and he solved my problem in a hurry by taking out a razor blade and lancing the blisters to the bone without the use of an anesthetic. I nearly jumped out of my parka, but, surprisingly, my toes healed within a few days. My treatment in no way equaled the ordeals of the men who had frostbitten toes removed in the same manner, also without the administration of any anesthetic.

While the Chinese medic was lancing my toes, he noticed that I had no toenails on any of my toes but made no comment. I had tried to take proper care of my feet during the forced march. When we arrived at Kanggye, however, I had taken off my shoe packs and socks, which had been reduced to not much more than shreds of material, and was shocked to discover that I had lost every one of my toenails. I looked in my boots, shook them out, and finally turned my stinking socks inside out. Out of each sock fell five toenails. No doubt, the medic had seen many similar cases among his countrymen. Loss of toenails is a common aftereffect of frostbite. Luckily, mine grew back within several weeks.

The wound to my knee appeared to be healing fairly well. A large scab had formed over it, and whatever type of grenade fragment was buried in there wasn't hurting me very much. After the blister treatment, I thought it would be in my best interest to leave well enough alone. Besides, there were plenty of men with much more serious problems than mine.

Later, I learned that most of the Chinese medical personnel in our area were not yet doctors but medical school students. They had been pulled away from their studies at colleges and universities in China and sent into Korea to help in the war effort. I believe that most of the POWs shared my feeling that, while treating us, the Chinese medics' intentions were good and they were doing the best they could with what they had available to treat us. With proper equipment and medicines, however, we probably would have received better medical treatment.

When we complained to the Chinese about the lack of good care, their answers were always the same, as they were about our meager rations. The best medical gear and food went to the frontline troops, and those in the rear had to make do with what was left.

Our food consisted mainly of sorghum seed and, occasionally, soybeans. The tiny sorghum seeds were soaked in huge cooking pots of water until the seeds swelled to the size of a grain of rice; then they were cooked for several hours and the water was drained off. The cooking usually left some residue that stuck to the sides of the pot; actually, it was baked on. This delicacy was much sought after by the POWs. When each squad sent its men to get chow, they always tried to get some of the "burnt," as it was called.

The soybeans were always welcomed. They were much more palatable than the tasteless sorghum seeds, and although many of us did not realize it, they were very rich in nutritional value. We had our soybeans served in one of three ways: regular, bean sprouts, or parched like a peanut. We still had seen no rice.

It was the responsibility of each squad leader to assign two men to get the squad's meals each day, and we all took turns. We received our ration of food in a small cast-iron pot; there wasn't usually too much of it. The Chinese had issued small bowls, and we divided the portions equally, right down to the last seed or bean. The dividing of food was closely watched, with all of the others standing over the man serving the food. Accusations of being shorted could, and did, lead to real fights if the squad leader didn't maintain close control. Once or twice, the Chinese cooks tossed a fish head or two in some type of gruel, and it was not unusual to see men almost on the verge of fighting over the eyeballs.

Surprisingly, on Christmas Eve, only three days after our arrival at the camp, we received word that we were to have a

Christmas party that evening. The party would be held in a large meeting hall, and there would be presents for all of us.

Just after dusk, we marched by squads to the meeting hall and lined up outside. We had to await the arrival of the Chinese troops because they, too, had been invited to attend the party. While we were waiting outside, some of us were witness to an incident that indicated just how little military rank meant to the Chinese, even among their own troops.

A Chinese Communist sergeant had marched his unit to the entrance of the meeting hall. He was waiting for word to move the men inside when a young lieutenant brought his troops right up to the hall's main doorway and began moving his men inside. The outraged sergeant gave a yell, ran over to the lieutenant, grabbed him by the tunic collar, and shook him like a rag doll. In a "universal" language, he told the lieutenant that he wasn't going to pull that kind of crap on a sergeant. The CCF troops in both units seemed unimpressed by what was taking place and acted as though the incident was nothing out of the ordinary. (I could not help but think, "There goes the Chinese equivalent of a Marine Corps gunny!")

We finally managed to get inside the building, a large, barn-like structure that had been used before the war as a grain storage house. It had a dirt floor and was not heated. Rows of pine logs had been laid on the deck, two feet apart, to serve as benches. The place was quickly filled with more than two hundred prisoners and Chinese soldiers. To our surprise, the Chinese had actually tried to decorate two Christmas trees with red paper balls, and they had placed a few wreaths of pine clippings along the walls. Two large banners proclaimed "Merry Christmas," and there were a few lighted candles in various places.

Several placards also hung on the walls; one read: "If it weren't for Wall Street, you would all be home with your families on Christmas Eve." I must admit that, like a number of other men, I wasn't exactly sure what this was supposed to mean. This night was intended to be the beginning of our "reeducation," however, and, in the coming weeks, we would damned sure find out what the Chinese had in store for us.

The Chinese political officers, whom we had come to recognize, kicked off the ceremonies by welcoming us, remarking on how well we were being treated, and commenting repeatedly about how much trouble they had taken to provide the party. They told us that we would soon be treated to a most important speech from a very high-ranking officer.

We never did find out just how high ranking this officer was, but he was damned long-winded. His speech was loaded with Marxist doctrine and heavy doses of well-rehearsed examples of propaganda on the causes and conduct of the Korean War. He denounced General MacArthur and President Truman. He told us that we were the victims of Yankee imperialism and that the Wall Street warmongers had sent us to Korea as nothing more than cannon fodder.

He went on to explain that neither he nor any other Chinese harbored any ill feelings toward us. They welcomed the opportunity to teach us how wrong our government and the governments of the Allies were, and he promised that we would learn, in the coming months, all about the glories of Communism.

Of course, his speech was given in Chinese. After every few sentences, he paused while his words were translated into English, which meant that the original speech, just over an hour long, required more than two hours to be presented. (This was to be the normal pattern of our "reeducation" over the coming months.)

We learned many more things on that memorable Christmas Eve. No longer were we considered to be, or referred to as, prisoners of war. We were now "liberated friends," meaning that we had been liberated from "the yoke of Yankee imperialism." The Chinese called themselves the Chinese People's Volunteer Army (CPVA). This was later shortened to the Chinese People's Volunteers (CPVs). We were told that every one of their soldiers serving in Korea had volunteered to come from China and help their Korean cousins. This explanation reminded me of how our first sergeants "volunteered" us for unannounced work details.

The Chinese presented another startling revelation that night—contrary to our belief that North Korea had started the war, it was actually South Korea who had attacked across the thirty-eighth parallel on 25 June and invaded the sovereignty of North Korea. The North Koreans, the Chinese explained, had no alternative but to defend themselves and their country. The fact that they had "defended" their country damned near down to Pusan had no apparent bearing on the case. The Chinese also ignored the fact that South Korea had fewer than 100,000 troops, less than four infantry divisions, guarding the thirty-eighth parallel when the invasion began, whereas North Korea had amassed seven infantry divisions and one armored division in its attacking force (division size on each side was similar). This point was later raised to our Chinese educators and immediately dismissed as propaganda fed to us by our imperialist government. The Chinese persisted in using this example during the coming months. In fact, one of their favorite questions during our study periods was: "Who is the aggressor in Korea, and why is South Korea the aggressor?" It became a standard joke among all of the POWs.

As the Christmas Eve speech wore on, the translator continued to emphasize how "well" we were being treated. We were sitting on the logs, which were no more than eight inches in diameter, with the result that our collective asses were very close to the ground and our knees under our chins. The outside temperature was far below zero, and we had to stomp our feet continuously in our efforts to keep warm and to keep our blood circulating, which added to the din of the hall. The guards passed out a few cigarettes to each man, our "presents" from the Chinese. Most of us lit up and soon created a thick haze within the confines of the building.

When the speech was over, a few pieces of candy and some peanuts were handed out to promote the party atmosphere, and then the Chinese asked for volunteers among the POWs to speak or sing. Some of the British Marines belted out a few well-known songs. The party definitely wasn't going as well as the Chinese had expected. They offered a couple more cigarettes as a bonus to anyone who wanted to get up and say something. When they had no takers, they asked if anyone had anything to confess—for instance, had anyone withheld any information during the initial interrogation? Well, there sure weren't any takers for that request, so they asked if anyone would like to talk about how well he, or we, had been treated, so far.

I'll be damned if a soldier from my own squad didn't stand up and tell a story about being captured by the Germans during World War II and having to stand at attention for so long that he urinated in his trousers. He compared his experience with the Germans to the Chinese who had been treating him so well! Naturally, the other POWs took exception to this man's story and starting booing him to sit down. The Chinese put a stop to this in a hurry. We were hesitant to display any outward signs of hostility because we still did not know anything about these people or their policies.

The soldier got his cigarettes and was treated like a celebrity by the Chinese, but he had sealed his fate with the rest of us. We didn't trust him after that moment and were particularly careful about what we said in his presence. With the dubious distinction of being his squad leader, I had to be extremely careful. Fortunately for him, he was removed from our squad after a couple of months.

This soldier would later make propaganda speeches for his captors and went so far as to write surrender leaflets, some of which were actually printed and scattered over Allied lines. His actions, however, would come back to haunt him—the guy had put his name on them! Some five years later—after seventeen years of service in the U.S. Army—he would be the subject of a general court-martial, be tried and convicted of collaboration with the enemy, be sentenced to two years at hard labor and reduction to the grade of private, with forfeiture of all pay and allowances, and receive a dishonorable discharge.

He knew while still in North Korea, however, that he had sealed his own fate. Not too long before he was repatriated in 1953, he reportedly told a fellow POW that he would "gladly settle for five years," meaning five years' imprisonment, for what he had done as a prisoner of war. This was also brought out at his court-martial.

And some of the stories he told while in the company of our squad simply didn't hold water. During his court-martial, representatives of the U.S. Army disclosed that they had no record of his ever having been a prisoner of the Germans during World War II.

I was one of dozens of former POWs who were called to testify during his court-martial. One of the saddest things about him, I thought, was that during our time together as POWs, I never believed that he had any Communist or leftist leanings. I always thought that he was nothing more than a man who would do anything to make things easier for himself. He certainly did get special treatment. Some evenings, he was called out of the squad's hut and, on his return, was picking his teeth and looking well satisfied. There was no doubt in my mind that he was getting extra food and other favors.

The "Christmas party" finally came to an end. Shivering cold and damned stiff from being forced to squat and sit for so many hours, we were herded back to our huts.

The men in my squad sat huddled together in the darkness of our room. We were hungry and miserable and thinking about what our families were doing this holiday season. Suddenly, out of the blue, we heard the Korean family singing in the adjacent room. The words and music were completely foreign to us, and we wondered what the Koreans would be singing about in this war-torn, godforsaken land. Surely they were not celebrating Christmas, but, frankly, we were too tired even to care.

Then they began to sing a tune very familiar to me—"Santa Lucia." I knew the song well and had played it often on the harmonica as a kid. The Chinese had not searched me, and, by sheer coincidence, I was still carrying a harmonica in the pocket of my field jacket. It took it out and began to accompany them. Their singing stopped for just a moment, but they began again and I accompanied them until they finished their song.

The wooden door between us opened slowly, and a face peered in at us. In the dim candlelight coming from their room, I held up my mouth harp for them to see. The door closed briefly, then opened again, and a hand passed a small porcelain cup to me. I tasted the contents and recognized it as soju, the Korean version of sake, a pungent rice wine. It was piping hot, and I passed the cup around so that each man could have a sip.

Even that tiny bit of wine seemed to help warm our bones. I passed the cup back and closed the door. This was all done very quietly so the guard on the porch would not hear us.

It finally dawned on us—these people were Christians, and they were celebrating Christmas! At some point in time, who knows how long before, a Christian missionary had taught them or their ancestors some Christmas carols, one to the melody of an Italian love song. For that brief moment in the frozen waste of an enemy country, there was a thin common thread between us—our celebration of the birth of Christ.

On Christmas Day, the Chinese gave us a break—sort of a holiday routine. For the first time since we had been captured, we received rice. It wasn't the white, long-grain variety that most Americans know but small-grain, brown, dirty rice containing small rocks and other bits of assorted debris. We had to be careful while eating it because the rocks could play hell on teeth and fillings.

The Chinese even threw in a few small pieces of pork with this meal, and our hopes rose slightly that perhaps the quality of our food was going to improve. We learned, however, that this holiday meal was only a scheme, one that would be used continuously to remind us of just how well our new Chinese "friends" were treating us. It was part of a well-orchestrated plan to lull us into a false sense of well-being, and they never stopped trying.

Most of us took advantage of the day off and tried to catch up on our sleep. We were still bone-tired from the forced march. It was good that we did rest because, the following day, the Chinese decided to get down to business with their political indoctrination course, our reeducation, as they called it. It was their attempt to brainwash us, that is, completely change our political views and our way of thinking.

About this time, the officer POWs, who had been separated from us during the march, showed up at Kanggye. They were immediately formed into a separate squad and kept in a distant part of the village. We saw them only during meetings or at other campwide functions.

The indoctrination course began when the POW squads

throughout the camp were paired off for intersquad discussions; the subject was the political speech given by the Chinese officer on Christmas Eve. A political officer presided over each meeting and asked for our views on what the officer had said that night. Naturally, we had all thought that his speech was a lot of bullshit, but we were reluctant to say so. Our Chinese instructor persisted in encouraging us to speak up. He assured us that we were free to voice our true feelings and no action would be taken against those who disagreed with the philosophy of Communism. He said that he welcomed opposing views.

Finally, Dickerson, whose squad was meeting with mine, broke the ice by saying that he thought it was all a bunch of BS. The instructor didn't understand until the term was explained to him. When he finally understood, he laughed and asked for other opinions. Of course, this opened up a tirade of comments, none of which were complimentary to the instructor or to his remarks. The instructor was absolutely delighted—this was exactly what he wanted. Now, the Chinese reasoned, they understood us and could correct our misguided views.

Evidently, the same reaction occurred throughout the entire camp. Within a day or two, we were herded back into the barn and subjected to more long-winded speeches designed to point out how wrong we were about the merits of Communism and about our own capitalistic, imperialistic form of government. This routine continued for several weeks. The more doubts we expressed, the more meetings and speeches we witnessed, and, although it could have been coincidental, our food rations dropped slightly in quantity and quality.

A camp schedule was soon established and followed closely from day to day. We were awakened shortly after dawn, or before dawn on clear mornings, and herded outside to join other squads in some form of physical exercise, usually a run or fast walk for a half hour. Because the majority of us were suffering from colds, this exercise plan created a great deal of coughing and spitting. The Chinese said that this was the purpose of the exercise—to help in bringing up the phlegm and getting rid of the cough. Whether this practice had any medical benefits is doubtful, but it certainly was rough on our weakened bodies.

During one of these morning runs, another incident occurred that only added to the mystery of our captors and their surprising conduct. One of the POWs was very sick and began to lag behind on the run. A Chinese guard came up from behind and gave him a shove that caused him to stumble and almost fall down. When he recovered his balance, he turned around and knocked the guard on his ass with one punch.

Oh, Christ, we thought. Now we've had it. That POW, and perhaps all of us, would catch hell, and we hated to think of what that could be.

One of the instructors came running up to see what the commotion was all about. When the guard explained what had happened, the lieutenant merely admonished the POW and explained that this was not the proper type of conduct. This left us shaking our collective heads in disbelief. We were pleased that no action was taken against the sick man, but we shuddered as we imagined what would have happened if the guards had been North Koreans.

One other morning, we took a particularly long walk northwest of the camp. About the time that we turned around to return, the guards were jabbering and motioning ahead. We couldn't understand them because most of the guards could speak no more than a few words of English. Someone asked one of the instructors what they were talking about, and he explained that we were very close to the Yalu River, the physical boundary between North Korea and China. We had no doubt that our guards wished they could keep going and head for home.

Interestingly, the lieutenant added that a very high-ranking American POW was being held at the border. Although we didn't think too much about it at the time, I was curious about him. If a map had been handy, we would have discovered that we were close to Manpojin. During the POW repatriations in 1953, Maj. Gen. William F. Dean, USA, commander of the 24th Infantry Division when he was captured early in the war, would show up after more than three years in captivity. He said that he had been held in solitary confinement during almost the entire period at a place close to the Yalu River. Since then, I have often wondered if the lieutenant was referring to General Dean that day.

After the exercise period, which was not always a daily event because of the extreme weather conditions, each squad received the morning meal. Usually, we had only two meals daily; only on rare occasions was a third meal served.

When breakfast was over, our studies or political discussions began. They were usually conducted in one of three ways: intrasquad, intersquad, or campwide. For intrasquad discussions, the squad leader was in charge and followed procedures set down by his instructor. During intersquad discussions, the instructor conducted the meeting. On the occasion of a campwide meeting, all of the Chinese officers, including the camp commander and his staff, attended, along with the guards and all of the POWs. The duration of this session depended on how many of the senior Chinese officers felt like speaking on a given day. The campwide meeting was also a great opportunity for the prisoners to get together and exchange information and for Major McLaughlin to pass along any message that he had for us. The Chinese did not seem to mind these sessions, as long as we did not talk during their lectures.

After three or four hours of lectures and discussion, we were given a noon break for an hour or two. Then, we went back to the lecture room for an additional three hours of lectures and discussion.

Our second meal was usually served just before dark. Afterward, we were allowed to take care of our personal hygiene needs. These usually depended on whether, or how badly, any man had dysentery, a constant and debilitating battle in the more severe cases.

Once in a while, a working party of POWs was assigned to perform some menial chore, usually to gather firewood for Mama-san. One such occasion is forever etched in my memory. There was no precut wood available, and a couple of guards called out my squad and marched us up the slope of a mountain to where a group of soldiers had felled some large pines. They had trimmed off the branches by the time we arrived.

Two or three of the Chinese lifted a cut tree, which was covered with snow, off the ground and placed it on the shoulder of one of the prisoners. Then, they gave him a push down the hillside. When it was my turn, they set a tree on me that was not much smaller than a telephone pole and gave me a shove. At the time, I was down to about 120 pounds, and I doubted if I could handle one of the pine branches, let alone the entire log.

I must have looked like a snowplow going down that hill. My boot heels dug into the snow, but my body was at a 45-degree angle as I leaned back to maintain my balance. Obviously, there would be no stopping until I reached the bottom.

At the end of this joyride, I picked myself up, grabbed the stump end of the pole, and managed to get it onto my shoulder. I was walking down an ice-covered path not more than a few yards from our hut when my feet shot from beneath me. I went straight down, and the log followed me. Fortunately, I had been on the side of the path, and a snowbank caught the end of the tree so that its full weight did not fall on me. As it was, the tree rapped me on the forehead, and the blow knocked me out momentarily. When I came to, Ernie Hayton, who had been dragging a tree behind me, was staring down at me and asking me what I was doing there.

Although I was tempted to tell him that I just felt like taking a short nap, I screamed at him. "Get this damned tree off of me!"

Ernie obliged. He stuck the tree on my shoulder, and we trekked back, most carefully, to the house. I had a knot the size of a goose egg on my forehead, but I felt lucky that my skull hadn't cracked.

The evening hours in our quarters were usually spent in total darkness, not only because of the lack of lighting but also because the Chinese strictly enforced their blackout rules. We had heard that the penalty for any Chinese soldier caught showing a light on a clear night, even while lighting a cigarette, was death. Continuously, we were cautioned not to move about on days when aircraft could be flying. Doors and windows on any building that could be lighted, even if only by candles, were carefully blacked out.

Often, we could hear the drone of high-flying U.S. Air Force B-29s overhead on their way to bomb border installations along the Yalu River. As the planes flew over, our guard on the porch stuck his head in the doorway and told us to stop talking. He was not only visibly shaken with fear, but he showed his lack of understanding about our aircraft because he thought that the aircrew could possibly hear us, thirty thousand feet below, and learn the location of American and British POWs.

Prisoners continued to pour into Kanggye. By the end of the year, almost 250 POWs were in the camp. Nearly 50 percent of these men came from two regiments, the 31st and the 32d Infantry Regiments of the Army's 7th Division. Almost all of them were survivors of either Task Force Drysdale or Task Force Faith, the dubious designation of the convoy that had attempted to reach Hagaru from the eastern side of the Chosin Reservoir. U.S. Army Lt. Col. Don C. Faith, Jr., had taken command of the convoy when the original commander of the 31st Infantry Regiment was killed in action. Faith, too, was killed shortly thereafter. He would be posthumously awarded the Medal of Honor for his actions (see appendix B).

As 1950 drew to a close, three questions remained unanswered: What was in store for us? What was the current tactical situation? How much longer would we remain as prisoners of the Chinese Communists?

My inner thoughts, of course, and those that helped to sustain me, were my concerns for my wife and infant daughter and my ability to survive and somehow be reunited with them.

# === 9 ===

# Reeducation, Chinese Style

NEW YEAR'S DAY, 1951, arrived. We were looking forward to nothing more than another tedious session in the barn, or at least some study periods, when the Chinese surprised us. They announced that we would observe the day with another holiday routine. Again, we received a little better meal of the usual dirty brown rice, but with a few pieces of pork added to it. This was accompanied, of course, by the usual announcement that our "new friends" had gone to a great deal of trouble to obtain this food and were making every effort to ensure that our treatment was lenient and fair. We were confused, caught off guard again, because we had not expected any special holiday treatment.

More important was the welcomed announcement that, on this day, we each would be allowed to write a letter home!

Each prisoner was given one small piece of paper, no larger than five by seven inches, on which he could write a message to his family. We were told to write the recipient's name and address on the top of the page, followed by the message. One man in each squad was provided with an envelope to address to his family. In his letter home, he was to ask that the other letters be forwarded to each family listed on the individual scraps of paper.

I addressed my squad's letters to my wife in San Diego. None of us had any idea as to how long it might be before the letters left our camp, but they did arrive in San Diego in March. The envelope bore no postage, but someone had written in ink,

"Prisoners of War Correspondence," in the upper right-hand corner.

Later, I learned that Sharon immediately forwarded the other letters, which caused a flurry of excitement among the families. Letters and telephone calls to her from the other families asked for more information about their loved ones. Of course, she was unable to provide this because she knew only what I had written in my letter, which was basically the same as the other nine letters. The Chinese had made it quite clear that, if they were not satisfied with the contents of a letter, it would not be sent. As we very much wanted to let our families know that we were alive and doing fairly well, we said so. We added statements, designed to please the Chinese, to indicate that our treatment was not as bad as we had expected.

Until the arrival of my letter, my family knew only that I was missing in action after receiving a telegram from Headquarters Marine Corps, Washington, D.C., that had been delivered on 2 January 1951, thirty-three days after I had been captured.

My name had been mentioned on a Chinese propaganda radio broadcast in February 1951. The broadcaster stated that I was a POW, and Headquarters Marine Corps notified my family of this fact. The Marine Corps indicated, however, that because there was no way to confirm my status, I would continue to be listed as an MIA.

Fortunately, my family had also received word from another source that I was probably a POW. Captain Clarke, the San Diego reservist who had commanded Company D tanks in Task Force Drysdale, had been wounded about ten days after I was captured. While awaiting medical evacuation, he was talking to another evacuee, Bill Harrison, the truck driver from our company who had chosen to stay in the ditch when we were captured. Corporal Harrison told Clarke that he had seen the Chinese take Hilburn, Hayton, and me at gunpoint. The captain had known the three of us from our service together in San Diego with the Reserve tank battalion. As soon as he reached home, he called our families and told them the story of our capture.

The Chinese never made any official attempt to notify our

next of kin or the U.S. government of our capture and subsequent POW status while we were held at Kanggye. They stated, conveniently, that they did not recognize or abide by the articles of the Geneva Convention, which governed the treatment and handling of prisoners of war.

For some reason, probably because she was so excited about receiving my envelope full of letters, Sharon didn't notify Headquarters Marine Corps (HQMC). It didn't take HQMC long to learn about this situation, however, when it began to receive letters and telephone calls from the other families who wanted to know more about their missing men.

A letter from HQMC officials to my wife stated that they had been informed of the letters and asked for the names of the other nine POWS, which she immediately provided. They cautioned her not to mention having heard from me in any letters to me because they believed that my letter might have been smuggled out of North Korea.

Those letters, written on 1 January 1951, were the only ones that we were allowed to write during our entire time at Kanggye, and we never did receive any mail while we were there. Upon verification of Sharon's receipt of my letter, however, HQMC changed my status from missing in action to prisoner of war.

On 2 January, our Chinese political indoctrination began unceremoniously in earnest, with another long political session in the barn, during which we were continually reminded that our "hosts" had gone to great lengths to provide us with our holiday meals and Christmas party. The Chinese also disclosed some of the details concerning the Kanggye prison camp and what their policies would be.

Kanggye was to be a "lenient policy" camp, which meant that we were to be well treated and adequately housed and fed and that the needs of those men requiring medical attention would be met. Of course, we had been promised these things since the day of our capture. Because the Chinese had failed to meet their commitments, it did not take long for us to realize that we were in for a long, hard winter. We assumed that our conditions were not going to get better, as there had been too many broken promises already.

The Chinese further stated that our condition was dependent on our cooperation in our studies and conduct. Those who cooperated would be rewarded; those who failed to do so would be punished. The prisoners who cooperated would be known as "progressives," and those who resisted would be labeled "reactionaries."

These two terms were later distorted by some authors and historians, who suggested that, whereas the progressives cooperated to the point of collaboration, the only true reactionaries were those who resisted to the extent that they suffered beatings, solitary confinement, and other forms of punishment for various infractions of the rules, including any escape attempts.

One writer, working on his graduate thesis, went so far as to suggest that all POW squad leaders were progressives, therefore collaborators, and had been selected for the position because of their cooperation. Nothing could be further from the truth.

These theories were certainly not borne out by the facts, at least not at Kanggye. Actually, there was no fine line of distinction between the groups, but there was also a third, middle-of-the-road group. This group, which included the majority of Kanggye POWs, neither accepted nor resisted the Chinese with any great degree of fervor. They simply listened to the lectures and appeared to accept them; read the study material presented; and seldom, if ever, commented one way or the other. The men in this middle group were those able to convince the Chinese officials that the POWs were cooperating, which, at least at Kanggye, made life just a bit easier—and food a bit more plentiful. This was done with only one purpose in mind—survival.

The instructors continued to hold out the lure of early release for men who "cooperated." If anyone could feign this cooperation without giving aid or advantage to our enemies, then so be it.

A good example of the misunderstanding of the term *progressive* came up some four years later during the general court-martial of a soldier who had been a member of my POW squad. During pretrial examination, I was asked by his lawyer, an Army lieutenant colonel, if I had not been a collaborator and even a member of a secret Chinese society.

I was dumbfounded and asked him what in the hell he was talking about.

He replied, "Were you not a member of the 'Goon-zo-yeh' and wore a badge to prove it?"

I practically laughed in his face as I explained what the term and the badge actually meant. Every POW squad leader was required to wear a small white patch of cloth containing some Chinese characters, that was sewn on the front of his jacket. The Chinese instructors who issued these patches explained that the characters read "Goon-zo-yeh," which meant cadre or leader. The patch identified us to the guards and other POW camp instructors. It also meant that we were allowed to move about in our own section of the camp, without armed escort, to visit other POW huts to discuss our studies or to take care of any administrative problems. Of course, there were no advantages to this privilege; we received no special favors or treatment, and escape was out of the question because of our location and the extreme weather conditions.

The study sessions continued, and we were now spending nearly five hours each day at lectures or group studies. We had no choice. Attendance was mandatory, and sickness was no excuse for missing a class.

We were now being provided with English editions of Chinese magazines and newspapers, in which the instructors marked certain articles for us to study. We had been surprised to learn that some major Chinese newspapers in Shanghai and Peiping had English editions. At times, we received these papers when they were only a week old. I could envision some poor coolie humping nearly a hundred pounds of newspapers on his back over snow-covered mountains and across icy streams—the Chinese version of the rural newspaper boy.

The Chinese stories and articles were pure propaganda— distortions of the truth to such a degree that, at first, they were actually humorous. Then, we realized that these disingenuous stories were all that the Chinese had to read and hear and that they were probably spread to other Communist-dominated countries throughout the world. Two particular news articles have stuck in my mind, perhaps because they seemed so absurd. One described the streets of Bakersfield, California, littered with the bodies of hundreds of people who had died of starvation. Why the Chinese had selected that particular city was anyone's guess, but we recognized it as pure crap. Being a native Californian, I knew the city of Bakersfield well and also knew that, if such a condition ever were to exist, our own media would be the first to spread the story.

The second preposterous story was about the "bravery" of Chinese soldiers on the battlefield in Korea. It detailed some of their acts of heroism that had earned certain individuals awards for gallantry. One particular incident concerned two individuals who had "jumped on the back of an American tank, ripped open the hatches with bayonets and threw in grenades, killing the crew." Anyone even vaguely familiar with armored vehicles, particularly tanks, knows that this would have been impossible. The hatch covers on a tank are covered with several inches of armor and have a strong inner locking device. A bayonet blade could hardly do anything but scratch the surface of the hatch before the blade broke. Of course, millions of people who were subjected to this type of propaganda did not know this.

It was apparent from the articles that the Chinese were not overly liberal with the presentation of their medals and decorations. The most coveted award was acceptance into the Communist Party, although the highest medal award for heroism was called the Military Hero's Decoration. Contrary to popular belief at the time, only a small segment of the Chinese population was offered the privilege of joining the Communist Party. Once they became party members, these people never had to worry about the source of future meals for themselves and their families.

We discussed the magazine and newspaper articles with our instructors and were encouraged to speak freely about what we had read. Although we were allowed to comment as we saw fit and the Chinese seemed pleased to hear any disagreement, we were beginning to catch on. The more doubts that we expressed about any phase of our studies, the more lectures we would hear in the barn, usually at night when subzero temperatures were at the lowest.

Major McLaughlin continued to be the source of our inspiration, and he passed the word to the squad leaders during our campwide meetings at the barn. At one meeting, the major told us, in no uncertain terms, "They [the Chinese] have the guns and the food. Play along, but do not do anything to disgrace yourself or your country."

That was all it took. The entire camp began to "understand" the teachings of the Communists. The doubts and disagreements dwindled, the barn lectures decreased in frequency, and the quality of our food rations improved a little. One prisoner remarked, "If they say black is white, it must be so, because they said so."

Around mid-January, my squad was moved to a house closer to the main road and other squad billets. The inhabitants of our new home were definitely not pleased to see us arrive. This meant that they had to live in one small room, while we occupied the other. Like us, they had no say in the matter.

A very old Papa-san lived there with his daughter-in-law and grandchildren. He made no effort to conceal his hatred for us. Our instructor mentioned that the old man had lost two sons in the war, which meant little to us. We intended to follow orders and not cause any problems with this family.

One day, the guard stuck his head in the door of our hut and motioned for me to gather my squad on the porch. There was a stack of firewood there, and the guard wanted it moved into the kitchen where it would be more handy for Mama-san. Papa-san was standing there, and he began to act like a sidewalk supervisor.

I bent over to pick up a piece of wood, and the old man could contain himself no longer. He kicked me square in the ass, and I went sprawling on my face, right in front of the guard. I was really pissed off and lost my temper. Picking up the small log, I started for the old man. The guard jumped between us and motioned for me to return to the squad's room.

About two hours later, I was called outside by Lieutenant Pan, one of the instructors. Pan was all business, and he let everyone know who was the boss. He had a mean look about him and gave the impression that, if allowed to, he could get extremely vicious. He never bothered us, however, as long as we followed orders.

Pan said, "Mah-foi [the closest he could come to pronouncing my name], guard tell me you have trouble with old man who live here." I explained what had happened, and Pan warned me not to have anything more to do with Papa-san. I wanted to protest because he made it seem as though the assault had been my fault, but I knew that it was useless and kept my mouth shut.

A few minutes later, I heard some commotion on the porch. I peeked out to see what was happening. Damned if the old man wasn't standing straight and stiff in front of Lieutenant Pan, with Pan's pistol pointed at his temple. I guess that Pan had explained, in no uncertain terms, what would happen if he ever screwed with prisoners again. From that moment on, every time the old man saw me outside he ran around to the other side of the hut and hid.

The family had a pig, a dog, and a chicken. They were usually in front of the house when it wasn't snowing. These poor creatures were always hungry—the people hardly had enough food to feed themselves, let alone their animals. It was surprising to watch them follow one another around as they waited for one to leave some droppings. As soon as this happened, the other two ran right over and gobbled up the offering. Being a city boy, I didn't know if this was normal behavior, but a few of the other POWs said that these animals did this only because they were so hungry. Nonetheless, their habits certainly helped to keep the yard clean.

The chicken caused us a bit of trouble one day. We were sitting in the room studying, when that hen began clucking. One of the men in the squad said, "I'll be damned if that old hen ain't laid herself an egg."

He knew that the bird roosted in a shed adjacent to our room, so he quietly went outside and returned a few minutes later with one white egg cradled in his hand. All of us looked like we had never seen an egg before. We gathered around and admired it as though it were a nugget of pure gold.

While we were in the process of deciding if or how we

should cook the egg, Mama-san started yelling and kicking up a hell of a fuss. She, too, had heard the hen clucking and knew damned well what it meant. By the time she checked the hen coop, her prize was gone. She had a pretty fair idea of what had happened. Evidently, our man had just beaten her to it and returned to our room unseen.

Mama-san's shouting brought the guard (he must have been asleep), and he came into our room with his palm outstretched. We gave him the egg. He handed it to the lady of the house, and, with a tirade of what were surely unkind remarks toward her houseguests, she headed back to her kitchen.

The incident was duly reported. Pan came down to the house that evening and called me outside. He royally chewed my ass and let me know that there had better not be any further incidents of this nature. Of course, this went along with one of the Chinese Communists' favorite slogans: "Take not a single needle or piece of thread from the people."

The Chinese repeated this slogan to us on numerous occasions. Supposedly, it meant that, under Communism, the people's possessions were their own and not to be pilfered, confiscated, or otherwise taken by government troops or anyone else. We knew that this was pure propaganda and certainly not practiced by the Chinese soldiers. We had seen many incidents of confiscation by the soldiers, and we would see plenty more. There is no doubt in my mind that if Lieutenant Pan, himself, could have gotten away with keeping that egg, he'd have had it for his next meal.

We hadn't been living in that house long when we discovered that the pig, although not very large, posed a real danger. The crudely constructed head outside was built pretty much in the same fashion as the last place—a thatched roof over four poles with logs laid out on which to balance.

Well, the family porker knew exactly when someone headed out that way and why we were going. He followed everyone there to catch whatever dropped to the ground, and he devoured it before it froze, which was only a matter of minutes in the subzero temperatures of North Korea. The problem was that the pig was overanxious. He came awfully close to those particular parts of our anatomy that hung down when we hunkered over the logs. We thought that it would be ironic as hell to have to tell our grandchildren that our major war wounds occurred when we were neutered by a starved pig. Keeping a large switch in the head solved the problem, but we had to swat continually at the pig while using the facilities.

Our guards seemed to be a fairly happy group. I guess they had every reason to be because they were several hundred miles from the front lines, where their comrades were being slaughtered by the thousands. Apparently, however, they received the same news as we did and had no idea of how badly their forces were doing. We heard only what the Chinese Communist propaganda machine wanted us to hear—severe defeats on our side and nothing but celebrated victories for the Communists. For example, those of us captured in late November knew nothing of the Allied withdrawal in December, except that the Chinese had informed us that "the enemy has been driven into the sea." Although we refused to believe this, some later arrivals at the camp confirmed that the Allies had pulled out of the Chosin Reservoir area and headed south. We would later learn from new prisoners that the 1st Marine Division had left the port of Hungnam and moved to the Masan area of South Korea.

I believe that another reason why our guards seemed so content was because they were not likely to be subjected to air raids in this small village, which was at least ten miles from the city of Kanggye. We usually heard only the B-29s, at thirty-five thousand feet or better, headed for the Yalu River. I do not recall any air attacks while I was held at Kanggye prison. If there were any antiaircraft units in the area, they were well hidden.

The average Chinese soldier came from a life of extreme hardship. Hunger and primitive living conditions were no strangers to him, and our guards were no exception. They had little or no formal education and were probably "volunteered" into the Army by CCF recruiters who came to their villages and persuaded them, through political and economic pressures, that it would be in their best interests and the interests of their families to enlist. In some cases, local officials in Chinese towns and villages had been assigned quotas to fill the ranks. As a general rule, families were required to furnish at least one male for military service; however, the average soldier was still expected to consider himself a volunteer. To say that this was a major step in his life would be an understatement. There were no provisions for discharge at the end of the war. The Chinese soldier remained in the army until he was killed, captured, or wounded or until he deserted.

Men from the same village usually went into the same company. The companies from the area were assigned to the same battalion and the battalions to the same regiment or division. Replacements also came from the same geographical area. This system had decided advantages. Not only was there camaraderie, but the soldiers spoke the same unique dialect. There were troops in our POW camp from different provinces who could barely communicate with one another because of the differences in their dialects.

Simultaneously with his military training, the Chinese soldier underwent extensive political indoctrination, and it continued during his length of service. Each company had a political officer who was usually equal in rank and authority to the company commander.

Like many CCF units, our guards carried a variety of weapons. The majority of the frontline troops who had taken us prisoner were armed with U.S. Thompson submachine guns, but most guards carried some type of rifle that was usually American, Japanese, Russian, or German. Two of the guards' favorites were the 1903 Springfield and M1 Garand, both manufactured in the United States. Their preferences depended largely on the availability of ammunition. No central ammunition supply point could handle ammunition requirements for such a variety of weapons. There was always an ample supply of .30-caliber ammunition lying around after the Americans pulled out of an area, and the Chinese also manufactured this caliber. It was not uncommon to see a Chinese soldier simply discard the weapon he had been carrying and grab a usable U.S. rifle because he knew that ammunition for it would be available.

An amusing incident involving an American weapon occurred

one day at our hut. Our guard was trying unsuccessfully to field-strip his weapon in order to clean it, and he was having a difficult time. It appeared that he didn't know how to remove the bolt correctly from the rifle. As we watched him fumble with the rifle, one of our squad members, an Army NCO, said, "Here, gimme that damned thing," and reached for the soldier's weapon. Amazingly, the guard handed it to him. The NCO removed the bolt and then proceeded, through sign language, to hold school on the proper way to disassemble, clean, and assemble a U.S. .30-caliber 1903 Springfield rifle.

This might seem a bit incredible, but the NCO could have done nothing with the weapon, even though the guard had a few rounds of ammunition in his cartridge belt. Given the severe weather, the terrain, and the presence of so many CCF troops, he obviously wasn't going anywhere. The Chinese guard was happy to have his weapon clean, the U.S. soldier was able to hold in his hands what many old-timers considered to be the finest bolt-action rifle that the United States ever made, and the rest of the squad enjoyed the show.

Most of our Chinese guards were not brutal, and some were friendly and helped us out in small ways whenever they could. This did not include giving us extra food, which they simply could not do. They had no access to any food.

One Chinese soldier stood more than six feet tall and was well built, certainly an uncommon sight among the guards in our camp. We named him "Big Boy" because of his mass, and he was an interesting character. He had worked as a chauffeur for the U.S. Army at the Shanghai International Settlement years before. He spoke some English and actually liked Americans. Of course, he never let his feelings be known when other Chinese, particularly the instructors, were about.

One day, he was in our room and began going through a chest of drawers left there by the family because they had no space for it in the next room. We had been warned not to touch any of the family's possessions and had not disturbed it, although we did peek into the drawers a time or two. As Big Boy began rooting around in the chest, he found a handsome brass spoon, a small pipe for smoking cigarettes, and a few pieces of heavy cloth that we were later able to use for patching our clothes and socks.

Mama-san never discovered her losses, at least not while we were quartered there, probably because neither she nor other members of the family were allowed in the prisoners' quarters. We greatly appreciated Big Boy's efforts to help us and made good use of the material. The brass spoon is my sole souvenir from those days in captivity. So much for the "take not a single needle" rule.

Big Boy stayed with us for some time, although, like the other guards, he was not always posted at the same house. In the coming months, we would have occasion to be very glad that he was around.

One amusing incident provided some insight into the simple peasant lifestyles previously experienced by most of our guards. After a study period one afternoon, I had one small piece of notepaper left, the usual five-by-seven size from a pad. I folded the paper into the form of an airplane, the type that kids made to sail across the classroom, much to the consternation of their teacher. The day was not terribly cold, and I walked onto the porch to give the fragile plane a toss. A light breeze caught it and carried it across the road and into a snowbank—an aero-dynamic masterpiece.

The Chinese guard was astonished. He had never seen anything like this, and he raced across the road to retrieve the plane. When he handed it back to me, I gave it a second flight and it sailed even farther. He retrieved it again. I showed him the correct method of throwing it and let him try his hand at it. He was overwhelmed, so I let him keep it and went back inside the hut.

Several hours later, after the guard had changed, I was called outside. The off-duty guard was standing there with half a dozen pieces of paper. I knew what he wanted, of course, and I carefully folded each piece into its proper configuration. We gave the planes at least one test flight apiece. The guard trotted off to his quarters, happier than a four-year-old, no doubt to share his new treasures with his comrades.

I wondered how he had managed to get the paper, a commodity not easy to come by. To this day, I marvel at how a simple toy, one that I thought every schoolboy must have tried his hand at making, could give such joy to a young Chinese peasant turned soldier.

Our food now consisted mainly of sorghum seed because the holiday season was over. This sorghum was very high in fiber content and inevitably resulted in our being gassed up, a condition, of course, that is most easily relieved by the passage of gas, commonly referred to as "parting wind." Naturally, Marines have their own terminology for this type of event—sometimes using the colloquial expression of "cranking one off" or, simply, farting.

Sometimes, lying in our room at night after the evening meal, with our bloated bodies suffering, we started the usual crescendo. Whoever began the medley was soon topped by a louder individual, and that call was answered by still another, until everyone in the squad had added to the tune. Fortunately, the diet of sorghum did not contain enough substance to cause the unpleasantry of offensive odors in a closed space. Also, it goes without saying that those men troubled with dysentery did not participate but conducted their business outside in the head.

One guard, a likable sort who never gave us any trouble, thought that these nightly rumbles were nothing short of disgraceful. Each time he heard such goings-on, he stood by our door and shouted, "Boohow," the Chinese equivalent of "bad," to let us know that this was socially unacceptable. Whether this was some Chinese social custom or just his opinion, we didn't know, but he protested with "boohow" whenever he heard us.

One evening, a squad member lying close to the door called the guard and cranked one off. Saying "fart" very loudly, he explained what the noise was. After two or three repetitions, the guard said the word. He pronounced it "faht" because he could not manage the letter "r." From that night on, whenever he had the duty at our hut and heard us, he exclaimed, "Faht, boohow!" This phrase became his nickname, a dubious title that he carried for the remainder of his time with us.

The instructors differed from our guards in that they were obviously educated, had language training, and came from a higher social class. I was always under the impression that, like many of the Chinese medics, they had been jerked out of col lege before they had a chance to graduate because their English-language abilities were sorely needed in Korea.

English proficiency varied from one officer to another; most of them displayed a fair knowledge of the language and could read it, but their pronunciation sometimes made them difficult to understand. I liken this to our pathetic attempts to learn Chinese—the Mandarin dialect, I believe—that we tried to pick up to get us through the daily routine. Some of the Chinese sounds were extremely difficult, much more so than Japanese phrases that most of us knew. As is usually the case, bilingual Americans fared much better in learning the language.

There were no formal language classes at Kanggye. Each man had to pick up the language on his own. I came out of captivity with a limited Chinese vocabulary, including the words for hot, cold, water, rice, and thank you but not much more.

Lieutenant Pan was a hard-core Marxist who appeared to be totally committed to the cause and seemed determined that we, too, would be thoroughly indoctrinated. He presented himself as serious, strict, and without any sense of humor. During our initial indoctrination, he had told us of the consequences for not cooperating—of being a reactionary. His most often used expression was, "You will be punished wissout mercy!" He repeated the phrase often, the word "without" pronounced with the "s" because he could not pronounce the "th." His attitude and mannerisms earned him our nickname for him, "The Snake," always spoken out of earshot.

Lieutenant Liu was quite the opposite. He wasn't nearly as aggressive as Pan, took a milder approach to his duties, and seemed less dedicated to the cause of Communism. Our nickname for him was "Egghead" because he was, at times, less than professional and also comical. Unlike Lieutenant Pan, he did not appear to be meanspirited.

With at least a dozen instructors in the camp at Kanggye, these two were the only ones that my squad knew very well. In spite of our harsh living conditions and the lack of a proper diet and medical care, we could have had it much worse. There was no doubt, as those of us who survived would later learn, that we were extremely fortunate to be in a "lenient policy" camp and, even more so, to be in the hands of the Chinese Communists, rather than under the control of the barbaric North Koreans.

# =10=

# A Cultural Affair

DURING THE FIRST week of February 1951, as we were herded into the barn for another learning session, someone noticed a group of four new American prisoners standing alone in a corner of the large building. I glanced over in their direction and did a double take, unable to believe my eyes. Among them was my buddy, Marine Cpl. Andrew "Chief" Aguirre from Baker-22! The other men were Cpl. Jim Glasgow, Cpl. Joe Saxon, and Pfc. Nick Antonis, also crew members of the tank to which I had tried to be assigned. All kinds of questions raced through my mind: How could a Marine tank crew get captured? When and where were they captured? Where was their tank commander, Sgt. Bob Dolby?

Fortunately, it took a few minutes for the Chinese lecturer to get to the podium. I walked over to Chief, and the first words out of my mouth were, "Chief, what in the hell are you doing here?"

He replied, "I'm a prisoner, Len, just like you." It was a good answer to a dumb question.

We had just enough time for him to tell me a few details of the tank crew's capture. Although I would not learn more until later, I knew that Aguirre's story was truly amazing.

During the night of 10 December, Company B tanks were the last vehicles in a long convoy winding its way south, down the narrow Funchilin Pass, from Koto-ri to Chinhung-ni. The brakes froze on one of the M-26 Pershing tanks located in the middle of the company column.

As the tanks in trace began to stack up behind the stalled vehicle, the tank commanders tried desperately to contact their platoon leaders and determine the cause of the holdup. Because of the mountainous terrain and winding road, radio contact was sporadic; some tank commanders could not reach their platoon leaders. A small platoon of Marines from the division's reconnaissance company, led by 1st Lt. Ernie Hargett, was covering the rear of the mechanized column, and most of the stalled tank crews were able to bail out and reach the portion of the column that was still moving. The crew of B-22, the last vehicle in the convoy, however, remained in their tank as they waited for the return of Sergeant Dolby, who had gone ahead on foot to learn what was causing the delay. By the time Dolby returned, Chinese Communist troops were swarming on and around his tank.

There were various accounts of the recon Marines banging on the hull of B-22 and yelling for the crew to abandon their tank, but, as Aguirre said later, "How in the hell did we know who was doing the banging, and if they were Marines, why didn't they use the TI [tank-infantry] phone?"

Like many tank models, the M-26 Pershing was equipped with an external telephone in an armored box on the rear of the tank. Infantry troops were trained to use this phone, which had a long extension cord, to contact the tank commander under combat conditions in order to direct the tank or to point out potential targets.

The B-22 crew finally dropped the escape hatch and slipped out from beneath their vehicle and, undetected by the enemy, tumbled down a steep incline into the darkness. Now led by Chief Aguirre, the crew were never able to catch up with the moving friendly forces, but they managed to elude the Chinese for two days. Aguirre had acquired a working knowledge of the Chinese language while he was on post–World War II occupation duty in northern China. The crew hid by day, and Aguirre slipped them past several enemy roadblocks and checkpoints in the dead of night by mumbling some familiar greetings when challenged. Their luck finally ran out when some alert sentries detected their ruse and took them prisoner.

Unlike the captives from Task Force Drysdale, who were

immediately marched northwest to Kanggye, Aguirre and his crew were taken in the opposite direction, almost to Hungnam, before they began their difficult trek to Kanggye. Although taken prisoner only twelve days after our group had been captured, they did not arrive at Kanggye for six more weeks.

They were a sorry-looking foursome after their long march and were just as tired and beat-looking as we had been when we arrived in camp. Their overall-type tanker's suits were smeared with black, oily goo. An enemy round had pierced the transmission housing of the tank while they were sitting ducks, and gallons of transmission fluid had drained onto the ground beneath their tank. When they exited the tank through the escape hatch, they had to slide through the mess to reach the side of the road.

Because of their late arrival at Kanggye, the tank crew was quartered in another part of the camp. My only chances to visit with them were during campwide education sessions at the barn. I couldn't get over the irony of the situation, and, even to this day, I still laugh about it. The tank crew that I had tried so hard to join was the *only* Marine tank crew captured during the Korean War. If I had been granted my wish, I would have ended up at the same place—Kanggye.

Early in January, the Chinese began to publish a camp newspaper, titled *The New Life*, and encouraged the prisoners to submit articles for it. They offered a reward of two tailor-made cigarettes to any individual whose article was selected for publication. The few collaborators among the prisoners jumped at the chance to get their stories published, but the majority were reluctant to write anything that could possibly help the Communists.

As time passed, however, more and more men began contributing harmless articles of gibberish to the paper. I even wrote a story. The subject was labor unions in the United States, and I offered my opinion of them. I had never had much love for unions, and my dad had fought them most of his life. For my effort, I received two cigarettes. To a smoker, the cigarettes were a treat, even though they were a Chinese brand. We had lowered ourselves to stealing tobacco from the Koreans, who dried it on their porches, and we wrapped it in whatever paper we could find or even in light cardboard. Then, we coaxed matches from the guards to light up.

I never saw or heard about the type of press that the Chinese had, but their newspaper stock was thin, even thinner than what we called onionskin paper used for typing carbon copies. Actually, I believe that it was rice paper. It proved excellent for wrapping tobacco, and the smokers in our group welcomed each new edition.

One day, Lieutenant Pan came to our hut to ask for our opinions about some of the articles in an edition distributed throughout the camp only minutes before. We were smoking the newspaper when he arrived. He knew that we couldn't have read the paper by then, and he questioned us on the contents. When we played dumb, he nearly blew a fuse. We were not so fast to smoke the newspaper from then on.

It is true that some rather hard-core material was written by the real progressives in camp. Two such articles were titled "Truman, a Swindler," and "We Were Paid Killers." President Truman, Gen. Douglas MacArthur, and John Foster Dulles were, by far, the favorite targets of these writers, and the Chinese were particularly pleased about their attacks. The authors of the articles, however, would have to account for their actions when, or if, they returned home.

Most of the articles, which we generally considered harmless, were motivated, no doubt, by the desire for a smoke or two. Some of them were even humorous. The editor of the newspaper, one of the Chinese instructors, sometimes added a cartoon to an article for additional emphasis, which also provided a bit of laughter, a scarce commodity in our prison camp.

A few years later, certain military "experts," authors, and so-called military historians would have a field day with these innocuous literary efforts and suggest that any articles written by us played right into the hands of the Communists. In 1957, the subject of *The New Life* even came up during congressional hearings on the treatment of American prisoners of war by the Chinese and North Koreans. It's easy to look back on history and find fault—to point out what the "man in the arena" should have done. Perhaps that is the low-cost benefit of 20/20 hindsight, particularly when one was not in the arena with him.

* * *

The cold weather continued into February. One effort to keep warm came close to costing the lives of eight of our squad members, myself included. Our room was always cold, and one of the men had the bright idea of making a hibachi-type of heating pot for the room. We found a container, filled it with ashes and dirt, conned Mama-san out of a few hot coals, and, within minutes, had the heater fired up. None of us had the slightest idea of what we were doing; a few minutes later, the room was filled with deadly carbon monoxide. One by one, we drifted off to sleep.

We attributed our rescue only to the grace of God. Two of the squad members had left the hut earlier to bring back the evening meal. When they returned and opened the door, we were all unconscious.

Ernie Hayton, one of the men on the chow detail, later said that he knew something was wrong as soon as he opened the door. Not only did the room have a strange odor about it, but we didn't jump up to get the chow. He and the other man dragged each of us out of the hut and laid us in the snow. When we finally came to and realized what had happened, we got rid of our "heater" in a hurry. This was the second time that Ernie had saved my life. I have no recollection of how long the pot had been in the room or how long we had been unconscious, but one thing was certain—we had survived a very close call.

The lack of proper medical care continued to plague the camp. The more seriously ill and wounded were hauled away to what our Chinese instructors said was a "complete hospital with beds and good care," but most of the patients who left Kanggye were never seen again. One of the MPs who had been captured with us said that, while he was in the "hospital," four or five POWs had died of dysentery alone within one week. The camp hospital was actually a bombed-out building, and the sanitary conditions were all but nonexistent.

The Chinese continued to say that they had absolutely no medicine for dysentery, the disease that continued to be the biggest killer of U.S. POWs. They repeated many times, "The best medicines and food go to the frontline troops." Yet, one incident left me completely confused as to the medical care situation. In early February, I began to experience swelling of the glands on both sides of my throat and was having increased difficulty in swallowing. This condition really gave me a scare, as I had experienced it twice before coming back into the Corps. Then, I had been treated by a doctor who gave me some pills and told me that, if left untreated, the condition could cause my throat to swell to the point of being unable to eat.

Our Chinese medic, accompanied by one of the instructors, came around one morning and asked if any of us were sick. I explained my problem to him, and he examined me but didn't say much. That evening, many hours later, the medic was back with some large pills in hand. I followed his instructions about when and how to take them. In just a few days, I was fine.

The interpreter with the young medic told me that the "doc" had gone all the way to a Chinese Army medical supply unit to get the pills. He pointed toward the mountains in the west and said, "It take him all day to climb mountain and come back for you!" I'll never know how much of his story was true, although, at the time, I had no reason to doubt him. Then again, he could have merely walked across the Yalu River to get the medicine.

If the medic did make a special trip, I will never know why he made it for me. I can only believe that it was because I was a squad leader or perhaps because he was a bit more conscientious than his fellow countrymen. Whatever the case, it was very frustrating to know that I had received special treatment when other men continued to die from the dreaded amebic dysentery. The Chinese were truly a strange people.

One day, the Chinese announced that we would all attend a "cultural affair" the next evening. This event would be held in a schoolhouse near the city. The next day, at dusk, we were herded out of the Kanggye camp and marched south to the schoolhouse, at least ten miles away. There was plenty of grumbling among the ranks, as we figured the barn sessions were bad enough, but there was nothing we could do about it— attendance was mandatory.

We finally arrived at the schoolhouse and were crammed inside, more than 275 of us, and those North Korean school-houses were just not built to accommodate so many people.

Our instructors carefully explained that this affair was part of our education and that it was very important to learn the cultural background of the people. Groups of small children came inside and sang their patriotic songs. A chorus of NKPA soldiers (mean-looking bastards) sang marching songs and recited patriotic poetry. In numerous speeches, local officials and top military officers congratulated us repeatedly for having surrendered and wished us success in our cultural studies.

All of this, with the exception of the songs, was translated into English, and the program lasted for several hours. As far as we were concerned, all of this crap was adding insult to injury. The second time they held one of these cultural affairs, nearly half of the cold-numbed audience got up, walked out, and started back to Kanggye without the benefit of the guards. Lieutenant Pan and his cohorts were incensed and even appeared to be slightly hurt that we could reject such quality entertainment. They conducted no more cultural affairs after this, however; the Chinese had finally taken the hint.

Close to mid-February, the study material became much more involved with the theory of Marxism. As we had been doing for weeks, we listened to the diatribes and made few, if any, comments. I'll admit that most of us were not theoretical thinkers in the first place, and we saw no good reason to begin now.

The Chinese had chosen this time to implement their plan to subvert and convert their prisoners of war. Essentially, their plan was a diabolical scheme designed to demoralize, break a man's spirit, and completely subjugate the individual, thus making him easier to control. This was the same system, with some variations, developed and proved so successful by the Soviets, and the Chinese Communists were using it to control their own masses. Although they were never able to implement their plan fully at Kanggye, they did use it in other POW camps in North Korea with some degree of success.

The first phase was to separate the leaders from the other prisoners, which they had done with us; however, because of the lack of importance they placed on rank, they considered only commissioned officers to be leaders.

Using several methods, they attempted to create a feeling of "aloneness" among selected individuals. One way was to institute a system of informing. They stated that it was each and every man's duty to inform on someone who was disrupting the system. Their actions reminded us of the Hitler Youth Movement, where young children informed on parents and friends who made anti-Nazi statements. They rewarded informers, although, for obvious reasons, this was done in private. The person informed on was seldom punished in any way. The Chinese attempted to show him the error of his ways and, if they could, have him admit his guilt publicly. This method of demoralizing a man, when properly employed, tended to create a sense of distrust among the prisoners. They became isolated and had a tendency to crawl within a shell.

A second method of control, which was also used at Kanggye, was self-criticism—the "confession is good for the soul" type of thing. Basically, it was the same idea as that commonly used in group therapy. Under these circumstances, however, if the individual exposed just a bit too much of himself, it could leave him with a feeling of "nakedness" and vulnerability. One reaction, and actually the best defense for this feeling, was to try to get something on others to even the score. The Kanggye prisoners of war made something of a joke out of this criticism business. They got up and "confessed" to all sorts of ridiculous things, and the Chinese, apparently convinced of their sincerity, gave little rewards for these endeavors. One night, I announced to all of Kanggye that I had lied to the Chinese Communists during my initial interrogation. When questioned about my political affiliation, I said that I had never voted, when, in reality, I was actually a registered Republican and had voted for Thomas Dewey in the 1948 presidential election! I received two cigarettes for my confession.

A third method of control involved mail. Although we received no mail at Kanggye, the Chinese later controlled all incoming mail by withholding the happy-type letters, those containing good news and family photographs. They delivered only those letters with bad news, such as a death, an illness, or some other type of family problem. This, too, was designed to sustain the "nobody loves me" attitude of the individual soldier in order to make him vulnerable and manageable.

One of the primary goals of this program was to ensure that there would be no internal organizations within the POW camps—no buddy systems and no escape committees. The feelings of isolation and loneliness, which the Chinese were able to maintain in some individuals, probably contributed to an affliction that would result in more than a few deaths among the POW population. The strange malady became known as "give-up-itis" for lack of a better name. It usually attacked the younger, more passive individual who tended to be homesick and unable to cope with the deprivation and other hardships associated with captivity. He became uninterested in food, failed to keep himself clean during bouts of dysentery, and resisted all efforts of assistance. Unless the man was force-fed and cleansed, he could literally crawl into a remote corner and die within a few days.

This happened to a young Army private in my squad. At the time of his capture, his mother had been scheduled to undergo a serious operation. He was extremely anxious to hear the result of the surgery and talked about it constantly. Despite our efforts to help and comfort him, he worried himself sick over the lack of news and eventually died.

Although the Chinese Communists had some degree of success with this cruel system in North Korea, they made a major mistake by misjudging the tenacity of their American prisoners. They would not accept that Americans enjoyed a particular way of life, which they were unwilling to replace with anything that the Chinese could offer. American military personnel, by and large, were patriotic individuals. But, more significantly, they possessed a sense of traditional values and ideals and were not as opportunistic or as materialistic as the Chinese wanted to believe.

The Chinese formed a peace committee at Kanggye. It was the first such organization in a Korean POW camp. I cannot recall the names of its members, but I do remember that Lieutenant Pan selected S.Sgt. Charles L. ("Charlie") Harrison to write a "Stockholm Peace Appeal" patterned after a document that had originated at a meeting of world Communists in Stockholm, Sweden, in early 1950.

Charlie, a Marine MP who had been with our convoy and

was one of the squad leaders, was a two-time loser. He had been captured by the Japanese at Wake Island when that garrison was forced to surrender in late December 1941 and had spent almost four years in a series of Japanese prison camps. A natural-born leader, Charlie was a guiding force in our section of the POW village because we did not see Major McLaughlin except during our barn meetings.

Charlie wrote the peace appeal under the direction of Lieutenant Pan. Being too innocuous, the document fell short of what the Communists wanted and Charlie was ordered to write it again. Several tries later, Lieutenant Pan ended up writing the document himself, only to have most of the POWs refuse to sign it. After much haggling, it was finally agreed that only the peace committee members would sign the document, but they managed to make their signatures illegible. Lieutenant Pan was not a happy man.

A problem of a different sort also plagued the camp at Kanggye—body lice. At one time or another, nearly every POW was lousy. It was a recurring nightmare. No sooner was a man rid of lice than he was exposed to them again and had to repeat the process of delousing himself. We had delousing parties, where we took off our jackets (when our room was warm enough to allow it) and turned them inside out. The lice laid their eggs in the seams of our clothing, and we tried to find the eggs and destroy them. If we managed to do this, it saved a great deal of time and pain later. When we were finished with our jackets, we began the process on our trousers.

The lice were miserable little devils. Some actually grew to a recognizable size, though not much larger than the tip of a pencil. They were usually quiet as long as the temperature remained cold, but as the temperature rose, so did the lice. They scurried around on our bodies, making our skin crawl, to say nothing of the terrible itching they caused. We grew accustomed to them, though, and became adept at catching them. A man could unbutton his jacket or his trousers, reach in, and nab one without even looking for his intended target.

It was extremely disheartening when we had rid ourselves of lice and destroyed their eggs, only to enter another building and get reinfested. We knew that the lice inhabited the piles of

Len Maffioli in San Diego,
April 1948.

Pfc. Leonard J. Maffioli,
4th Marine Division, 1944.

Platoon 960, Marine Corps Recruit Depot, San Diego, 1943. Len is the
third Marine from the left, second row from bottom.
(*U.S. Marine Corps photo*)

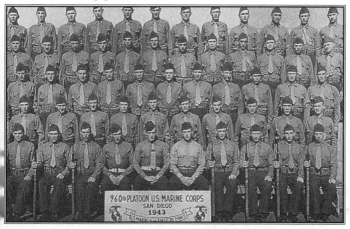

Near Seoul, Len guards his Jeep.

The escaped POWs, moments after being rescued by a tank section of the 7th Reconnaissance Company, 7th Infantry Division, U.S. Army, 25 May 1951. Len is at the far right.

Cpl. Frederick G. ("Fred") Holcomb, USMC. (*U.S. Marine Corps photo*)

Sgt. Charles W. Dickerson, USMC. (*U.S. Marine Corps photo*)

S.Sgt. James B. ("Smokey") Nash, USMC.
(*U.S. Marine Corps photo*)

M.Sgt. Gust H. ("Gus") Dunis, USMC.
(*U.S. Marine Corps photo*)

Cpl. Clifford R. ("Roy") Hawkins, USMC.
(*U.S. Marine Corps photo*)

Cpl. Ernest E. ("Ernie") Hayton, USMC. Len credits Hayton with saving his life on at least two occasions in Korea.
(*U.S. Marine Corps photo*)

Pfc. Theron L. ("Leon") Hilburn, USMCR.
(*U.S. Marine Corps photo*)

An "official" photograph of Len the day after his escape. The picture does not tell the whole story. Immediately after the photo was taken, all of the candy, cigarettes, and toilet articles were taken back by the Red Cross representative who had asked Len to pose for the photograph. (*U.S. Marine Corps photo*)

Len reenlists at Marine Corps Recruit Depot, San Diego, 1952. (*U.S. Marine Corps photo*)

Marine Sergeant Maffioli, 2 January 1953. (*U.S. Marine Corps photo*)

The Marine Corps Birthday Ball, Vienna, Austria, 1959.

Len laughs with Bing Crosby during a Marine Corps Toys for Tots program on the set of *Stagecoach*, August 1965.

Len (far right) and his brother-in-law Scotty (second from right) pose with a pair of marlin caught off San Diego from the *Marstan*, September 1966. (*Courtesy of The Marlin Club, San Diego, California*)

Len (at left) with 1st Tank Battalion, Vietnam, September 1967.

Len at a new school for Vietnamese children in September 1967.

Marine Security Guard Battalion graduation, Arlington, Virginia, November 1968. Len is in the front row, fifth from left.
(*U.S. Marine Corps photo*)

Consulate General Lee Dinsmore (front row, at left) and Master Sergeant Maffioli (at right) with members of the Marine Security Guard in Dhahran, Saudi Arabia, May 1969.

Len and Donna at the Marine Corps Birthday Ball, Kabul, Afghanistan, 1970.

Len greets Ambassador and Mrs. Robert G. Neumann at the Marine Corps Birthday Ball in Kabul, 1970.

Len (at right) with Royal Marine David L. Drysdale, son of Lt. Col. Douglas Drysdale of Task Force Drysdale fame, Marine Corps Recruit Depot, 1978.
(*U.S. Marine Corps photo*)

Master Gunnery Sergeant Maffioli, 1978.

Len salutes during retirement ceremony, Marine Corps Recruit Depot, San Diego, 1979.
(*U.S. Marine Corps photo*)

straw found in and near the animal shelters, and we tried to avoid these places at all costs.

From time to time when new prisoners joined our camp, they would be so lousy that we could see the lice crawling around on the outside of their clothing. Those men had been made to sleep in animal sheds while on the march. All of the other POWs avoided contact with them until they could properly delouse themselves.

The Chinese gave us some powder that they claimed was an insecticide, but it was useless. We tested it once by catching a large beauty, placing it in a small pile of the powder, and watching its reaction. Hell, the damned thing seemed to thrive on the powder. Several hours later, it still had no effect.

I don't know if the lice carried any type of disease, and I don't know of anyone who got very sick from them, but those little bastards could bite like hell. I still have a few small scars on my inner thighs from lice, and they were a problem that we could never solve.

By the end of February, something was beginning to happen at Kanggye. The Chinese suddenly took more interest in our health. Whereas the medic had usually come by once a week, his visits now became more frequent. Those men who complained of any type of sickness were asked repeatedly if they thought they could make a long journey.

Rumors began to fly throughout the camp that we were going to move, and, of course, the POW pundits had a field day with this story. Some said that we were all going to China for further education. Others claimed that we were headed south toward the front lines. One POW had it "from good authority" that we were all to be placed on a neutral ship and sent home. Finally, one cloudy day, we were marched into the barn for what our instructors called a "very special meeting." They seemed almost as excited as we were.

Once we settled down, the announcement came. The entire camp was to be moved to the south! The purpose of this move was to set up another POW camp where newly captured prisoners would be brought. Our job was to help these "newly liberated friends" get started on their routine of prison camp life and, of course, to help them with their studies of the Communist way. The Chinese did not forget the old lure of possible early release for those individuals who were most cooperative.

It goes without saying that all of the prisoners greeted this news with great enthusiasm. We immediately thought of the possibilities of escape or liberation by our own forces. Not forgotten, either, was the fact that, by traveling south, we would find a milder climate. Anything had to be better than the weather along the Manchurian border.

One of the biggest surprises was the announcement that we would travel by train and not be subjected to the forced-march routine that we had suffered during our trip to Kanggye.

We began packing up what meager possessions we had and constructed our packs to make them easy to carry. The Chinese cooks made up large batches of what they called "marching food," rice and soybean flour made into squares about two inches thick. This was far better fare than anything we had yet been given, but we were cautioned that it was to be eaten only when the Chinese could not obtain other food for us while we were on the move. Each squad was issued these squares, carefully counted out according to the number of men in the squad. We put them in long, socklike bags, often used by CCF soldiers, that we could hang around our necks.

Those POWs determined by the Chinese to be too sick for a long trip were transferred to that "good hospital with fine medical care" near our camp. Most of these men would not survive.

Finally, the long-awaited day arrived. Beginning at dusk, we were marched to the railyard at Kanggye and herded into old wooden boxcars. We were packed in so tightly that, if a man could sit down, he could do so only with his knees drawn up under his chin. The trip was not designed to be comfortable.

The day was 3 March 1951. Our group of prisoners had survived at Kanggye for seventy-one days. Not only had we seen many of our friends slowly die, but we had suffered physically and mentally. Now, we had no idea what lay ahead for any of us. But, one thing was certain—*no one* was sad to be leaving Kanggye.

# ===11===

# The Move South

OUR TRAIN RIDE south began as a miserable journey, although, by now, misery was something to which we had grown accustomed. The train's boxcars were in poor condition. I wasn't able to see the locomotive, but I can imagine that it was also in bad shape. After we pulled out of Kanggye, we hurried along at speeds that, at times, must have approached sixty or seventy miles per hour. When that old train ran downhill, it became a frightening ride as we rocked back and forth along the narrow-gauge rails. I was concerned for our safety, and I'm sure that I wasn't alone in wondering about the condition of the tracks, bridges, and rail switches. Trains and railroad tracks were favorite targets of Allied aircraft. The unwilling passengers rolling along in the pitch dark at high speed on this train had no way to know if a section of track or a bridge somewhere up ahead had been destroyed during the previous day.

We did feel a little better when, during a slowdown, we were able to slide the car's door open and see a railroad signalman—an old Korean civilian holding a dimly lit lantern. Later, one of the Chinese instructors explained that the North Koreans had an arrangement of signalmen, placed at given intervals of so many kilometers apart, who were responsible for knowing the condition of the track within their given areas. As a train rolled along, the engineer watched for the signal lanterns and, when given a proper wave of a lantern, kept the train moving. Fortunately, our train's engineer always got the go-ahead signal, and we never had to grind to a halt for any type of emergency.

Just before dawn at the end of the first night's ride, the train came to a stop. We were ordered out of the boxcars and marched to a small village, where we were housed for the remainder of the day. The train was hidden in a tunnel during daylight hours because the weather was fairly clear and the North Koreans did not dare to move it during daylight. That day, we were allowed, for the first time, to eat our "marching chow"—those tasty rice and soybean squares prepared at Kanggye.

That evening just before dusk, we were herded aboard the train to begin another leg of our trip. The second night's ride was pretty much the same as the first, except that some of the men were getting weaker and our living conditions became more miserable. The men with dysentery had nothing to use as a toilet but a few empty cans, and we were so crowded in the boxcar that most men just evacuated their bowels on the floor of the car. The stench grew to be horrendous, but we became accustomed to that, too.

At dawn on the morning of 5 March, the train stopped in a large railyard on the outskirts of a small city. We were quickly marched from the train, eastward, for about seven or eight miles to a small village in a narrow valley. The Chinese had not wanted to linger in the area of the railyard because of the obvious danger of prowling Allied aircraft, and we certainly had no objections to this prudent measure. From what we had seen, the North Korean railyards had taken quite a pounding.

Just how far we had traveled by rail or exactly where we got off the train was anyone's guess, but later studies placed our location at or near Kaechon, a large railroad junction located about fifty air miles north of Pyongyang. If that was the case, we had traveled a distance equal to about ninety-five air miles during the past two nights, but we still had one hell of a long walk ahead of us.

The Chinese guards found houses for us in this small village by using the same method of selection as they had at Kanggye. They forced the inhabitants of each house to move into one room and placed the prisoners in another. No one had gotten much rest during the trip, so it wasn't long before we had all drifted off to sleep. Early the next morning, we were rousted outside and formed into new squads, assigned to quarters by squad, and then notified that we would attend a lecture by some "high commander" at a local schoolhouse that day.

Around noon, we were marched to the schoolhouse and ushered inside, where we all sat on the floor. Lieutenants Pan and Liu were jabbering away, along with another instructor, and they appeared to be anxious. We figured that we were about to receive some important word. Inasmuch as we had been told that we were moving south to help set up new POW camps and that there was a possibility of our early release, we knew that something was about to happen. Besides, the Chinese hadn't brought us south for nothing.

We could have been flattened with a feather when Lieutenant Pan translated the commander's first few sentences. The Chinese had just received instructions from their high headquarters to send all but sixty prisoners back up north. Astonished at this news, we just stared at one another like zombies as we tried to comprehend what this could mean; why it was happening; and, more important, who among us would make up the sixty prisoners. It just didn't make sense. After the Chinese had gone to all the trouble of moving 270 POWs nearly one hundred miles by rail, this new decision shocked us all. We could not understand the Chinese or their inability to reason. To the best of my knowledge, they never explained their decision. Obviously, someone at a very high level had screwed up badly.

While the Chinese officer continued with his speech and Pan translated it, we were lost in our thoughts and concerns until we heard that the sixty men chosen to remain would continue to move south toward a position near the Chinese front lines. That statement earned our immediate attention. As each of us started hoping or praying that we would be among the "lucky 60," Pan ordered the guards to march us back to our huts, where we would be notified of those selected to make the trip south. Walking back to the houses, we discussed this latest "bombshell" that had been dropped on us. The 210 men not selected would have to endure their miserable journey back to the north, and we assumed that the trip back to Kanggye would be by train. The Chinese had not said otherwise.

A short time later, one of the instructors came to our hut and called outside about half of the members of my new squad, including myself. He told us that we were to go back to the schoolhouse, where we would meet the other prisoners who had been selected to travel south. To this day, it is difficult to explain the mixed feelings that came over us. We were relieved that we had been selected, but we also felt regret for our friends who would not be going with us.

When our group assembled, we could finally see who had been chosen. The four other Marine truck drivers from my company, Charles Dickerson, Ernie Hayton, Roy Hawkins, and Leon Hilburn, were there, as were Chief Aguirre of tank B-22, Charlie Harrison, Marine 1st Lt. Frank E. Cold of the U.S. 7th Marines, and Royal Marine Rueben Nichols. In all, twenty-four U.S. Marines, one Royal Marine, and thirty-five U.S. Army soldiers had been selected to continue the march south.

Those returning north included Major McLaughlin and all of the other officers, AP photographer Noel, and the rest of the enlisted soldiers and Marines. They would be force-marched to various prison camps in Pyoktong and Chonsong along the Yalu River. Several men would die along the way. Gone for them was any hope of liberation, escape, rescue, or release.

A short time later, the prisoners who were returning north were brought into the schoolhouse. We were allowed a few minutes to say good-bye to our friends and to wish them good luck. Not a few tears were shed by these brave men. Little could we have realized, at that moment, just how many of them would not survive the coming years of brutal captivity.

That evening, our group was marched off to another village and billeted there for the night. Two days later, we began a forced march that would take nearly two months and cover an estimated three hundred miles.

We walked during the night and slept during the day in whatever type of shelter we could find. Although we hadn't come as far south as we had hoped, the early spring-like temperatures were much less severe. Some of the hilltops of higher elevations were still covered with snow, but others were bare.

The melting snow and mud added to the drudgery of the march, but there was less danger of frostbite.

When houses in a village were available, the Chinese requisitioned our quarters in the usual manner. With only sixty prisoners to manage, they had fewer problems in finding the necessary seven or eight huts, compared with the number needed on our previous march. Unfortunately, some of us frequently had only animal pens to sleep in, and we were again covered with body lice.

By far, the biggest difference between this trek and the forced march to Kanggye was in the pace. It was not nearly as frantic; we normally covered no more than eight to ten miles each night and had longer breaks. We also had the advantage of being accompanied by some of the guards who had been with us at Kanggye, and Lieutenants Pan and Liu were still with us. Also, the false promises each night of good food, a warm house, and a hospital for the sick were gone. I'm sure that even Lieutenant Pan realized by now that no one believed his bullshit.

We first moved toward the east, somewhere in the vicinity of Tokchon, but soon started south toward the village of Yangdok. On this leg of the march, we began to see the effects of the war on the villages and towns and particularly on the civilians. This area had changed hands several times. It had been taken by the ROKs, who were then routed out by the CCF. The local people had little or nothing left; their food and livestock had been confiscated by the CCF and NKPA. Many of the houses had been leveled, and others were badly damaged from artillery fire. Children roaming the area looked like they were as hungry as we were.

For the first time since our capture, we began to notice a change in the attitude of the civilians. They appeared to have mixed feelings toward us. Some of them acted as though they'd like to be friendly, but, in the presence of the Chinese, they didn't dare. I believe this change in attitude was due to their having been robbed blind by the Communist troops, whereas the ROK soldiers had not been barbaric in their dealings with these people.

Early one morning, following a good night's march, we

were billeted in a house. The Papa-san of the place stood in the room while the guard ushered us in. When the guard left, the old man went around the room and shook hands with each of us to let us know how he felt. His feelings were quite a contrast to the hatred shown to us by other people in North Korea.

We normally stayed in a village anywhere from a day to nearly a week, depending primarily on how much food was available. As these people didn't have very much, we subsisted mainly on only sorghum and millet. There was no rice.

One day, our Chinese guards "bought" a pig from a local farmer. We could tell by the anguished look on the poor man's face that he was getting screwed in the deal because he had to take what was offered. I'm sure that payment was in the form of Chinese currency, which was totally useless to the farmer. We welcomed the very small pieces of pork, however, that showed up in that evening's portion of sorghum gruel.

While we were on the night marches, the Chinese began to practice air attack drills. We were now in the north-central area of North Korea, and Allied air activity was nearly continuous during periods of good weather. Also, there was beginning to be more of it. The threat of an air attack was constant, particularly now that jet fighters had been introduced to the battlefield. Unlike propeller-driven aircraft, they could be over us long before we heard them. The air attack drill consisted of several whistle blasts—the signal to freeze—no matter where we were or what we were doing at the time. If we were crossing a stream or a river, so be it; we froze on the spot.

This defensive measure was incorporated into the march because, often on a night mission, an Allied aircraft dropped an illumination flare and then flew back to bomb or strafe any visible targets, particularly those that appeared to be moving. If we remained stationary, it was much more difficult for the attacking pilot to determine that we were beneath his aircraft. These air attack drills were a good idea. A plane dropped a flare over us one night while we were on the move. Lieutenant Pan blew his whistle, and we froze. The pilot evidently didn't see any worthwhile targets because he moved on.

Early one morning, after another long night's walk, we were

settling down in a house and getting ready to flake out (sleep) when Marine Pfc. Leon Roebuck said, "I don't feel well at all."

He laid down and was soon unconscious. He had complained of a fever and stomach pains for several days and had been eating snow to cool himself off. We immediately yelled for our guard. Somewhere, the Chinese found a medic who came to our room with a small first-aid kit. I helped open Roebuck's clothing. The "doc" felt around and remarked about Leon's stomach. I felt his gut, and it was as hard as a rock. It was soon apparent that he wasn't breathing.

Muttering something, the medic took out a long hypodermic syringe, filled it, and drove the needle directly into Leon's chest, in or near his heart. There was no effect—Leon Roebuck was dead. I notified Charlie Harrison, who was in the next room. He went in to remove Roebuck's dog tags, placed one tag in Leon's mouth, and kept the other one.

I still carried my GI missal, the little prayerbook given to Catholic servicemen, and I located the Twenty-third Psalm, which I read over Leon's lifeless body. We then carried him outside to a place that the guard had selected near the entrance to the yard and returned inside. The next morning, as we were marched away, we noticed that Leon's body was frozen stiff. The nighttime temperature had dropped well below freezing.

Leon Roebuck had been captured with us on the morning of 30 November 1950. A truck driver for Service Battalion, 1st Marine Division, he had been part of Task Force Drysdale. He was the only black Marine in the column, a damned good Marine and close friend to many of us.

Some forty-one years later, I had a strange and emotional experience. After attending an MIA/POW Recognition Day ceremony at March Air Force Base in Riverside, California, my wife and I stopped in at the Officers' Club for a drink. The bartender, a black woman, greeted us cordially and asked what we wanted to drink. As we ordered, I casually mentioned that we had come from the ceremony and told her that I had been a POW during the Korean War. She said that she had lost her favorite uncle in Korea. As she turned to make our drinks, she added, "The name was Roebuck."

Without even thinking, I blurted out "Leon!"

She quickly spun around and asked how I knew his first name. I explained to her that not only had I served with her favorite uncle, but that I was with him when he died.

His niece told me that Leon had suffered an attack of appendicitis while he had been home on leave, just before leaving for Korea. She was not sure if he had been operated on before leaving, and it could be that he had died from peritonitis.

A second Marine, Pfc. Hans Grahl, one of the MPs who had been captured with us, also got very sick during the march. Chief Aguirre helped to carry him for several days. When Grahl became too ill to proceed, the Chinese ordered Chief to leave Grahl and continue the march. He was never seen again, and we presumed that he died shortly afterward. We were now down to fifty-eight POWs, twenty-two of us Marines.

After more than a week on the move, we came to a small town, where we were to stay for a couple of days. We heard the sound of a bombardment in the east as we approached, and the ground literally shook when we got closer.

Most Koreans spoke Japanese because that language had been mandatory during years of Korea's occupation by Japan. Charlie Harrison, who had learned Japanese during his four years of imprisonment during World War II, and U.S. Army Cpl. Saburo ("Sam") Shimomura found out what was happening. Sam was a nisei (Japanese-American), originally with a U.S. Army intelligence unit but attached to the 1st Marine Division as an interpreter.

Charlie and Sam found a Korean civilian who was not afraid to talk to them. He told them that we were close to Wonsan— the very place where we had made our administrative amphibious landing back in October. According to our calculations, we had walked a distance equal to nearly 100 air miles since we left the train. Because we had followed a zigzag route, we probably had walked more than 150 miles as we crossed the narrowest part of the Korean peninsula from west to east. We learned later that the constant rumbling sounds came from the 16-inch guns of the USS *Missouri* that were shelling the Wonsan area.

When it became apparent that not all of the POWs were of the same strength and stamina, the Chinese split up the group.

The smaller group, the men who were slower, walked for longer periods of time in order to maintain the distance made by the main body. Some of us referred to the smaller group as the "sick, lame, and lazy squad." The number of men in that squad varied from five to ten members. With my dysentery acting up again, I was assigned to the smaller group, as was Chief Aguirre. When it became known that the "sick" squad had it a little easier, more men managed to get themselves assigned to it. Several interesting incidents, some amusing and others quite serious, involved our group.

One day, while we were walking along a mountain road in clear weather, we stopped in a forested area that kept us well concealed from the air. We were sitting alongside the road when a North Korean unit came by. The leader saw that we were Caucasian and halted his men. He approached a POW and, in the only English he probably knew, asked, "Why did you come to Korea?"

A Marine (I can't remember which one), who happened not to be in the mood for stupid questions, answered, "To kill North Koreans!"

The NKPA officer stood there seething. He pointed his burp gun (small submachine gun) at the Marine and began ranting and raving. With our guards and the Chinese lieutenant sitting with us, he had to know that we were prisoners, but he continued to press the point until the instructor barked a command at him. He glanced over and saw that the instructor had his German Mauser machine pistol pointed directly at him. There was no doubt as to who was in charge, and the North Korean unit left in a hurry.

On another day, the sick squad was crossing a wide, open plain with no mountains or covered terrain close by. The weather was clear, and I guess the only reason that we were walking was to make up for lost time. There were six of us, plus a pair of guards. I was carrying a large bucket, similar to a coal scuttle, that contained our chow.

We were halfway across the open area when a U.S. Navy fighter showed up overhead. Obviously on the lookout for targets of opportunity, it wasn't very high, perhaps a thousand feet or lower. We figured that we had really had it, this time.

The pilot saw us—he could hardly have missed us—and we all wished that we were wearing something other than Chinese quilted uniforms. We put our hands over our heads, as though that would have done any good, but the guards motioned for us to hit the deck and remain motionless. I remember trying to hide behind that bucket. A foolish feeling still comes over me when I realize that the bucket would not have provided any protection whatsoever. I wanted to dig a hole and hide in it.

The plane came in lower and began to circle. As we lay there, we prayed that the pilot would consider us a waste of ammunition. We made a point to look up at him in the hope that he could see our Western features.

We would never know what kept him from strafing us. Perhaps he saw our faces or even our hands in the air for that one brief moment; when he saw no weapons, he might have guessed that we were noncombatants. Whatever the reason, he flew off toward the hills, where some idiot opened up on him with an automatic weapon. We watched the show as he climbed, circled back, and then made a couple of strafing attacks before dropping a single bomb. He played around with his target for no more than five minutes and then flew off for home, probably low on fuel and ammunition. Whoever that Navy pilot was, we thanked him, as well as God.

One afternoon, during the best weather that we had encountered in North Korea, four or five of us were sitting on the porch of a house where we were billeted. We were enjoying the warmth of the sun on our faces when two North Korean officers appeared. They were toting burp guns and were followed by two fairly attractive young girls, also in uniform. They were resplendent in their sharp dress—a good-looking foursome. The Chinese uniform, whether officer or enlisted, was baggy and shapeless, with no styling whatsoever. The wearer looked like, as commonly referred to by Marines, "Joe Shit, the rag-man." The North Korean uniform, patterned after the Soviets', gave the wearer a much more tailored appearance.

When the NKPA officers spotted us, they suddenly stopped, unslung their weapons, and began to yell at us. Apparently, they were ordering us to surrender.

The guard was taking a nap in our room, and we called for

him to come out. We pointed to the North Koreans, but we weren't particularly concerned—we hadn't even bothered to get up. I don't know exactly what the guard said, but it must have been something like, "You dumb assholes, they already *are* POWs, shove off!"

The two girls burst out laughing and pointed at the officers, who reslung their burp guns and marched off. The girls were still giggling. I didn't know that a Korean could get red-faced with embarrassment, but those two definitely did.

The house where the sick squad was billeted was a little better than most, by Korean standards. It was protected by a walled compound, with four houses joined together in a U-shape and a small courtyard in front. Papa-san had two oxen, which probably made him one of the wealthier Koreans in the region. There was a small beehive, similar to the type used in the United States, on the porch in the center of the compound. The weather had warmed to the point that some honeybees were using the hive. One of the Chinese guards, a new kid whom we didn't know very well, began to watch the bees with great interest. Perhaps he came from a province where they didn't have any bees, but, whatever the case, he decided to see what would happen if he plugged up the entrance to the hive.

He placed some twigs in the entranceway. It didn't take long for the bees to decide to attack him. They stung the kid at least four or five times on his neck and face, but he put up a brave front and tried to act as though the beestings didn't hurt. I believe that our laughing probably hurt him more. Finally, much the wiser, he pulled out the twigs and left the area for a while until the bees calmed down.

At this same compound, we were to get a special treat—our first in months. Standing on the porch one day, I was playing my harmonica and entertaining our guard when a young boy who lived in the house came over to listen. Not more than ten or eleven years old, he seemed fascinated with the mouth harp, probably because he had never seen or heard one before. By his gestures, he wanted me to give it to him, but I refused. Then, he indicated that he only wanted to try to play it, which I also refused. Suddenly, I had an idea.

The Mama-san of the house had cooked up some yud. The

aroma wafting across the compound had been driving us crazy. Yud is a Korean candy made from molasses and formed into patties of varying size, but they were usually about four inches in diameter and half an inch thick. We hadn't had any sweets since the Christmas party at Kanggye. There were only five of us in the sick squad, so I figured what the hell. Using sign language and the word "yud," I told the kid that, if he brought me five patties of the candy, the harmonica was his.

He had to wait until nightfall, while the candy was cooling and all was quiet, to scale a wall and conduct his raid. The next morning, there he was with candy in hand and wanting his mouth harp. He got the harmonica, we each got a delicious patty, and I thought that would be the end of the story. For some reason, I hadn't given any thought to the fact that the old gal might miss some of her goodies.

We hadn't heard such a commotion since the missing egg caper back at Kanggye! Mama-san was yelling and crying, and, of course, we Americans were the first ones to be accused because no one dared to point a finger at our Chinese guard. He was able to testify in our defense, however, as he knew that none of us had left our room that night. The evidence was gone, having been consumed within five minutes of receipt.

All this time, the kid, feigning innocence, was blowing on his new harmonica. For some unexplained reason, Mama-san didn't seem to tie in the missing candy with his new possession.

Later, I regretted the deal. The kid had no musical talent whatsoever, and we had to endure the noise for the rest of the time we were there.

Just before we left the compound to move out again, the five of us were on the porch. We saw some Chinese bartering with a farmer for an ox that he obviously did not want to sell. They gave the farmer some kind of currency and slaughtered the animal on the spot. When they carried the meat up the road, we walked out to the entrance of the compound and peered around the wall to see where they were going with it. Not surprisingly, they took it straight into the hut where the Chinese prepared the food for their troops. We wondered and hoped if we might be lucky enough to get a few pieces in that night's chow.

Later, while Chief Aguirre and I were still on the porch, we saw two Chinese soldiers carrying a dog, very much dead with its legs tied together and strung on a pole, in the same manner that hunters would carry a dead tiger. Being curious, we looked around the wall and watched them carry that poor mutt to the hut where the food was prepared for the prisoners. Sure enough, that evening, there were some small pieces of meat mixed in with our sorghum. When the other squad members commented that the beef was a little stringy, neither Chief nor I had the heart to tell them what they were actually eating. Besides, we all needed the protein.

We finally moved out of the area. The sick squad hated to leave because we had enjoyed the most comfortable quarters to date, and it had been a restful stay. We walked for several days toward the southwest until we came to a village where, our instructors said, we would spend the next few weeks.

We set up camp and again resumed our studies. This time, they consisted primarily of lectures and meetings. As usual, the latter were in the local schoolhouse. We hadn't been in the village for more than a few days when Lieutenant Pan announced an important meeting. When we all assembled in the schoolhouse, Pan dropped the biggest bombshell yet. He announced that one-half of the prisoners were to be released! These men would be taken to the front lines and turned over to Allied forces.

When we finally quieted down, Pan said that the names of those selected for release would be announced the following morning. He then followed up with a lecture about the glorious cause for which these men were being sent home—to continue the fight for "world peace."

The purpose of the delay in announcing the names of the fortunate men, we assumed, was to let us all sweat it out. One of the favorite tactics of the Chinese was to lower our morale. Few, if any, of us slept that night.

During the waiting period, Lieutenants Pan and Liu and the other instructors visited with the squads. Each prisoner was asked why he would like to be included in the group to be freed. Although this might have sounded like a stupid question, we had to be extremely careful in our answers. Wanting to see one's family or to eat some decent food again was not what they wanted to hear. The Chinese had already explained many times that a "true friend of the people" and a "champion in the cause for world peace" would not care whether he were sent home, just as long as he could continue his work against capitalism and Allied aggression.

Dawn finally broke. After breakfast, the guards marched us down to the schoolhouse for the much anticipated news. When we had finally settled down, Lieutenant Pan called off the names of twenty-nine men and told them to move to the right side of the room. All others were to move to the left side.

We must have been a sorry-looking lot. All of us looked at each other and wondered which group had been selected to go home. It seemed logical that those who had their names called first were the ones to go, but logic didn't always apply when the Chinese Communists were running the show. I was particularly worried because the four tank battalion drivers from my unit were on the right side of the room, and I was on the opposite side.

Lieutenant Pan, that arrogant bastard, was obviously enjoying himself. He said that one of the two groups was to be released and then asked aloud, "Who shall go, the men on the right side, or the men on the left?" He then turned to the Chinese commander standing beside him, and they both laughed as they scanned the groups of anxious faces.

After nearly ten minutes of toying with us, Pan finally announced that the group of men on the right side of the room would be allowed to go. Those of us on the left side had a difficult time trying to control our tears, which resulted more from anger than disappointment. If the bastards wanted to send someone home, more power to them, but they didn't need to get everyone's hopes up! That was our impression and our attitude.

Lieutenant Liu led the group of "unfortunates" to our quarters, while the others stayed at the school to discuss the details of their release with Lieutenant Pan. I let Liu know, in no uncertain terms, just what I thought of their system and all of the bullshit they had been handing out. He then explained how we had been selected.

In my case, it was because of my good work as a squad leader. I was needed to help with the new prisoners. On the other hand, Charlie Harrison, although considered a good squad leader, was being released because of his four long years in Japanese captivity, and they feared that he was beginning to crack under the strain. Even in our disappointment, we had to laugh at that one. Good old Charlie had outfoxed them again by convincing the Chinese that he would be of greater value to them in the United States.

The next several days were busy ones. We attended several "peace rallies," during which several of us were delegated to make speeches to our departing friends and assure them that we would continue the fight in Korea. On the other side, Harrison and a couple of others assured us they would continue the fight at home.

Lieutenant Pan was the one who "volunteered" individuals to give their speeches. For instance, he said, "Maffioli [or Harrison], write a speech and I will correct it and you will give it." Oddly enough, although we never did specify what we were going to fight for, the Chinese didn't seem to catch on.

These rallies were serious business. The messages on large banners read, "Farewell Party for American POWs Going Home" and "Fight for World Peace." The Chinese had cameramen present, and even a newsreel team from China covered the events.

The men who were headed home were also given propaganda and "surrender leaflets" to pass out (urging Allied troops to surrender) when they returned to Allied lines.

There was some delay in the departure of the "freedom" group. Lieutenant Pan charged the delay to difficulty in making the proper arrangements for the men's release. While they waited, the men in the freedom group received some pretty good meals, while we ate the same old fare.

Finally, the word came for them to leave. After many good-byes and requests to contact our families when they got home, the rest of us watched them shove off. The lucky devils—we wished them all Godspeed, but we didn't get much time to dwell on them. That same night, the twenty-nine of us left behind were headed in a different direction.

At daybreak the next morning, we appeared to be heading south and probably had been during most of the night. We couldn't help but wonder about the other bunch. How far had they gone, what route had they taken, or, how far away were they from the front lines? That was something the Chinese never mentioned anymore—how far away the fighting actually was. This was probably to discourage any escape attempts; the weather was much better and we were now closer to Allied units than at any time since our capture.

We rested during the day and hit the road again that night. We could only wonder, as we walked through the darkness, just how far it was to this new camp, where we would be expected to help out with the new POWs.

# ═══12═══

# Escape

PLODDING ALONG NIGHT after night, we knew that we were getting closer to the front lines. We could hear the distant sounds of booming artillery and other heavy weapons. Occasionally, we saw probing searchlight beams as they bounced off the low-lying clouds—a method used by Allied forces to illuminate the battlefield at night.

We all continued to lose weight and grow weaker because of our meager rations. The Chinese guards again formed a sick squad, and my recurring dysentery qualified me for membership.

We saw more and more CCF units heading in the same direction as our group and, on a few occasions, even marched along with them. This was a variation to the former rules of march. We had always moved as an independent unit and had been kept safely away from CCF and North Korean troops.

One night, we came upon a Chinese unit that was using oxcarts to haul equipment toward the front lines. The oxen were fairly slow, and we were able to keep up with the unit. Several of us recognized a very large Chinese soldier—it was Big Boy, our former guard from the POW camp at Kanggye! When we called to him, he immediately recognized his nickname and came over to greet us. Big Boy saw our condition and gently loaded each of us onto an oxcart. No one, including our guards and instructor, seemed to be paying much attention to us, and we were able to get a much appreciated ride for

183

several miles. Then, we parted company with Big Boy for the last time.

Later, our squad was on the outskirts of a small village, where we came upon a group of North Korean soldiers with two American pilots whom they had captured only a few days before. Our Chinese lieutenant immediately halted the group to question the North Koreans, and we were able to speak to the pilots. One of them was Marine Capt. Mercer R. ("Dick") Smith, who had been flying with Fighter Squadron VMF-311.* Dick told us that it had been more than a little rough traveling with the North Koreans. To emphasize the point, he rolled up the right leg of his flight suit and showed us several stab wounds around his knee, where the North Koreans had bayoneted him. (Dick, a veteran pilot of World War II, had killed a North Korean guard during an escape attempt, and his present guards were ready to kill him at the slightest provocation).

The second pilot was also in pretty bad shape. His face had been badly burned as he tried to bail out of his plane, and the thick scabs over his eyelids were encrusted so heavily that he could barely open his eyes. He identified himself as U.S. Navy Ens. Thomas Biesterveld, assigned to an aircraft carrier in the Sea of Japan.

Our Chinese guards took control of the two pilots, despite the protests of the North Korean soldiers. Smith and Biesterveld eventually would be in the same camp as the rest of us, but we would not see them there.

Captain Smith would survive some twenty-eight months of captivity, remain in the Marine Corps, and fly during a third war in Vietnam. The two of us would meet again more than forty-two years later in La Jolla, California, and recount the events of the day that we met in Korea. Unfortunately, Ensign Biesterveld would never return from captivity; reportedly, he died from infection of his wounds.

We had been on the road a little more than a week and rested only one day before moving again. One night, we were on a

*See appendix C for excerpts from an interview with Smith.

short break when we heard the recognizable sound of American voices. Immediately, we thought that these must be some new prisoners that the Chinese were bringing to join us on our march. It was several minutes before the men came close enough for us to see their faces, but, before that, we recognized some of their voices. They were the original group of twenty-nine POWs who had been with us at Kanggye and were supposed to have been released earlier. A more disheartened group of men I had never seen. They were able to give us some of the incredible details of what happened to them before we began to move again.

The group had been force-marched south to a point just behind the front lines, when the Chinese decided that it was too dangerous to release the men and they were brought all the way back. They told stories of begging their Chinese guards to let them take their chances in traveling toward the front lines, but the Chinese refused to listen. Since then, they had covered a distance of some sixty to seventy miles.

What was particularly frustrating for these men was the fact that their release could have been accomplished in several ways. The Chinese soldiers possessed captured and abandoned American field radios; many of the POWs had some military communications experience and could have made radio contact with an Allied outfit. Any unit commander could have arranged a temporary cease-fire in the area and checked out the authenticity of the POW radio traffic. The best solution would have been a prearranged meeting, with the Allies notified in advance of a POW party coming through the lines at a given date and time. The Chinese had the means to accomplish this, but all of the POWs' requests were refused as being too dangerous. This was another blatant example of the insincerity of the Chinese claims—of pure deceit.

Several days later, we arrived in a large valley. We were told that it was our new home. In fact, it would become the site of the new Chinese POW camp. A sizable village in the valley had a small river running through it. With the snow gone and the weather warmer, we were allowed to take our first baths in more than five months.

The Chinese claimed to have captured a large number

of Americans during the spring offensive of 22–23 April.
They informed us that these captives would be brought to the
new camp.

We spent the next several days resting and cleaning up the
area for the new occupants. In early May, the Chinese brought
in the first group of about one hundred U.S. Army soldiers,
who had been prisoners for two weeks or less. When they were
free to move about the camp, we asked them hundreds of questions. Other than what the Communists wanted us to know, this
was our first news from the outside world in more than five
months. We were surprised to have the new prisoners verify
that the Allies had completely withdrawn from North Korea
and that Communist forces had recaptured Seoul and the
port of Inchon. The Chinese had told us many such things, but
we had refused to believe them. We also learned that Allied
casualties had been nowhere near as high as claimed by our
Chinese hosts, whereas Chinese losses had been incredibly
high.

Many of the new POWs had been wounded before or during
their capture. The few Chinese medics did what they could for
the prisoners, but they were hampered, as usual, by the lack of
medicines and medical equipment.

Although we did not know it at the time, our new camp was
located in the vicinity of Chorwon, one of the three points of
what became known as the Iron Triangle; the other two were
Pyongyang and Kumhwa. The area within this triangle was
comparatively flat and had fairly good roads, by Korean standards, that were used by the CCF as an MSR (main supply
route) for supplies and personnel. Also unknown to us,
Chorwon was a scant twenty air miles from the thirty-eighth
parallel.

Because the weather had cleared considerably and this
strategic area was heavily patrolled by Allied aircraft, we could
not stay in the village during daylight hours. Each day at dawn,
we walked into the nearby heavily forested hills, where classes
were held, chow was sent up at noon, and our drinking water
was brought up in old wooden buckets.

Actually, the camp was located in a beautiful area. Had it not
been for the miserable living conditions and our circum-

stances, the experience would have been pleasant. While the new POWs were undergoing interrogation, the rest of us were assigned to make up rosters of the new personnel. We made duplicate copies, which would later prove quite useful to U.S. intelligence officials.

During the next several weeks, U.S. prisoners continued to pour into the camp. Our POW population soon numbered more than three hundred. Many were soldiers from the 24th Regiment of the 25th Infantry Division, an all-black unit.

Because there was not enough food in the area to feed this many men, the Chinese organized food-gathering parties. These groups had to leave camp at dusk and walk some ten or twelve miles to a Chinese food distribution point. They drew supplies for the camp and returned before the first light of dawn. The pace was so fast that the prisoners sometimes had to run to keep up, a severe strain to their systems. Many were still weak from the effects of malnutrition, and others suffered recurring intestinal problems.

Hilburn, Hawkins, and I were among those chosen to make the first trip to the food distribution point. Accompanied by half a dozen Chinese guards, we started out at dusk and reached the distribution point at about midnight. Chinese troops were coming in from all directions to draw rice and flour for their respective units. Frontline troops had priority status, and we were issued only soybean flour.

While we were waiting to have our bags filled, a lone plane flew over. The pilot obviously saw a light somewhere and dropped a bomb. Fortunately, the impact wasn't too close to us, but the exploding bomb must have hit some of the hundreds of Chinese troops milling about. We managed to return to camp before dawn, but it was one hell of a physical strain. Each of us had to carry sixty pounds of soybean flour.

The interrogation of the new POWs was finally completed, and they began their "reeducation," much in the same manner as we had done at Kanggye. It was still the same old Communist crap—lies, exaggerations, and grossly distorted claims, especially of Chinese victories. We had given the new POWs a few tips on how to avoid long lectures, but, unfortunately, the rest of us had to attend the lectures, too, and listen to the same old rhetoric.

The house where my squad was billeted was also used for food preparation. One cloudy afternoon after finishing our classes in the forest, we were allowed to return to the village, where several of us planned to flake out in our hut. As I entered the little house, I noticed that the gruel in one of the huge iron kettles was completely black on top. It was covered with large black flies—one of the disadvantages of warmer weather. Most of us were soon asleep. When I awoke, I noticed that the kettle was empty; its contents had been dished out to the squads for the evening meal.

In just a few days, nearly half of the camp population had come down with amebic dysentery. Within two weeks, men began to die from the effects. I will always attribute these deaths to the pot of gruel covered with flies. I have no doubt that the idiotic Chinese mess cooks did not bother to take off the top portion of fly-infested food before serving it to the POWs that evening.

As usual, no medicine was available to treat this common ailment, and the Chinese Army had not established any field hospitals in the area. The sick men remained in the camp until they either recovered or died.

It was a gut-wrenching sight to watch men, weakened to the point of physical exhaustion, try in pathetic desperation to drag themselves off to the head. We tried to help them, but they often could not endure the short trip and relieved themselves wherever they lay or stood.

One day, I was in the head when an American soldier dragged himself inside, hunkered down beside me to relieve himself, and fell over dead. I noticed that he had passed nothing but blood—bright red, tinged with a white froth. This was the point at which the sick began to die.

I never did learn the medical term for this advanced condition, if there is one. As my fellow POWs continued to die horrible deaths, I realized that two weeks was usually the longest period of survival for any man with this wretched condition. Ironically, the Chinese seemed almost immune to these unsanitary conditions, probably because they had a built-in resistance through generations of exposure. It was not uncommon, though, to watch Chinese soldiers leave the head and see intestinal worms, as thick as a pencil and at least a foot in length, slithering around in the spot they had just left. The Chinese walked away, seemingly unconcerned, yet apparently in good condition.

Also disturbing was the fact that the Chinese officials, our instructors included, did not show any concern about the illness or the soaring death rate in our camp. They made no promise of a "good hospital with medical care," and the Chinese medics had discontinued their periodic visits to the POW squads to ask if anyone needed medical care. There seemed to be a total indifference to the problem, a complete reversal of their earlier attitude.

The Allies began Operation Ripper on 7 March 1951. This offensive plan called for the IX and X Corps, which included the 1st Marine Division, to drive toward the thirty-eighth parallel on the central front. The objective of the plan was to keep the enemy off balance and prevent a buildup for a new North Korean/Chinese spring offensive. A previous operation, code-named Killer, had not achieved admirable results in the kill ratio, that is, the number of enemy dead versus the number of friendly KIAs.

The POWs knew nothing of these operations or their results, although the Chinese continued their gross exaggeration of battlefield successes and claimed near-annihilation of several American divisions, including the Marines. In reality, unless a high-ranking officer, referred to as one of the "high commanders," came into the area, Lieutenants Pan and Liu and even the camp commander probably did not know a hell of a lot more about the conduct of the war then we did.

The final objective of Operation Ripper was to be the tactical development of a semicircle stretching from Uijongbu on the west, to Sapyong-ni on the north, and to a point west of Hongchon on the east. Sapyong-ni and Hongchon were just south of the thirty-eighth parallel.

The Marines encountered only light resistance during the first week of the operation, and the 1st ROK Division found that its capital city of Seoul had been abandoned by the enemy

(The city had changed hands four times in nine months.) This was a psychological blow to the Communists. Our instructors were always bragging about reoccupying the capital. The advancing Allies inflicted extremely heavy casualties on the Communist forces, and the Marines had secured the town of Hongchon by 15 March.

As it had done in the past, the CCF used NKPA troops to fight the delaying actions, which allowed the Chinese to withdraw and regroup. The NKPA had been truly used as cannon fodder, the term the Chinese had used in describing our fighting for the "Wall Street warmongers."

The Marines continued to advance so rapidly that the final objective was changed to a line farther north, and the drive was continued as Operation Rugged. By 10 April 1951, the 1st Marine Division was deployed along what was known as the Kansas Line, an imaginary line running generally northeast from near Uijongbu, through Hwachon, and to the east coast. Allied troops were now well above the thirty-eighth parallel again. Men of the 7th Marine Regiment, while attached to the U.S. Army's 1st Cavalry Division, had been among the first troops to cross the parallel on 4 April. The advance was then halted, and the Marines consolidated their positions with Maj. Gen. Oliver P. Smith's command post as Sapyong-ni.

On 22 April, as the Chinese launched their spring offensive, the 1st Marine Division was fighting in an area generally northwest of Chunchon, along the Pukhan River, and stretching as far north as Hwachon, site of a critical reservoir whose floodgates controlled the depth of the Pukhan and Han Rivers.

As the Chinese offensive advanced southward, the Allies withdrew to predetermined positions to the south, in keeping with the policy of trading real estate for heavy enemy casualties. The Marines continued the withdrawal until they were between Chunchon and Hongchon to the southeast. Chunchon was ten miles south of the thirty-eighth parallel and Hongchon about twenty-one air miles below it. These were their general positions on 19 May 1951.

\* \* \*

On the same date, while we were all attending a lecture, the names of eighteen Marines, including mine, and one U.S. soldier were called out. When we had assembled away from the rest of the POWs, Lieutenant Pan came over to us and announced that we had been chosen to move to another location, but he made no mention of where we were going. Of course, this news started a great deal of speculation as to what was in store for us and, in particular, why only Marines had been selected. The lone soldier, Sam Shimomura, was still considered to be a Marine by the Chinese.

Lieutenant Pan led us to a schoolhouse about two miles away at the far end of the valley. He told us that we would receive a talk from the camp commander the next day and be informed of our ultimate destination. The Chinese were back to their old trick of letting us sweat it out, hardly conducive to a good night's sleep.

During the night, we continued to speculate openly on why only Marines had been selected. Only four Marines in the camp had not been selected: T.Sgt. Chester Mathis and T.Sgt. Albert Roberts, both MPs; my buddy, Chief Aguirre; and Pfc. Daniel Yesko.

The following morning, we were more than a little surprised to receive a special meal of rice with pork, the best chow, by far, that we had eaten since we had come south. We couldn't help but get the feeling that we were being "fattened up" for the kill. Unfortunately, several of us in the group, myself included, were feeling so damned lousy that we couldn't enjoy the meal. I was getting very concerned because my dysentery had reached the serious stage.

While we were eating, Lieutenant Pan, grinning like the proverbial Cheshire cat, walked among us and asked each of us where we thought we were going. To humor him and let him have his sadistic kicks, we gave such answers as Moscow, Shanghai, home—any place that came to mind. At this point, we were in no mood to play along in his game.

Lieutenant Liu showed up and made a point to ask me where I thought I was going. When I replied that I felt too sick to give a damn, he said, "You will feel better when you hear the news."

Mulling over his words, I wondered what the hell he meant and hoped that he might be implying good news. Then, Pan decided to make the announcement himself because the camp commander had failed to show.

Lieutenant Pan said that we were to be taken south and released to an American patrol. We would leave the next day! This news was another bombshell, of course, but we were remembering what happened to the last group of men who were supposed to have been released. We remained skeptical. When Pan told us to get ready to leave, gave us some administrative details, and explained that we would be traveling by truck, things began to sound more serious.

We whispered among ourselves about the possibility that, this time, the Chinese meant what they said. As soon as Pan left, our chances for escape became the main subject. For several weeks my World War II buddy, Ted Wheeler, and I had been discussing an escape plan. We had scrounged a piece of broken mirror from somewhere and some matches from a guard, and we had stored a tiny bit of extra chow. Just how valuable all of these items would be, we didn't know, but escaping was worth a shot. The two of us had vowed not to return north without an attempt at escape. I knew it had to be soon—I was down to a weight of about one hundred pounds.

As we lay in our hut that afternoon, a lone American propeller-driven airplane came overhead. The pilot must have spotted something that caught his attention, probably CCF troops on the hill above us. Flying low, he made several strafing runs and came straight toward our hut on each run. We were lying prone on a straw mat when we heard something hit the thatched roof. Knowing that the straw offered no protection, we figured this was a hell of a time to get killed, especially by one of our own. When the pilot left the area, we discovered that brass shell casings and linkage from his machine guns had hit the roof.

Later that afternoon, we walked over the hill to another small valley and boarded a truck just before dusk. So far, so good—at least we were not going to have to hump the hills this time. The date was 22 May, and our journey—one of the most miserable in my memory—began. It began to rain heavily. All nineteen of us were crammed in the open bed of the truck. The underpowered vehicle was unable to climb most of the muddy hills, and we had to climb out and push it. Somehow, we made it through the night. Early the next morning, we stopped and camouflaged the vehicle, then caught some sleep in the surrounding foliage.

By the end of the second day, the skies had cleared. We were about to experience a thrill that none of us would ever forget, an event that came frighteningly close to ending the trip right then and there.

The night was pitch black. The truck was rolling along at a pretty fair clip when we heard an aircraft start into a dive. The truck driver had the headlights on, certainly not a common or a particularly safe practice in this part of the country. We immediately knew what was happening. The pilot had found a target of opportunity—and a moving one, at that! We began pounding on the top of the cab, yelling "airplane," and telling the driver to turn off his damned lights. Luckily, Lieutenant Liu was sitting in the cab and understood what we were saying.

To this day, I firmly believe that the only thing that saved us was the driver finally turning off his lights. He continued to drive on at the same speed, and the attacking pilot fired two rockets that hit the road directly behind us. The screeching sound of the incoming rockets was terrifying. We felt the concussion from the explosions, but no shrapnel found its mark. The petrified driver continued to move on, as he followed the light-colored dirt road through the darkened countryside.

On the morning of the third day, we left the truck and were met by a new party of Chinese guards and a lieutenant. Speaking English flawlessly, the lieutenant introduced himself and said that he would lead us the rest of the way to the front lines. We told Lieutenant Liu good-bye—he had been with us for nearly six months, from the time when we first arrived at Kanggye. He wished us all "success in your new work," meaning, of course, spreading the word of his Communist teachings to our families and friends. In a way, we were sorry to see him go. He had always been fair, never brutal. If there were any such thing as sincerity in the POW camp, he probably came as close as any of the Chinese to having that trait. I had always tabbed him as one of those young men who possibly had been attending college somewhere in China and studying English, among other subjects, when he was drafted into his job, and I think he actually believed that we were headed home. We had been given surrender leaflets and other propaganda materials to pass out to friendly troops when we met them.

Our new lieutenant surprised us with his announcement that U.S. Marines were known to be fighting south of us and that the Chinese intended to capture a large number of them. He added that we would be there to greet them and help to transport them back to the camp we had just left—the real reason for the all-Marine detail!

I doubt that the lieutenant's news came as much of a surprise to any of us. We were now conditioned, mentally, to roll with the punches and to "believe it when we saw it," but it did let the wind out of our sails for a while. Wheeler and I were walking together, and we reconfirmed our commitment to make a break for it if we started north again, with or without new prisoners.

Late that night, we reached a river. While the lieutenant and our guards discussed whether or not we could cross the river, the prisoners were ushered into a house. The sounds of artillery fire and sporadic gunfire were becoming much more audible. It was quite apparent that the front lines were much closer than the Chinese had thought. We believed that this was the reason for all of the discussion.

What was more apparent, however, was that a big operation was taking place. We began to see hundreds of Chinese infantrymen hurrying back northward and many wounded men loaded on oxcarts. There was little wonder that the lieutenant was fearful of continuing the march and crossing that river. While he and the guards were discussing the situation, I was lying down in the hut, praying long and hard that we would cross the river that night, and believing that it would probably be our best chance ever to make a break for it.

The Chinese finally made their decision, and we crossed the river. We went only a short distance before we were confronted by another river. Fortunately, both rivers were fairly shallow, about armpit deep. We figured that we had crossed two forks of the same river, but we had no idea of our geographic location. Later, we learned that we had crossed just above the confluence of the Pukhan and Soyang Rivers. Because the crossings were so close together, we had been slightly northwest of Chunchon.

After the second crossing, we kept moving at a pretty good pace. I was feeling terrible, but I was able to keep up with the rest. My adrenaline was really flowing as we got closer to the Allied units, and my buddy, Ernie Hayton, was there to give me a shove forward if I faltered.

Just before dawn, we came to a small village of only five or six homes. We were ushered into a hut, but I found it much too crowded and moved outside to an oxen shed. Fifty-two-year-old M.Sgt. Gust H. ("Gus") Dunis joined me there. Lice or not, we needed some room to stretch out and rest.

I awoke about noon to the sound of artillery shells landing in the valley, not too far away. Apparently, we were pretty close to the action. The other prisoners were still in the house. With artillery shells walking up and down the valley, the Chinese guards had taken shelter in some dugouts in a small hillside less than thirty or forty yards from the house.

As the incoming artillery rounds continued to get closer and closer, I began to hear the unmistakable sounds of small-arms fire in the nearby hills. Suddenly, a North Korean soldier raced past the oxen shed and ran up to the dugouts. He talked excitedly to our guards, and they immediately came streaming out of the protective holes and went running over the hill. Meanwhile, the lieutenant came barreling back to the house, grabbed his gear from the porch, and, without saying a word, ran off in the same direction that the guards had taken.

Gus and I were lying in the shed and watching all of this activity. We were wondering what the hell was going on. The men inside the house knew nothing about what had just happened. The tempo of the incoming artillery fire increased. Gus and I watched an American OY spotter plane flying overhead while the pilot directed the fire. We were soon hugging the straw and wondering if we should try to find better cover.

After nearly half an hour, I went into the house and spoke to Harrison. "Charlie, our guards and that lieutenant took off half

an hour ago, and they never came back. We're out here alone!"
(Although there were senior men in the group, including a
commissioned officer, Harrison was the obvious leader.)

Harrison peered outside. Realizing that this might be our
one chance, he decided that we would wait in the house until
dark, no more than an hour away. If the Chinese did not return
by then, we would take off.

Darkness fell with still no sign of our guards. Literally hundreds of Chinese troops were straggling back from the direction of the front lines. This movement didn't appear to be an
ordinary withdrawal; it looked more like a rout. The Chinese
were very disorganized as they called out for their units and
their comrades. To our immediate south, something big was
definitely happening.

It didn't take Charlie and the rest of us long to realize that,
with this huge movement of enemy troops, the house was not
the safest place to be. Some of the Chinese troops would surely
want to use the house for shelter or at least check it out. Obviously, we were in an extremely precarious position: eighteen
Caucasians and one nisei, all dressed in quilted Chinese uniforms, unarmed, with no idea of where we were and with no
CCF guard personnel to explain who we were. We didn't want
to consider the possibilities of being discovered by retreating
CCF infantry.

We moved into the three dugouts that our guards had used.
There was barely room for six or seven men to hide in each
one. Much to our surprise, some local villagers arrived and sat
down in front of the dugouts. As the night wore on, we had several close calls when CCF troops passed by us; some even
stopped to talk with the villagers. It was pitch dark inside the
dugouts—we could not see each other's faces—but we were
certain, at one point, that our guards returned to look for us. We
owe our lives to those Korean men and women who sat by the
dugout entrances and denied having seen any Americans.

Close to midnight, Charlie decided that the caves were no
longer safe, and we moved out over the hill and down into a
grain field. We laid between the rows of grain and tried to get
some sleep, but we were much too hyped up even to close our
eyes, that is, all except Ernie Hayton. I had to keep nudging

him to stay awake for fear that his loud snoring would give away our position.

Just before dawn, we moved back to the valley and into a badly shelled house with no roof and only three remaining walls. At first light, we could see Chinese stragglers still streaming out of the hills to the south, headed our way, and the small-arms fire began to increase.

While the rest of us remained in and around the house, Charlie and Sam Shimomura left to see if they could find a civilian who would take a message from us to the nearest friendly unit. Conversing in Japanese, they found an old woman who said she would go, but they were reluctant to send her for fear that she would be injured. She insisted, saying that the Americans would not harm an old woman, and she and a young boy took off down the valley.

The OY spotter plane returned not long after dawn, and the artillery fire began almost immediately. The plane was not too high this time. It continued to circle the valley as the pilot called the shots and reported the results. This was another concern for us because the roofless house did not provide any overhead cover. If the OY pilot came over the house at a low altitude, he would probably notice the large group of men, dressed in Chinese uniforms, all huddled together—a fine target of opportunity. He could easily adjust his cannon fire to complete destruction of the house and us with it.

The house, at one time, had been a little fancier than most. The walls were eight feet high and had been covered with wallpaper, but the constant shock from hits and nearby misses had loosened the paper and it was falling off in many places. Someone suggested that we cut the wallpaper into strips and lay out a message in a nearby dry rice paddy. Someone else had a small knife, and we began cutting the wallpaper into strips about a foot wide. We laid them on the deck inside the house, as we decided just what our message should be.

We fashioned the letters POW and the number 19. After arranging the pieces into a well-defined eight-foot message, we all stood around looking at each other and wondered who was going to lay out the letters in the open. Artillery and small-arms fire was getting closer.

"Hell, I'll go," I said, and I soon found myself joined by Ernie Hayton, Sgt. Morris L. Estess, Cpl. Calvin W. Williams, and Cpl. Frederick G. ("Fred") Holcolmb. We wanted to go home! Each of us grabbed a letter or a figure—I ended up with the four pieces of the W—and ran out into the paddy.

Automatic weapons immediately opened up on us from the hills, and artillery fire was walking up the valley floor again. It was coming in much too close for comfort, but we were too excited and too busy to pay much attention and kept working until we completed the message.

The place where we were had been the site of an Allied artillery unit, probably during Operation Ripper, and there were lots of empty shell containers lying around. We grabbed some of them and formed the letters RESCUE below the panels of wallpaper before hightailing it back to the house. Again, Lady Luck was with us. No one had been hit by shrapnel or gunfire.

We were still waiting for the pilot in the OY spotter plane to notice our message when the old woman and the young boy returned. They had obviously contacted two different friendly units because they brought back contradictory messages. One read, "Proceed to Chunchon," and the other read, "Stay where you are friendly infantry coming." The fact that the woman and boy had returned so soon was encouraging—friendly forces must be close. While we were wondering what to do next, the OY spotter came zooming down, read our message, waggled his wings that he understood, and flew away.

There we were with three escape or rescue possibilities, and we weren't sure which one offered the best opportunity for success. We remained in the house to wait it out and suddenly realized that the artillery fire had stopped.

A short time later, the spotter plane was back. I took off my filthy gray undershirt and tied it to a stick. I ran out in the open and waved it frantically at the pilot. He dropped a red, white, and blue streamer with a message pouch attached. I ran out to pick it up and carried it to Charlie Harrison. Inside was the message, "Have radioed three tanks to pick you up. Line up on panel. If any wounded, have them lay on panel."

We went streaming out of the house and down to the rice

paddy. At this moment, we had our closest call with getting wiped out by our own forces. Three M-4A3 Sherman tanks from the 7th Infantry Division's Reconnaissance Company came around a bend a little way down the valley. As the recon lieutenant explained later, he expected to find nineteen Americans waiting to be rescued, but, when the tanks rounded the bend, all he saw were men in Chinese uniforms, complete with ear-flap hats. He gave his crews the command, "Get ready to open up with the fifties [.50-caliber heavy machine guns]— they don't look like Americans to me!"

The lieutenant picked up his binoculars to get a better look. At that very moment, somebody in our group yelled, "Get rid of these hats!" We whipped them off—the tank leader saw this. Recognizing our features as American, he commanded the tanks to hold their fire. As I have often thought since then, if the lieutenant had first seen Sam Shimomura's face, we would have really had it!

We were lined up on our message panel in two rows, in military formation, when the tanks roared up. They were the prettiest sight we had seen in six months. The first two in line were named "Double Trouble" and "Nightmare." The names were painted on their turrets.

It must have taken most of us more than a full minute for everything to sink in. Suddenly, we were laughing, crying, joking, and babbling on and on with each other and with the Army tank crews.

Nightmare, hell! This was a dream come true! We had made it. We were rescued. We had survived. We were free!

# —13—

# Welcome Back

WE HAD TO be a most sordid-looking group—emaciated, odoriferous, filthy, and ragged, but, above all else, we were hungry. The tankers were carrying several extra cases of C rations on the back of each tank. They threw a few of them down to us and said, "Here, help yourselves!"

Needing no encouragement, we began ripping open the cases and tearing into the contents. We wolfed down such tinned delights as hamburgers with gravy, frankfurters with beans, sausage patties, and ham and lima beans. All of these foods were far too rich for our delicate systems, which had processed nothing but grains during the past six months. We began throwing up everything we had eaten, but this did not deter many of us. We merely ate another can, tossed it up, and started all over again. The tankers also had packs of good, fresh American-made cigarettes, and those of us who smoked were soon lighting up and puffing away on real tailor-made smokes.

While we were talking with the tank lieutenant and his crewmen, some of the villagers began to gather around us. The artillery and small-arms fire had stopped. We learned that we were on the outskirts of Chunchon, South Korea, about ten miles below the thirty-eighth parallel. We had been in "friendly" country for two or more days without realizing it, and this explained the willingness of the local civilians to hide us the night before.

We asked the lieutenant about the Marines, and he said that they were fighting in the Hongchon area, some twenty miles to our southeast. It was here, and in later conversations with military intelligence officials, that we were able to figure out the apparent confusion by the Chinese Communists as to why we had been brought to this particular area.

As a result of the lack of communications and current intelligence information, the Chinese officials in our POW camp had no definite knowledge of where the various Allied units were fighting at any given time. They must have assumed that, because the 1st Marine Division had been in the Chunchon area when the CCF launched its 22-23 April spring offensive, it must still be there. With this in mind, they chose that destination for us. Although Lieutenant Pan and his fellow officers had promised us release, we knew that the new Chinese lieutenant had no such intention. He had made it quite clear that we were headed toward Chunchon to greet the newly captured leathernecks and help to escort them to our former POW camp at Chorwon.

To show our gratitude to the South Korean villagers for their help, we gave them articles of clothing that we would no longer need, and the tank crewmen left them some of their C rations. These people didn't have much left after their village had been occupied by the CCF and NKPA twice within the past eleven months. I was still carrying my cold-weather parka. Although filthy, it was still in fairly good shape. I gave it to a little old Papa-san who had helped us that night, and he quickly put it on. It dragged on the ground, but he was as happy as he could be, no doubt already thinking about next winter.

One of the tank crewmen had a small camera, and he took some snapshots of all of us gathered on and around the tanks. I gave him my name and address, and, several months later, I received a letter from him with three small prints enclosed, which I later had enlarged. To my knowledge, they are the only existing photographs recording the events of that memorable day.

Interestingly, only seventeen of us appear in the photographs; Charlie Harrison and Frank Cold are missing. I can only imagine that they were standing behind one of the tanks and talking with the tank commander. Meanwhile, overhead were at least half a dozen Allied aircraft, including a pair of

Australian P-51 Mustangs. I guess they had heard the spotter plane pilot's radio message and had come to have a look at what was happening on the ground.

I often wish that I could have met the OY pilot. We didn't know who he was until his name, U.S. Army Capt. Edward N. Anderson of Lawton, Oklahoma, appeared in the news releases about our rescue. I was the one who had the most contact with him when I waved to him and retrieved his dropped message, but we all wanted to thank him personally for saving our lives.

Through Harrison and Shimomura, we again thanked the villagers and were then lifted aboard the tanks for the short ride into Chunchon. We were taken directly to a small airstrip where nineteen small planes had been flown in—one for each of us—and we were flown to the U.S. Army's 7th Infantry Division command post. (See appendix D for the names and units of the nineteen escapees.)

Lt. Gen. James A. Van Fleet, Eighth Army commander, and members of his staff greeted us. This was first-class service! I hadn't seen so many stars moving around since we had run across General MacArthur and his band of straphangers at Inchon.

The U.S. Army debriefers from G-2 (Intelligence Section) asked us a lot of questions, and we turned over the rosters of U.S. Army personnel that we had copied at Chorwon. It was evident, however, that most of us needed immediate medical attention. We were soon loaded into field ambulances and taken to the 1st Marine Division command post outside Hongchon. I suppose that we could have been flown there directly from Chunchon, but the brass must have wanted to take a look at us first. We said good-bye to Sam Shimomura when he was dropped off at his parent Army command. Forty years would pass before I saw Sam again, when Chief Aguirre and I had lunch with him in San Diego and spent the afternoon talking about unhappier times gone by.

Maj. Gen. Gerald C. Thomas was at the 1st Marine Division's CP to greet us. He had relieved General Smith as division commander only a month before. Several of Thomas's staff officers were with him to welcome us back into the fold of the Corps. It was great to be home.

The division staff had notified the various units that some of their MIAs and POWs had appeared, but the problem was complicated. During the past six months, some unit officers had been killed or wounded, many had rotated back to the States, and others had been promoted and were no longer in their former jobs. In the case of the five truck drivers from Service Company, Colonel Milne, our battalion commander, had been relieved by Lt. Col. Holly Evans. Our company commander, Captain Morell, had been promoted to major and kicked up to battalion executive officer; Maj. Douglas Haberlie was our new company commander. When several tank officers showed up to see us, we didn't know any of them. Besides, what officer does a Marine corporal usually know beyond the platoon leader and company commander? We were too busy and too elated with the prospect of going home to care.

We soon underwent preliminary physical examinations at "Easy Med" (E Company, 1st Medical Battalion). Then, we were issued new dungarees and had the pleasure of watching our filthy Chinese clothes, which we had worn for half a year, burn in a huge bonfire. Good-bye, lice!

General Thomas gave specific instructions to his Headquarters Battalion mess chief to feed us at any time that we were hungry, day or night. We put away stacks of hotcakes, dozens of eggs and steaks, and whatever else was available. After receiving large doses of stopgap medicines for our dysentery, we were soon able to tolerate better-quality foods.

The division's public information office was there in force, and plenty of photographs were taken of us in the chow line and at every other opportunity. We were interviewed, and telegrams were immediately sent to our next of kin.

American Red Cross representatives also offered us assistance, but my opinion of the Red Cross changed one day when I was walking past a Red Cross official who suddenly grabbed me by the arm. He asked, "How about a picture, Marine?" He had a cardboard box, filled with PX items, sitting on the ground. I thought that he might give me some of the items, so I agreed to the picture. He asked me to hold my arms out in front of me and loaded me up with a variety of toilet articles, cigarettes, and candy bars. After he snapped the photograph, he took back everything but a single toothbrush and a tube of toothpaste. He said, "Thank you," and walked away. Obviously, I have never forgotten the American Red Cross.

I still have an 8 x 10 copy of that black-and-white photograph—it's a real beauty. I was up to about 110 pounds and wearing new dungarees that were much too big for my skinny frame. The cover on my head would have slid down over my eyes except for my protruding ears, and I was forcing a smile that didn't quite mask the sick look in my eyes.

A couple of news correspondents were also there. They interviewed us and took some photographs, which were wired to the various U.S. news services in the States and published nationally.

After a week at the division CP, we were flown to Pusan and admitted to the U.S. Navy hospital ship *Haven*, anchored in the Pusan harbor. We were there only a couple of days, but I remember that those of us who felt well enough were taken into the city to view a USO show. I also recall that Jennifer Jones, the popular movie actress, visited the *Haven*. When she learned that former Marine POWs were on board, she came down to our hospital ward to see us—talk about a boost in morale!

When the doctors discovered that several of us needed more advanced medical treatment than that available on the *Haven*, we were flown to Japan and admitted to the U.S. Naval Hospital at Yokosuka. We received complete physical examinations and learned that we were all suffering from the effects of malnutrition. In addition, the majority of us had contracted some type of gastrointestinal problem, primarily caused by the amebic dysentery that we had all suffered at one time or another during our captivity. Unfortunately, mine was one of the more advanced cases, and it had not cleared up by the time I reached Yokosuka.

At the naval hospital, we were finally able to get some rest and begin regaining lost body weight. Also, for those who felt well enough to go off base, liberty was available. For the majority of us, this was our first liberty since the previous September when we had been in the port of Kōbe, Japan.

It was at least a week before I dared to venture more than a block away from a head, but Ted Wheeler and I did hit the beach one day and even downed a few tall bottles of good-tasting Japanese beer. That was not the best medicine, however, for stomach problems such as ours.

We were issued new khaki uniforms and also received a special pay advance, according to our rank. We all had at least six months' pay on the books, less the allotments taken out of our regular pay and sent to our families each month. We would have to wait for the full amount owed us until our individual records were located and corrected, but the advances were hefty enough that we were able to splurge on gifts for our families and ourselves at a large post exchange in Yokosuka.

I purposely do not mention much about my wife, Sharon, or our baby daughter, Debby, in the telling of the six months of my captivity. During that time, I had tried not to think of them because I believed that it wasn't mentally healthy for me to do so. To be consumed with thoughts of my wife, daughter, and the rest of my family seemed to lower my spirits and morale. Most of the other POWs felt the same way and, purposely, did not talk about their families. We saw what can happen to a man who becomes obsessed with worry about his loved ones. At Kanggye, the young Army private who had literally worried himself to death over his mother was a striking example.

At Yokosuka, now that we were free and preparing to go home, however, we talked about our families constantly. They were foremost in our minds because we were that much closer to being with them. We were now able to send them telegrams, and a few of the men even managed to place international telephone calls to their families. That was not always easy to do during the early 1950s, long before the days of long-distance direct dialing. A MARS (Military Amateur Radio System) station was located at Yokosuka, and we were allowed to have personal messages sent by ham radio operators and relayed to our home areas, where they were telephoned to our families. We hadn't been in one location long enough since our return to Allied lines to receive any mail. We didn't write any letters because we hoped to arrive home before mail could get there.

We were collectively debriefed and questioned again by

naval intelligence officers. They were particularly interested in the political indoctrination courses to which we had been subjected. We were the first "graduates" of the Chinese Communist course to return to the Allied forces and therefore the first to provide accurate details of the reeducation process.

The 1st Marine Division Board of Awards sent representatives to interview us for possible personal decorations. Fourteen of the eighteen Marines in our group had been wounded before or during capture. The awards representatives took our statements, obtained signatures of witnesses, and forwarded their recommendations for the Purple Heart to higher headquarters.

They also recommended the Silver Star for the five of us who had run out into the rice paddy with our message panel. This award was subsequently "reduced" to the Bronze Star, a common but contemptible practice by unknown military administrators. Similarly, several of us had recommended Charlie Harrison for the Silver Star for his exemplary leadership and heroism in exposing himself to artillery and small-arms fire while trying to arrange for the civilians to carry our message back to friendly troops. This recommendation was also reduced to a Bronze Star, which, like ours, was awarded at ceremonies after our return to the States (see appendix E). When I consider the many decorations awarded to service personnel who participated in the four-day operation known as Desert Storm, I am convinced that, in comparison, Charlie Harrison would have been recommended for, and probably received, the Navy Cross.

Among our visitors at the Yokosuka hospital were Maj. Dennis Aldridge, executive officer of 41 Independent Commando, Royal Marines, and another officer from his command. They were seeking information about their missing Marines, especially those who might have been captured. Until that time, there had been no official word on their fate since that night in Hell Fire Valley. Some twenty commandos had been captured with us, and we were able to provide the officers with the names of most of them.

On 16 June 1951, we traveled by bus to Haneda Air Force Base, where we boarded a chartered aircraft for our trip home. There were only sixteen of us. My hometown buddy, Leon

Hilburn, and S.Sgt. James B. ("Smokey") Nash were not well enough to travel with us. I don't recall exactly what Smokey's medical problems were, but Leon had complications from gastrointestinal infection that resulted from his recurring bouts of dysentery. These men were disheartened, to say the least, and we hated to leave them behind.

Our first refueling stop was at Wake Island. This was an emotional moment for Charlie Harrison. He had been captured there nearly ten years before when the Japanese overran the island. After lunch, we had a chance to look around. Charlie said that postwar bulldozers must really have been at work, for they had completely changed what he remembered of the place. The island was barely recognizable to him. This was the first visit to Wake for me, as well as for most of the other men. What stuck in my mind was the visible wreckage of dozens of Japanese Zero fighters, still littering the sides of the runways six years after the war's end.

Our next stop was Honolulu for another refueling and then on to Travis Air Force Base in northern California. We went from Travis by bus to Treasure Island, a Marine and Navy headquarters located in San Francisco Bay. There, we were assigned temporary quarters while awaiting orders to our new duty stations. We had been notified that the Commandant of the Marine Corps had directed that we be given our choice of new duty stations, so far as practical. This opportunity meant that Hayton and I could, and did, choose our hometown of San Diego, as did Gus Dunis, whose family also lived there. As it turned out, most of the Marine POWs were reservists and due to be released from active service.

At San Francisco, our uniform issues were finally completed, and everyone was able to make those long-awaited telephone calls to families and friends. Two days after we arrived, there was a banquet in our honor at the Marine Memorial Club on Sutter Street, and we enjoyed a wonderful evening of wining and dining in that great establishment.

My aunt and uncle, the Hubberts, lived just across the bay. They picked me up after the dinner and took me to their home in Albany. Two days later, my father drove my mother, Sharon, and little Debby up from San Diego, and many tears

flowed freely during that family reunion! Sharon looked prettier than ever, and my little girl, who was ten months old, was
just beginning to walk. She was also talking up a storm, but
Sharon was the only one who understood most of her secret
vocabulary.

My mother and father were beaming with pride and relief.
They were extremely thankful that their son had returned
safely from his second war.

We got together with all of our relatives living in northern
California, those aunts and uncles we had not seen in years.
Their great Italian meals helped to put a few more pounds on
my bones, although I still had to take it easy on the rich pasta
sauces. We returned to San Diego a few days later, and I was
finally home.

At a round of parties and dinners, I saw the rest of the
family—my sister Marion and brother-in-law Scotty, my
brother Sonny, and Sharon's folks.

Some of my school buddies were still around. Bud
Wilkinson, Farris Kolbeck, Art Alford, and I got together to
hoist a few beers and talk about old times. All of them were
married and had at least one child; some were planning to
enlarge their families. These get-togethers were all dreams
come true from those darker days in captivity, and I relished
every moment.

I was on a thirty-day leave, with orders to report to the
Marine Corps Recruit Depot at the end of it. By that time, however, I was ready for the hospital again. My stomach problems
were far from over, and the amebic dysentery still was not
cured.

After admission to the U.S. Naval Hospital at Balboa Park,
I underwent every test imaginable at that time. I had tubes run
up and down me and barium pumped into me from both ends.
Also, I was introduced to that opprobrious medical device, the
proctoscope, more commonly referred to as the "Silver Stal-
lion." I was placed on a bland diet, seemingly one of the
"gastro-doctor's" favorite prescriptions, but that didn't seem to
help much either.

After more than a month of treatment, I was deemed fit to
go on "rehab," a rehabilitation program that allowed for over-

night liberty as long as I was involved in some menial job within the hospital—a polite way of saying, "No work, no play." My promotion warrant to the rank of sergeant came in during this time.

I had plenty of visitors. My parents came to the hospital whenever they could, and Sharon and little Debby came often, but I wanted to go home at the end of the day. To accomplish this, I volunteered for work in the Veterans Administration office. After four hours of work each day, Sharon picked me up at the hospital's main gate at 1700.

Another month passed before the doctors at Balboa declared that I was fit for full duty. Uncertain as to what my job would be, I reported to the Marine Corps Recruit Depot. Although discharged from the hospital, I didn't feel physically ready for active duty. Release from the hospital, however, meant that I was.

My father was again seriously hinting about my giving the dry-cleaning business another try. Sharon wanted me home for a while to resume our family life, with which I wholeheartedly agreed. MCRD had a limited number of billets. More than likely, I would be transferred to Camp Pendleton and have to commute seventy-five miles round-trip each day from Ocean-side to San Diego. So it was, on 1 October 1951, that I was released from active duty and retained on the rolls of the in-active Marine Corps Reserve.

# ═══14═══

# The Aftermath of Korea

THE KOREAN WAR would rage on until 27 July 1953, when an armistice ended thirty-seven months of hostilities. More than 4,200 U.S. Marines would lose their lives, and another 26,000 were wounded.*

Three months prior to the cease-fire, 150 American POWs were repatriated during an operation dubbed Little Switch, in accordance with an agreement between the Allies and Communists to release sick and wounded prisoners.

Among these POWs were 15 Marines and 3 Navy hospital corpsmen who had been attached to the 1st Marine Division. All but one of these men had been captured subsequent to 1 October 1952; all of them had been wounded and were in poor condition. They deservedly received the "red carpet" treatment on entering Freedom Village, the name given to the collection point in South Korea. They received immediate medical screening and care, and the more seriously wounded were evacuated by air to a hospital. Also, the men underwent many hours of interrogation during their debriefing sessions. Although they had little knowledge of enemy military matters, they were able to furnish U.S. authorities with the names of at least 115 Marines still known to be in Communist hands. Fol-

---

*All casualty and prisoner of war figures in this chapter are from Lynn Montross et al., *U.S. Marine Corps Operations in Korea, 1950–1953*, 5 vols. (Washington D.C.: Historical Branch, G-3, Headquarters Marine Corps, 1954–72).

lowing military and medical clearance, they were flown home via Hawaii in three groups.

Another small group of Little Switch returnees was flown directly from Japan to Valley Forge Hospital near Philadelphia, Pennsylvania, for further interrogation. They were considered possible security risks because of reported collaboration and other charges. No Marines were in this group.

On 5 August, nine days after the armistice took effect, the first POWs repatriated under Operation Big Switch entered Freedom Village. This operation was designed to release all remaining Allied POWs. Although the POWs were encouraged by the fact that the prisoner release started so soon after the cease-fire, the release of prisoners stretched out for more than a month. The last remaining Marine returned on 6 September 1953.

Operation Big Switch returned a total of 3,597 Americans, including 157 Marines, for a total of 172 Marines recovered during the two operations. More than 82,000 Communists were also repatriated.

During the repatriations of August and September 1953, I anxiously watched the television news coverage of the lists of returnees and saw the names of many friends and acquaintances. Maj. John McLaughlin, WO Felix McCool, and AP photographer Frank Noel, members of my original POW squad, survived the thirty-three months of brutal captivity, as did the only four Marines who were not chosen at Chorwon to accompany us to Chunchon: T.Sgt. Chester Mathis; T.Sgt. Albert Roberts; Pfc. Daniel Yesko; and my good friend, Chief Aguirre.

Many of my friends failed to come home. Among them were Cpl. James Glasgow (the only tanker who did not survive) and Royal Marine Rueben Nichols; both were victims of the dreaded amebic dysentery.

The routine in handling Big Switch returnees was similar to that in Little Switch. They received immediate medical screening, press interviews, tailored uniforms, delivery of all mail from home, and access to recreation and refreshment areas when they were finished with immediate processing.

Unlike those in Little Switch, however, the men in the latter group were transported home on board U.S. Navy ships because of their large numbers. Their interrogations were conducted and completed prior to reaching the United States. In addition, a two-week sea voyage allowed for rest, recuperation, and good food. The Big Switch POWs were in much better physical shape to meet their anxious families.

The debriefing and interrogation sessions had revealed cases of animosity between ex-POWs, with charges and countercharges, lots of bitterness, and accusations of being "progressive."

On 31 December 1953, five months after the cessation of hostilities and three months after the last POW had returned home, some branches of the U.S. Armed Forces started to write "presumptive finding of death" letters to the next of kin of many MIA personnel. Such a letter stipulated that, although an actual or probable date of death could not be established, a presumptive finding of death was required in order to terminate pay and allowances and to settle death gratuity payments by insurance companies.

This action followed the interrogation of all returned POWs and took into account the report of an investigation made by each MIA's immediate commander concerning the circumstances of his disappearance. In other words, if the MIA had been missing for a certain period of time with no news of his fate, it was presumed that he was not going to return and was probably dead. Dropping the missing and presumed dead from the rolls was not new. It had been practiced at the end of both world wars.

These letters caused considerable uproar among the families of the missing men. Many of them formed or joined "families of missing" groups and began lobbying for more answers, action, investigations, and, in some cases, resumption of full pay and allowances until a loved one returned or his remains were found and duly identified.

There was considerable justification for the reaction of the American public and families of missing men when the figures on the Korean War were tallied up and published. More than 8,000 men were unaccounted for. The figure of 8,140 is still used today by the media, activists, family groups, and some veterans organizations. This number is misleading because it encompasses several thousand known dead, including those who perished in POW camps and on death marches, whose deaths were confirmed; those who died in air crashes and losses at sea; those whose bodies are known to be in temporary UN cemeteries in North Korea; and battlefield deaths where the bodies were destroyed by explosives or are otherwise nonrecoverable.

Over the years, the main problem faced by the U.S. government has been in trying to determine how many of the more than 8,000 missing, known as bodies not recovered (BNRs), are truly unaccounted for. A report published by the Department of Defense Prisoner of War/Missing in Action Office (DPMO) in 1993 reduces this number considerably as a result of extensive research by Dr. Paul M. Cole of the Rand Corporation. In close consultation with the U.S. Army's Central Identification Laboratory—Hawaii (CILHI), Dr. Cole calculated that the number of those actually missing was just over two thousand. From time to time, sets of human remains are returned by the North Koreans and received at CILHI for identification. The BNR count is further reduced when the remains are determined to be American.

At the time of this writing, CILHI is reviewing its BNR casualty files in order to establish a new data base. Upon completion, this data base should be able to provide a name-by-name list of the truly unaccounted for.

For a better understanding of the BNR situation, one need only recall the fate of the almost twelve hundred soldiers of Task Force Faith, the column of some twenty-five hundred men that disintegrated while trying to reach Hagaru from the east side of the Chosin Reservoir on 1 December 1950. About 1,050 of the men managed to reach Allied lines. Another 250 possibly ended up in prison camps, although fewer than 100 showed up at Kanggye, the nearest POW facility. This leaves twelve hundred unaccounted for. The Marine reconnaissance patrol that reached the remnants of the convoy several days later counted more than three hundred dead bodies in the trucks. Those three hundred men are truly BNRs, as are the remainder of the missing, although none of the deaths are confirmed by name. This breakdown is necessary because some activitists have suggested that many of these missing men are being held in North Korea, China, and even former Soviet states as slave labor.

Equally shocking, and perhaps more tragic for the families of POWs, was the release of the final statistics on prisoners of war. A total of 7,190 Americans are *known* to have been captured during the conflict. Of this number, 2,701, or 38 percent, died in captivity—the highest death rate that the United States has ever known in any war, before or after Korea. Almost *four* out of every *ten* prisoners failed to survive!

As to specific causes of death, untreated combat wounds, frozen extremities, malnutrition-related diseases, and execution (conducted primarily by the North Koreans) claimed the lives of hundreds of prisoners. Undoubtedly, however, the largest killer was the insidious amebic dysentery that raged untreated throughout the camps. It is estimated that between twenty to thirty POWs died daily during peak periods of this disease.

Another sickness that claimed more than a few lives was the aforementioned "give-up-itis." All of the deaths in the POW camps were tragic, in that they probably could have been prevented by proper medical care, but there was particular sadness in seeing a fellow American just give up. Few Marines, however, were afflicted with this malady.

The U.S. Marine Corps survival rate figures were much more favorable in comparison to those of the other services. Of the 221 Marines known to have been captured, 194 returned, resulting in a 12 percent death rate. The considerably higher survival rate of the Marines was later attributed by investigating authorities and war analysts to three major factors: training, discipline, and esprit de corps.

A total of 21 Americans, all U.S. Army personnel, refused repatriation. The main reasons for their decisions to stay with the Chinese (in my opinion, no sane person would opt to stay with the North Koreans) were fear of vengeance by fellow POWs, the possibility of prosecution by U.S. military authorities for misconduct while POWs, or promises of jobs and wives in China. A few reportedly got the jobs and wives, and all eventually returned to the United States.

As a result of the lengthy and comprehensive interrogations of the returning POWs, the U.S. Army investigated almost fifty cases of various types of misconduct for possible courts-martial. Of these, fifteen courts were conducted, with the results varying from dishonorable discharge to a letter of reprimand to acquittal.

The Marine Corps had no courts-martial. It conducted one court of inquiry on a senior officer, and one enlisted man was discharged from the Corps for fraternizing with the enemy. In fact, a U.S. Senate committee that investigated the Communist treatment of American prisoners reported: "The U.S. Marine Corps, the Turkish troops, and the Colombians, as groups, did not succumb to the pressures exerted by the Communists or collaborate with the enemy, and therefore deserve the greatest admiration and credit."*

In 1955, as a result of the high POW death rate in captivity and the number of returning POWs who required disciplinary action, President Dwight D. Eisenhower signed an Executive Order that established the Code of Conduct—a set of guidelines for the armed forces in combat and during captivity. The code was modified in 1976 and certain requirements were deleted, but its principles remain intact today.

Over the past years, several groups and some individuals, including self-described authors and historians, have sought to discredit our escape at Chunchon on 25 May 1951 by claiming that we were, in fact, released by the Chinese Communists. There is a tendency to believe, "What difference does it make—you got the hell out of there, didn't you?" However, several published reports suggest that the Chinese released only progressives, and progressives were collaborators; there-

*U.S. Senate, Permanent Subcommittee on Investigations of the Committee on Government Operations, *Hearings on Communist Interrogation, Indoctrination and Exploitation of American Military and Civilian Prisoners*, 84th Cong., 2d sess., 1957, S. Rept. 2832, 23.

fore, we must have been collaborators. Nothing could be further from the truth.

It is true that our instructors, Lieutenants Pan and Liu, had claimed that we were to be freed, but we had long since learned not to believe them. The fact remains that the new CCF officer who took us from the truck to the outskirts of Chunchon specifically stated that we were to be used to escort newly captured Marines to the prison camp at Chorwon.

I, along with many others, have never believed or ever will believe that the intention of the Chinese Communists was to turn us over to a friendly patrol. My belief is based on the following facts:

- We were abandoned *behind enemy lines*, with no means of self-protection, when our armed guards and escorts panicked during the artillery barrage. Because we were wearing Chinese uniforms, we were subject to immediate execution if recaptured.
- Our armed guards returned that evening to look for us while we were hidden in the caves by friendly civilians.
- The Chinese Communists had previously promised to release the twenty-nine POWs who had been selected just before we reached Chorwon, but they were taken all the way to the front lines, only to be brought back.
- Our original group of sixty POWs, who continued south after the train ride from Kanggye, was told that we would be used to help set up new POW camps, which we did at Chorwon.
- Only U.S. Marines and Sam Shimomura, who was attached to the Marines, were selected for this detail when we headed for Chunchon.

The official five-volume Marine Corps history, *U.S. Marine Corps Operations in Korea*, details our escape and labels it as such. In addition, the Bronze Star citations for Charles Harrison and the five of us who laid out the rescue message in the rice paddy all list our return as an *escape*. The facts clearly bear this out.

# =15=

# Looking for a Home

SHARON AND I rented a home in Pacific Beach, only a block away from Bird Rock, which separated the little seaside community of Pacific Beach from the more prestigious neighborhood known as La Jolla.

As a dutiful son, I had returned to work at my father's dry-cleaning plant, but, after several months, my father and I mutually concluded that his business was not for me. He realized, as did I, that the business world just wasn't in my blood. To my credit, I had tried to learn every facet of the dry-cleaning operation, as well as a good deal about the laundry part of the business, but I somehow failed to grasp the management part of the operation. I didn't possess the necessary business acumen, so I bid the business world farewell.

Knowing that I didn't want to drive a laundry truck for the rest of my life—nor did my father expect me to—we again parted with no ill feelings when I left to search for a new line of work.

My longtime friend Bud Wilkinson had been working for the past five years at the Hormel Meat Company, and he steered me to an opening at the Cudahy Meat Packing Plant, then located off Morena Boulevard between San Diego's Old Town and Bay Park Village. I was thinking of getting a truck-driving job that would last long enough to make ends meet while I looked for something better. When I arrived at Cudahy, however, someone in the personnel department told me that I would be working on the loading docks and hauling sides of beef from the meat racks onto the delivery trucks. Hell, some of those slabs of meat weighed more than I did! When I was told that I'd be required to join the meat-cutters' union, I remembered the troubles that my father had experienced with labor unions and knew that the meat industry was no place for me.

I kicked around the idea of going back to school, perhaps even enrolling in a junior college or trying to get accepted at San Diego State University. With my less than stellar high school record and lack of college preparatory courses, however, I knew that the only chance for me would be a junior college. I was eligible to use the GI Bill, but that program offered slim funding. I would have to find a part-time job with a decent salary. Although I wasn't afraid of hard work, I needed to decide on a career that would allow me to stop bouncing around and get on with my life.

Then, I began to think about the Marine Corps. I had really enjoyed my time in the Corps, and I missed it, although I could have done without my six months as a guest of the Chinese Communists. Sharon and I talked it over, and she agreed to support anything I wanted to try.

When I was working for the Veterans Administration (VA) office, at Balboa Naval Hospital, I had learned about the possibility of collecting disability compensation because of my stomach problems. My dysentery had finally cleared up, but I was experiencing acid indigestion to the point that I was beginning to take Tums and Rolaids as though they were candy. In dealing with the bureaucracy of the VA, I learned that it worked at two speeds, slow and stop. If I were to need follow-on medical care, it would be slow in coming from the VA.

I reasoned that if I had been found physically fit for release from the naval hospital and returned to duty, I should be found fit for reenlistment in the regular Marine Corps. If I were to get sick again, the Department of the Navy would help to take care of me and my family. There were more positives than negatives in my decision to reenlist. I loved the Marine Corps because I truly enjoyed the stability of military regimentation and the sense of duty. Also, there was opportunity for advancement for those who busted their butt. I also needed a job. Only a few months after I returned home, Sharon became pregnant with our second child. But, by far, the greatest single factor was that I was not happy with the civilian lifestyle.

With all of these considerations stacked up in my mind, I visited the local Marine Corps recruiting office to check out the details for possible reenlistment. The first good news was that I would retain the rank of sergeant, a significant factor, and I was likely to go to Camp Pendleton for duty. I made my decision on the spot. I had a physical examination and completed all of the required paperwork. On 27 March 1952, I reenlisted in the U.S. Marine Corps and was able to drop the "R" from USMCR. I was now a regular Marine.

I was sworn in at the Marine Corps Recruit Depot and immediately issued orders for duty at Marine Corps Base, Camp Pendleton. Upon reporting in, I was assigned to the Tracked Vehicle Training Battalion (TVTBn), Supporting Arms Training (SAT) Regiment, a unit of training schools for Marines assigned to tanks, amphibian tractors, and field artillery located at Camp Del Mar.

I had no sooner checked into my new outfit than Sharon checked into Mercy Hospital in San Diego. Within hours, our second daughter, Marsha Jeanne, was born. Although we were eligible to use a naval hospital, either at Balboa or Camp Pendleton, Sharon preferred her family doctor and Mercy Hospital. I took several days' leave when my wife and daughter were discharged from the hospital, and, with the help of Sharon's mother who lived across the street from us, we settled into a new lifestyle.

When I reported to my new outfit, I had believed that I would finally get into the tank crewmen business, but my hopes were quickly dashed when the records clerk discovered that I had an MOS 3531, the truck driver's job number. My MOS had been changed during the Korean War because that was the duty I was performing at the time of my capture.

I explained to 1st Lt. Guy Kelly, the battalion adjutant, that I wasn't interested in becoming a truck driver again. When I asked about the tank company, Lieutenant Kelly explained to me, in no uncertain terms, that I was there for duty in my MOS as a buck sergeant, and I was not eligible for any formal school, which would require approval from CMC (Commandant of the Marine Corps).

Then, I happened to mention the magic word "typing" and said that I had gained some experience as a company clerk during World War II. The lieutenant introduced me to a typewriter, gave me a piece of paper, and told me to type something. I was a little bit rusty, but my performance was satisfactory and TVTBn had found itself a new clerk. Strange, how that MOS 3531 suddenly became so unimportant!

The battalion, and the regiment for that matter, was full of officers and enlisted instructors who had completed tours of duty in Korea. Many were combat veterans who had fought in the 1st Provisional Marine Brigade at Pusan, Inchon, Seoul, and Wonsan and in the Chosin Reservoir campaign. I saw many familiar faces, those of men I had known years before and those who had been in the 1st Tank Battalion. In fact, the battalion executive officer was Roughhouse Taylor, former commanding officer of Company C tanks in Korea and now a major.

When the word got around that I was one of the battalion's five truck drivers who had been captured, I took a lot of good-natured ribbing about my joining the wrong army, giving the Chinese my truck in the hope that I'd be issued a new one, and similar wisecracks. Several Company B veterans were around, and I liked to remind them that, if they had come only a few hundred yards farther north that night, I wouldn't have had to spend six months dining on Red Chinese cuisine.

As soon as I was snapped into my new job, the chief clerk suggested that I should do something about changing my MOS, still recorded as 3531. He explained that the motor transport (MT) field was notoriously slow in promotions. A Marine could rise in rank to buck sergeant, as I had done as a driver, but that was as far as it went. Marines in the grade of staff sergeant or above didn't drive vehicles but were assigned as section leaders or dispatchers. Because there were far fewer billets for those jobs, the opportunity for promotion simply was not there; in fact, it was not uncommon to see motor transport Marines retire after twenty years of service as either staff sergeants or technical sergeants.

This was a situation that I did not welcome, and I wasn't very interested in motor transport. Following the chief clerk's suggestion, I requested a change to an MOS in the administrative field. My request was approved, and I became an administrative clerk.

I was still commuting from San Diego to Camp Pendleton, so I went to the Base Housing Office to request military housing. My name was placed on the waiting list, and, within a few months, my family and I moved into one half of a Quonset hut, the Marine Corps version of a duplex. The housing unit, known as Homoja Housing, was located just inside Camp Pendleton's main gate. Our new home was quite small—two tiny bedrooms, small kitchen and living room, and a bathroom barely able to contain the shower-tub and pot. It was suitable enough for a small family, however, and the rent was more than reasonable. Best of all, Homoja Housing was less than two miles from my work.

Shortly after I had reported to the base, the Camp Pendleton newspaper, *The Scout*, ran a story about my having been a prisoner of war, my reenlistment, and my new assignment to TVTBn. An old boyhood friend, Igor Mougenkoff, who had grown up with me in Old Town and also attended Point Loma Junior High School, read the article and gave me a call. We got together one evening after work to renew our old friendship.

I learned that Igor had joined the Marine Corps in 1942 at age sixteen and decided to stay in. During the years, we had lost track of one another. He was now in the adminstrative field as an instructor at the Administrative School Company on board the base. With only ten years in the Corps, he was already a master sergeant (at that time, a pay grade of E-7), the top grade in the Corps. No doubt, the administrative field presented an excellent opportunity for making rank.

Igor was married and living with his family in nearby Carlsbad, and we began to get together on weekends. One day, he asked me if I would be interested in becoming an instructor at his school. I laughed at his offer and explained that I had been working in my new MOS for only a short time, but he shrugged off my concern. He said that an instructor, like many other teachers, only had to stay one lesson ahead of his students.

I thought his suggestion might be worth a try, and he arranged an interview for me with the school's officer in charge. I was accepted, and my transfer was effected immediately.

This was a Marine Corps School funded by HQMC, and the students were assigned directly by CMC order. Most of them came directly from recruit training. The curriculum consisted of two clerk-typist courses that ran simultaneously for a period of six weeks. Each course accommodated fifty students and usually included women Marines, which necessitated a different style of instruction because most of the usual jokes about Marines were not allowed. Besides basic typing and naval reports and correspondence, the curriculum also included classes in the new Uniform Code of Military Justice (UCMJ).

I began teaching basic typing (military forms and reports) and later specialized in SRBs (service record books) and OQRs (officer qualification records). Several weeks after I started teaching, I was accepted into the Instructor's Orientation Course, a class designed to teach effective teaching skills. Although only a two-week course, it was one of the best that I ever attended. It taught self-confidence, as well as the art of classroom instruction.

My fitness reports reflected my enjoyment of teaching. In December 1952, I was promoted to staff sergeant. I had made it to Marine SNCO (staff noncommissioned officer) and finally wore a coveted "rocker" on my chevrons, with a total active service of only four years.

Soon after my promotion to staff sergeant, Sharon and I learned that she was pregnant again. In the naval hospital at Camp Pendleton, our handsome baby boy, whom we named Leonard James, Jr., was born on 12 August 1953. We thanked God for my promotion because our half of that Quonset hut was getting crowded with little people.

Unfortunately, the Marine Corps decided to disband the Administrative School, and I was reassigned to duty at the SAT Regiment office as chief administrative clerk. A warrant officer selection program had just been completed, and two of our well-known tanker master sergeants had been selected.

They were Gene Viveiros, who had been with Capt. Max English's A Company tanks in the fighting from Pusan to Inchon, Seoul, Wonsan, and further north; and Willy O. Koontz, who had been a platoon sergeant with Company B tanks. The regimental commander called the two men into his office, and I typed their warrants. They were then sworn in, presented with their warrants, and congratulated.

Not being one to mince words, Koontz turned to me and said, "It ain't gonna do you any good to go outside and stand by the door, Maffioli. You ain't gettin' no dollar." This referred to the age-old custom of presenting a dollar to the first person who salutes a Marine who has just received a warrant or commission. The cheap son of a gun never did pay off, but Koontz was no slacker. He proudly wore the Navy Cross for his heroic actions on Saipan while serving with our old 4th Marine Division, and, in my opinion, was an outstanding example of a Marine.

In the spring of 1954, I was assigned to the Naval Ordnance Test Station at China Lake, California, for duty with the 1st Provisional Marine Guided Missile Battalion. The base was located in the Mojave Desert—the high desert—220 miles from San Diego and 175 miles from Oceanside. Sharon and I packed up our two daughters and brand-new son, along with our few belongings, and headed east to China Lake. Deserts are noted for extreme temperatures during the summer months, and this one was no exception. It was a rough trip in our old Plymouth sedan, well before the days when air conditioning was a common feature in automobiles.

At China Lake, base requirements dictated that all visiting personnel be met at the gate and escorted. The base security did not acknowledge decals from other bases because of the nature of the work at the base, where missiles used by the Navy and Marine Corps were tested. After a telephone call got us in, I drove Sharon and the children to the base bowling alley, where they could enjoy a sandwich and a cold drink in air-conditioned splendor, while I went about the tedious process known as "checking in." Luckily, base housing was available when we arrived. Although declared "substandard" by the U.S.

Navy, it was no worse than what we had become accustomed to at Camp Pendleton.

I replaced a staff noncommissioned officer, a master sergeant, who had been the battalion's chief administrative clerk. With this job came the grandiose title of battalion personnel sergeant major; the senior man in the office was *the* sergeant major.

This guided missile business was a brand-new ball game for me. The base was loaded with technicians, both officers and SNCOs, most of whom had engineering degrees. The men in the lower grades were graduates of the guided missile school in Pomona, California, which was owned and operated by the largest civilian corporation producing guided missiles at the time. This company had a hell of a scheme. It trained the students at government expense and advised them, on completion of their three or four years of active duty, to apply for work with the company at very attractive salaries. With our battalion reenlistment rate at nearly zero and the Marine Corps losing money as each of these highly trained technicians failed to reenlist, the commanding officer notified CMC. In turn, CMC warned the company to knock off its recruiting practices or significant changes would be made before the next guided missile contract came up for renewal. The company, so warned, stopped its illegal practice.

The young Marines assigned to China Lake were what we called "whiz kids." I held their record books and was amazed at their GCT (General Classification Test) scores. This test was the military's equivalent of the IQ test, and the personnel assigned to our battalion had some fantastic scores. A lieutenant colonel had an extremely high score, and most of his men did almost as well on the test. My test score placed me in mental group 1, but, compared with the scores of the whiz kids, I felt like a contender for village idiot.

The Marine Corps had the Terrier guided missile, a product tested and rejected by the U.S. Army, for several years, but it finally switched to the Hawk missile, a smaller, more accurate weapons system that was easier to handle. The U.S. Navy then ended up with the Terrier missiles on its ships for several years.

\*     \*     \*

I had just been promoted to technical sergeant when I wrote a letter to CMC and requested a retraining assignment in OF (occupational field) 1800, tanks and amphibian tractors, with tanks as my first preference. In my letter to CMC, I stated that I wanted to enter a combat field and also desired to qualify for first sergeant and sergeant major, positions that were not available to an administrative SNCO.

Lieutenant Kelly, the battalion adjutant who had persuaded me to switch to pounding a typewriter when I reported to TVTBn at Camp Del Mar, was now stationed at HQMC. I dropped him a line and said how much I would appreciate anything he could do in pushing my request through the proper channels. Much to my relief, he responded that he had "put in a good word" for me.

Sure enough, about four months later, I received orders directing me to Camp Pendleton for retraining toward MOS 1811, tank crewmen. In June 1956, we packed up the family again, and I reported to Camp Pendleton. Thanks to a close friend, we were able to rent a house in nearby Carlsbad for a reasonable price. Debby was almost six years old, and ready for the first grade. Marsha was four years old and Jimmy nearly three. Sharon had more than a full-time job keeping these three children in tow, but now they could play in a nice-sized yard instead of desert sand.

I was assigned to the 1st Tank Battalion and sent to Baker Company B to begin training. Because I had always been interested in tanks, I picked up my training fairly quickly. I had to study dozens of field and technical manuals, but the work was interesting.

When I had reported to the tank battalion, Company B was the only letter company then at Camp Pendleton. The rest were participating in a DESFEX (desert field exercise) at Twenty-Nine Palms. As soon as they returned, we loaded our tanks onto flatcars and sent them to the railroad siding at Baghdad, located off Highway 40 at the northern limits of the Twenty-Nine Palms base. A few train guards stayed with the tanks, and we boarded trucks for the trip to the Palms. We then made the trek across the desert to meet up with our tanks.

I could not have picked a better time to join the tanks. We

practiced cross-country movements, tank gunnery, and live firing of all weapons systems.

We were positioned in the boondocks, several miles from the center of camp, known as "mainside," and enjoyed a spartan existence in the field—C rations and no showers. On Holy Saturday, a group of us took a truck to mainside to attend Easter Midnight Mass at the base chapel. Inside were dozens of post troops and their families, all dolled up in their Easter finery, but they were soon sniffing the air and stepping away from us. Within a few minutes, we had one small section of the church to ourselves—not realizing just how offensive we smelled. The following Monday, the word came out to our company commander that it would not be necessary to send us in for church services. The chaplains would come to us.

I had been assigned as platoon sergeant of the 1st Platoon. Because I was a retrainee, the staff sergeant who had been filling the billet stayed with me and helped to get me snapped in. He was extremely knowledgeable, a fine instructor, and damned patient with me, considering that as a staff sergeant he had been replaced by a technical sergeant retrainee.

We were at the "Stumps," as the base at Twenty-Nine Palms was commonly called, for one month before returning to Camp Pendleton. The battalion command post was located at Camp Las Pulgas, and our tracked vehicles were maintained at a facility, known as the tank park, located at Camp Las Flores several miles away. We enjoyed an excellent mess hall at the tank park. Those Marines who didn't have their own automobiles were trucked between the two camps each day. Again, I found a good number of Marines in the battalion who had been in Korea with me. Many of them were now back in their former companies, and it was like old home week to meet again as we swapped sea stories and caught up on old times.

I was finally tested, and I received my long-awaited tanker MOS. Adding to the moment was the announcement that a Tank Unit Leader's Course was being offered for staff NCOs and senior sergeants, and the battalion training officer got a slot for me as quickly as possible. This six-week course, centering on the operation and maintenance of tanks and tank units, provided excellent training.

When I was getting ready to report back to the battalion, the word came out that Company B personnel were being transferred to form the nucleus of the new 1st Anti-Tank Battalion. It had a completely new weapon called the Ontos, a Greek word meaning *the thing*—and a thing it was!

The Ontos was a small, strange-looking, lightly armored tracked vehicle, with six 106-mm recoilless rifles mounted offset on top of its outer frame. A true tank-killer, if the occasion ever presented itself, it could deliver its fire with exceptional accuracy. Two .50-caliber "spotting" rifles, mounted on the two top 106s, were used for firing tracer or smoke rounds to get on target. Then, the bigger guns went to work. Considered something of a novelty, the Ontos was frequently referred to, by tankers and infantrymen alike, as a "kiddy car," but it was fast compared with a tank and could zip up and down hills at a fair clip.

We formed up the battalion and began to train—always the hallmark of the Marine Corps. The three of us who were the former platoon sergeants from Company B were now assigned as first sergeants for the three new letter companies. The three tank platoon leaders from Company B were assigned as company commanders in this unit, and my company commander ended up on the new battalion's staff. All of these tanker assignments were only for forming and training purposes, however; the battalion would subsequently end up with infantry MOSs in those remaining billets.

It was great fun for awhile. Then, the battalion adjutant, a gung ho type of warrant officer, asked me to take over Headquarters and Service Company as the "first shirt" (first sergeant) because this company was, according to him, in one hell of a mess. We negotiated awhile. The letter companies were short of platoon leaders, and I wheedled a solemn promise from the warrant officer that I would get a platoon of Ontos when the new man reported to the company.

I worked my ass off trying to get the company squared away—my administrative experience really helped—and a qualified first sergeant finally reported for duty. The adjutant kept his promise, and I took over a platoon in Company B, where I had been the first sergeant a month earlier.

\* \* \*

Like so many other career Marines, I probably had spent too much time trying to get that company squared away and not enough time taking care of my personal life. My marriage was now in serious trouble, and the situation in the Maffioli household was not well or happy. My wife and I had purchased a new home in the Cabrillo Heights area of San Diego, and I was commuting again in the hope that our differences could be worked out. This was not to be. One of the major problems was that my wife did not wish to remain in the Oceanside area but wanted to be closer to her own family. After several trial separations, we became more and more incompatible. Ultimately, we filed for divorce. I ended up with a car, which I sold just before leaving for the Pacific, as my sole possession. Without doubt, this was the most difficult and saddest period of my life.

In the fall of 1957, I received orders directing me to the 3d Marine Division, located on the island of Okinawa. I reported to division headquarters in early February 1958. As I had hoped and expected, I was sent to the 3d Tank Battalion and assigned as Company B's first sergeant. I hadn't been on board for more than a month when the entire division left Okinawa for the Philippines to participate in Operation Strongback. It was quite an experience to see the entire division on maneuvers—something that the budget did not often allow and that was impossible on Okinawa because of limited training areas.

When Operation Strongback was completed, our company stayed in the area between Cabanatuan and Dingalan Bay for additional tank gunnery practice. I had an introduction to the excellent San Miguel beer brewed in the Philippines, and, at ten cents a bottle, we had the local distributor's truck making frequent runs to our company's encampment.

On our return to Okinawa, the battalion sergeant major asked if I was interested in managing our camp's SNCO club. As new as I was to tanks, I realized that the training restrictions on Okinawa left little opportunity for training with our tracked vehicles and also that company first sergeants did not operate with the tanks in the field, so I agreed to manage the club.

We were billeted at Camp Hansen, and we surely did not have much of a building to call a club—a beaverboard hut, with a corrugated tin roof held down by several steel cables to help prevent the next typhoon from carrying it away. In fact, Camp Hansen was still a tent camp; every time Okinawa was threatened by typhoon conditions, a warning was sounded and all of the camp's tents were struck and stored until the storm passed. This was a tremendous amount of work until large Quonset huts were finally constructed and placed on solid concrete foundations.

The SNCO club was open for noon sandwiches and soft drinks, and, during the evenings, we served beer, hard liquor, and good dinners. We had bingo one evening each week, and we showed movies. Kin Village was located just outside Camp Hansen's main gate. At the time, the village was very small and its mayor allowed only teahouses, no bars. The percentage of tea-drinking Marines was extremely low, and the troops had to travel to Yaka Beach, a U.S. Army recreation center, or to the town of Ishikawa, the nearest place with civilian-style bars, bartenders, waitresses, and other amenities. Unless anyone owned a motor scooter or wanted to hire a cab, our club was it.

My assistant manager was a tanker staff sergeant. We traded duty between days and nights, which allowed each of us time to explore the island on my Lambretta motor scooter. Most of the Marine SNCOs had motor scooters. We had some great times running them around the island and visiting various camps and clubs.

A civilian manager also worked in the club. Kenyu, an Okinawan native, handled nearly all of the paperwork, including the periodic reports, and his assistance made my life easier. This was the first and only "skate" (easy) job that I ever had during my service in the Marine Corps.

The months on Okinawa flew by quickly, and a welcome break from the island was a five-day R&R (rest and recuperation) to Hong Kong. Each Marine was allowed one R&R during his thirteen-month tour of duty on Okinawa. We flew from Okinawa on R4Ds, the Marine Corps designation for the C-47 "Gooney Bird." En route, the plane's radio went out, and we landed at T'ainan, Taiwan, for repairs. While the radio was being fixed, we had time only to enjoy lunch. That was my only visit to Taiwan.

Hong Kong was a fantastic liberty port. I had never imagined a place like it. Everything was inexpensive. It had magnificent hotels, spectacular nightclubs, and beautiful women. Another tanker and I had teamed up for this R&R, and we also visited Kowloon on the mainland. We traveled to the area know as the "New Territories" and gazed across the boundary separating the British colony from Communist China. It was something of a struggle to board our aircraft for the return trip to Okinawa, commonly referred to as "The Rock."

One day, the battalion administration chief came into the SNCO club for lunch and asked me if I had ever applied for duty with the State Department. I answered, "Yes, several years ago. Why?"

He smiled, and said, "Because, you lucky SOB, your orders just came in assigning you to school at Henderson Hall!"

At first, I could not believe what I was hearing. When I realized that he was serious, I jumped up and started to yell like a banshee.

Embassy duty, as it is commonly referred to by Marines, was the most sought-after duty in the Corps. Officially called Special Foreign Duty with the Department of State, it was actually security guard duty at American embassies and consulates throughout the world. The waiting list for embassy duty was extremely long. It was not unusual for Marines to wait several years before being selected; some never were. The screening process was particularly stringent. This duty required a spotless record and, in the case of SNCOs, strong leadership abilities.

I considered myself extremely fortunate. At one time, I was considered ineligible because both parents had to be native born, but this requirement had been changed. Several months later, I learned that my divorce had actually helped my selection. Single SNCOs were needed for posts considered to be hardship tours of duty.

The Marine Security School was operated by Company F, Headquarters Battalion, at Henderson Hall in Arlington, Virginia. It was located close to the Navy Annex, which housed Headquarters Marine Corps. In early March 1959, I boarded an

Air Force transport plane at Kadena Air Force Base on Okinawa and began my homeward journey. I had thirty days' leave before reporting to my new school.

# ═══16═══

# New Posts and Stations

I SPENT THE majority of my leave with my parents, who now lived in Anaheim, California, and I also visited a number of old family friends. I even managed to spend a few days working at my father's new dry-cleaning plant and helping him and my brother with their work. On several occasions, I drove down to San Diego to see my children, but it wasn't the same and never would be again. Sharon had remarried shortly after our divorce was final, and the three children had begun to grow accustomed to their step-father. My sister and brother-in-law, Marion and Scotty, lived in my old stomping grounds of Pacific Beach. We had a few get-togethers there and enjoyed several memorable meals at their yacht club.

In early April, I left California for Virginia. During the six-week course, our classes covered such subjects as the security of classified material, protection of personnel, weapons training, emergency first aid, fire-fighting techniques, foreign policies and procedures, and protocol and etiquette. Staff non-commissioned officers also received additional training on security locks and administrative matters.

I was to be assigned to duty as NCOIC of a Marine Security Guard (MSG) detachment, which could consist of as few as five Marines or as many as thirty. With a few exceptions, there were no Marine commissioned officers at many of these posts, and the assigned NCOIC was, in most respects, the commanding officer of the detachment. Although personally responsible for the actions of individual Marines assigned to the post, the NCOIC did not have authority to administer any formal punishment, according to the rules and regulations of discipline under the UCMJ.

The course was tough and demanding. The instructors applied an ample amount of stress to determine if individual Marines measured up to the exacting requirements and rigid standards necessary for independent duty in a foreign country; of course, they also looked for leadership abilities in the SNCOs. In addition, all MSG students faced two screening boards conducted during the first and fourth weeks of the class. Consisting of Marine Corps officers and State Department officials, the boards were designed to cull those students considered unacceptable for this particular type of independent duty.

The MSG students who remained after the screenings were fitted for dress blue uniforms and then taken to Washington, D.C., so that each could purchase an appropriate, though modest, wardrobe of civilian clothing. Many posts required civilian clothes to be worn on and off duty, usually at the insistence of the host country. To ensure uniformity, daily personnel inspections were conducted in all issued Marine Corps uniforms.

A week before graduation, we learned our individual assignments. I could hardly believe my ears when I heard that I had been selected for duty at the American Consulate General in Munich, Germany. Munich was considered an "accompanied" post, which meant that quarters were available for dependents. Early in the course, when we learned of the available posts, I didn't think I stood any chance of being assigned to such a "plum" job as duty in Munich.

Following graduation, I put my personal affairs in order and began marking my baggage for Munich. In less than a week, our passports and visas were ready. Those of us headed for different posts in Europe hopped a train for Trenton, New Jersey, and took a transatlantic flight from McGuire Air Force Base to Rhine-Main Air Base in Frankfurt, Germany.

The Marine Security Guard Regional Headquarters for all of Europe was located in Frankfurt. We were met at the airport and transported to headquarters, where we reported for duty. I took a train from the Bahnhof (train station) on the following day and enjoyed an interesting and scenic ride to Munich. It was early summer, and the weather was fine.

Munich had seven watchstanders, sergeants or below, who stood post inside the consulate during nonworking hours. The NCOIC was normally posted on duty during the hours that the consulate was open for business.

On a typical business day at an embassy or consulate, the NCOIC arrived at the facility by 0730. He reviewed the night guard's duty log for time and frequency of the guard's rounds and noted any entries regarding unusual occurrences. If all was in order, the guard was relieved and the NCOIC began the daily routine of attending to administrative matters. His office was usually located in or near the lobby so that he was available if the receptionist needed assistance.

He made periodic personal checks of the building and, during the lunch hour, inspected office spaces for any classified material left unsecured. If he found any security violation, he immediately issued a violation notice against the responsible individual.

At 1630, the Marine on first watch reported in, assumed his post, and manned the reception desk to check out employees and to check in keys, which he logged in the appropriate logbook. When he had checked out the last employee, the guard locked the building's main entrance and began his security rounds. Entering all office spaces, he looked primarily for unlocked safes and filing cabinets; these, of course, were viewed as serious security violations. If a safe or filing cabinet was open or not properly locked, he immediately issued a security violation. At midnight, this guard was relieved by the second watch.

The NCOIC was also considered to be an assistant to the post security officer, who, at the larger facilities, was a specialist in that capacity. At smaller facilities, security was an additional responsibility of one of the Foreign Service officials. At posts with very large buildings or more than one building, two or more MSGs might be on duty at the same time.

Munich is a truly beautiful city. It is famous for its beer, as well as a host of other attractions. I enjoyed Saturday afternoons on the patio of the Hofbrau Beer Garden, where I mixed with the German people and tried to learn the language. The many cultural attractions include internationally known museums of history and fabulous art galleries. Just outside of Munich is the infamous Dachau extermination camp, which has been preserved as a reminder of the dark days of Germany's history during World War II.

I had no sooner started the formal language instruction required by the MSG Battalion for all Marines when I received word that I was being reassigned to the American Embassy at Vienna, Austria. The post and quarters at Munich were needed for a married NCOIC arriving with his wife and family. While I admit to being a bit disappointed in leaving Munich, as I had already made some good friends, I couldn't complain about my new assignment. Vienna is considered by many to be one of the most beautiful and interesting cities in the world.

There was just one unknown. Vienna had a master sergeant, one pay grade higher than mine, as the NCOIC of the detachment, and he still had a considerable amount of time remaining on post. I would fill the billet of assistant NCOIC, but that did not appear to be a problem. I need not have worried about the new assignment; within several months of my arrival in Vienna, the NCOIC was relieved as unsuitable and I took over the detachment.

The Marines in Vienna lived in style. The State Department rented a two-story villa in an area known as the Nineteenth District, a very upscale neighborhood. The Marine House had eight bedrooms topside for the thirteen watchstanders, and spacious grounds with beautiful trees.

As the staff NCOIC, I was eligible for my own quarters in the nearby American apartments, but I chose a basement apartment in the Marine House. I had acquired a German shepherd pup, and it was much easier to raise him there, particularly with a huge yard in which he could roam.

I bought a new Opel station wagon, a German General Motors product, and took road trips into Yugoslavia, Italy, Switzerland, and Bavaria during short periods of leave. The Bavarian Alps are only a few hours away, via good roads, and I spent many enjoyable weekends at Berchtesgaden, Germany, where the U.S. Army Special Services managed several hotels at rates of $1.50 per day for service personnel. This area is beautiful during both winter and summer.

The Marine Corps Birthday, 10 November, is celebrated by Marines throughout the world in one fashion or another, and the Marine Security Guards are no exception to the tradition. In many foreign cities, the birthday ball is considered to be the most important social event of the year for Americans. The occasion is often used to reciprocate the dinners, cocktail parties, and other social obligations incurred by the Marines during the year. The ball is always paid for by the Marines of the detachment.

In 1959, our birthday ball was held in a two-hundred-year-old Viennese palace, and, in 1960, at the Schoenbrun Palace in the suburbs of Vienna. Each ball was a beautiful, formal affair, with the military in full-dress uniforms, civilians in tuxedos, and the ladies in formal gowns. I will always recall our 1960 birthday ball because it was the only opportunity that year for me to wear my uniform; as the Marine NCOIC in Vienna, I wore only civilian clothes on duty.

Vienna was the gateway to the Iron Curtain. This was probably the most interesting aspect of duty at this post. Our security officers traveled to the Iron Curtain countries to inspect our embassies for planted listening devices, commonly referred to as "bugs." Occasionally, they had some interesting stories to tell about where the bugs had been planted.

In 1959, the Marine Corps made some sweeping changes in the enlisted rank structure when the armed services created two new enlisted pay grades of E-8 and E-9. Prior to the changes, the highest enlisted rank in the Corps had been master sergeant, E-7. The Corps brought back the pre-World War II ranks of lance corporal (E-3), gunnery sergeant (E-7), and master gunnery sergeant (E-9). The rank of first sergeant was now E-8, as was master sergeant, and sergeant major was at the top of the pay scale as E-9. The grade of technical sergeant no longer existed. In April 1960, after four and a half years as a technical sergeant, I received my warrant promoting me to gunnery sergeant.

*  *  *

As always at a great duty station, my two-year tour passed all too quickly. One day in February 1961, I received orders to report to the 1st Marine Division at Camp Pendleton.

After putting my dog, Mike, on a plane to Los Angeles and driving my little Opel to Bremerhaven, Germany, for shipment home by the U.S. Army, I took a train to Frankfurt and caught a U.S. Air Force transport plane out of Rhine-Main Air Base for the States. I visited my family in Anaheim during a short leave and then reported to division headquarters. Once again, I was assigned to the 1st Tank Battalion as Company B's gunnery sergeant.

Several months later, I was reassigned to the battalion's Operations and Training Section (S-3), where my billet was assistant S-3 chief. This job provided excellent training and experience; any staff-level position was considered at that time to be a career-enhancing position. Six months later, I was sent to the Supply and Logistics Section (S-4) to learn how the "bullets and beans" were procured, handled, and distributed. I soon learned that, without a well-trained logistical team and a well-planned resupply scheme, all of the tank battalion's efforts, either offensive or defensive, would be doomed to failure.

In September 1962, my father passed away after a long illness. I loved my father dearly and always wished that I could have pleased him by working with him. My brother Sonny, who had been running the business during my father's illness, took it over and did well with it.

I spent many weekends with Marion and Scotty. They lived in San Diego and enjoyed themselves as members of the Southwestern Yacht Club on Point Loma and on board their thirty-one-foot Chris Craft cabin cruiser, the *Marstan*. Usually during the months of August and October, they cruised the coastlines of Mexico and southern California in the pursuit of marlin or albacore. During the weekends, I was often on board with them.

Typically, a fishing day began well before dawn. Our first stop was at the bait barge, located near the entrance to San Diego's bay, to pick up several scoops of bait fish, sardines or anchovies, that went into the boat's bait tank along with the flying fish used exclusively for marlin. Then, we cruised out to the fishing grounds, about ten to thirty miles from Point Loma. Our destination was usually determined by the previous day's big bite.

During the long day of fishing, we cruised first to the north and then to the south, parallel to the coastline, at a trolling pace not usually exceeding seven or eight knots. Scotty always monitored his CB radio and listened to the chatter of other anglers as they reported their good luck or missed opportunities. We returned to the docks well after dark. If the weather was good, as it usually was, we headed out again early the next morning and repeated the process. During my weekends on board the *Marstan*, I caught only two marlin, along with dozens of albacore, but, catching fish or not, I never had a bad day out on the Pacific Ocean.

After two years of duty with the 1st Tank Battalion, I received orders to Recruiters School, located at Parris Island, South Carolina. My assignment there was quite a surprise because I had completed a tour of independent duty only two years earlier, but I had always wondered what recruiting duty would be like and was eager to find out. I knew several Marines who had served as recruiters; each had his own opinion of the job. Now, it would be my turn to find new recruits for the Corps.

In February 1963, I was best man at my brother Sonny's wedding, when he married Margie Pearson, of Santa Ana, California. Four days later, I left the West Coast in my little Opel and headed east for Parris Island.

Recruiters School lasted just six weeks, but it was a real challenge. We had two personnel inspections each day, at 0700 and 1300, which meant that we always spent our lunch hour pressing uniforms and shining shoes. The comprehensive course emphasized salesmanship, public speaking, and public relations, along with the required classes on new Marine Corps administrative forms and reports.

Choice of duty station or assignment to a particular Marine Corps District (MCD) depended on each Marine's class standing. I did well enough to get the requested 12th District, which encompassed the seven western states. Generally speaking, the structure consisted of the recruiting stations (RSs), also referred to as main stations, and recruiting substations (RSSs), which were under the control of the local RS. Each RS had an officer in charge, with rank dependent on the size of the station. The RSSs were usually operated by a Marine with a grade of sergeant or higher. At that time, Recruiting Station Los Angeles (RSLA), with Lt. Col. William ("Bill") Fagan as OIC, consisted of fifty RSSs and one hundred recruiters working within an area of responsibility that stretched from Santa Barbara to the Mexican border. RSLA was to be my new duty station.

I was hoping that I would be assigned to recruiting duty in my hometown, something that the Recruiting Service tried to do when practical, but that was not to be. The billets in San Diego were filled, and I was assigned to RSS Inglewood, California, as the NCOIC, along with one other recruiter. Inglewood was located about thirty miles west of Anaheim, where my mother still resided, and I moved in with her. She had plenty of room and welcomed my company.

I have often said that any Marine who completed a four-year tour of duty as a recruiter in a large metropolitan area, such as Los Angeles, could undoubtedly fill a book by writing about those unique experiences alone.

One of my first applicants was a young man only seventeen years of age, and both parents had to sign a consent form, which is a legal document, allowing him to enlist at that age. If only one parent or guardian signed the consent form, a statement entered on the reverse side of the form had to explain the reason for the one signature and documents had to be provided to substantiate the reason given. Details of these documents are also entered on the consent form.

During a telephone conversation, the mother of this young lad had already informed me that she had not been married to the boy's father. I told her to come to the recruiting office, and we would prepare the necessary paperwork. When she came in, I asked her if she had any idea of the whereabouts of the boy's father.

She looked me square in the eye and said, "Sergeant, not only don't I know where he is, I don't even know who he is!"

She signed the paper, I accepted it, and the kid left for boot camp.

About a month later, the mother of another young man was sitting at my desk. While preparing the enlistment forms, I noticed a discrepancy between the boy's date of birth and the dates on their divorce papers. I started to suggest that we could discuss the matter in private.

She interrupted, "No, he might as well know it now." Turning to her son, she said, "Eddie, your father and I weren't married when you were born."

The kid looked up at her and, with a grin on his face, said, "You mean I'm a bastard?" His grin seemed to indicate that it was almost a badge of distinction.

It's difficult to explain the look on a young man's face when his mother, at a Marine Corps Recruiting Station of all places, decides to tell him that he's adopted, when he had grown up believing that she and his father were his natural parents. Why some parents do not explain these things to their children is hard to comprehend.

The NCOIC at RSS Downey, located about ten miles from downtown Los Angeles, called me one day and said that he would prefer duty at Inglewood, and, if I agreed, we could swap duty stations. The OIC approved the request, and this move put me twenty miles closer to home.

In 1965, the military situation in Vietnam began to heat up when the 3d Marine Division went to the Republic of Vietnam from Okinawa. The draft kicked in at a faster pace. The Downey recruiting station was just around the corner from the local draft board, and my assistant and I caught the young men as they headed there to register for Selective Service. Enticing them into our office, we explained the evils and pitfalls of waiting to be drafted. We did a land-office business that year. Our recruiting station topped all of those in the entire 12th District, and the district presented me with a diamond ring for being the top recruiter in southern California. During one month, with a quota of twenty men, our station had managed to ship thirty.

In addition, I had been selected for promotion that year. In September, I received my warrant for master sergeant. These achievements did have their drawback, however. I was now the chief recruiter for RSLA, which meant that I had to drive to and from the Los Angeles office every day, a distance of thirty miles each way. Under good conditions, the trip took at least an hour. Using Interstate 5 all the way, I drove at one of two paces: slow or stop-and-go.

My new assignment also required periodic travel to the sub-stations, and I had to interview all applicants for enlistment. The job kept me busy and often required ten to twelve hours a day. It was also interesting and rewarding to be involved in the selection process of the young men and women who would become the future of our Corps.

Because of the rapid buildup in personnel, the Marine Corps began accepting draftees again, for the first time since World War II. Marine Maj. Cliff Delano, assigned to the Armed Force Examining and Entrance Station (AFEES), was in the same building with the RTS. On the days that the Corps received inductees, I assisted him with their processing.

After mental and physical examinations, the draftees were assigned to one of eight groups, starting with 1-A, which indicated mental group 1 (the highest) and physical group A (no physical impairments). The groups ran from 1-A through 4-B, which was the lowest mental group and some slight physical defects.

Naturally, the Marine Corps would have preferred all 1-As, but the AFEES required that we had to accept an equal number of men in each category on the days that we received draftees. For example, if the Marine Corps was getting 25 percent of all draftees on a given day, we had to accept the same percentage within each group. When Major Delano and I entered the room, usually containing about one hundred men, we explained that 25 percent of them would end up in the United States Marine Corps that day. When the groans and moans subsided, I asked for volunteers. This didn't always work out too well because no one liked to be the first to stand up, so I started the practice of walking up and down the line of draftees while they were waiting to enter the room. I asked quietly if any of them were interested in joining the Marine Corps. Usually, there were at least one or two brave souls.

Taking one of them aside, I coached him a little and told him that, when I asked for volunteers in the big room, he should jump up and say, "Hell, yes. I'll go!" That was all it took to break the ice, and several more men usually volunteered. The idea, of course, was that a volunteer was much more desirable, and more likely to become a better Marine, than a randomly selected individual.

One other duty associated with the draft was the witnessing of those men who refused to be inducted into the Armed Forces. After they had completed the examination process, they were taken to the swearing-in ceremony. They were given two chances to take the oath of enlistment! If a man still refused after the second time, he was considered to have refused induction. He then had to write a statement, which he was required to sign as I witnessed his signature. The usual reasons given for refusal were religious or philosophical, but, more often than not, it was just plain fear. We could see it in the men's faces. These "refusees" were subject to federal prosecution and usually sentenced to three years of imprisonment.

The days that we spent trying to fill induction quotas were long ones. By the time these new enlistees and draftees were placed on the Greyhound bus that took them to the Marine Corps Recruit Depot in San Diego, it was usually close to 2200, which meant that we had been on the job for sixteen hours.

Recruiting duty in the Los Angeles area, particularly while I was assigned to RSLA, had a lot of advantages connected with Hollywood, television shows, the theater, and professional football games. The Los Angeles Rams, members of the National Football League, insisted on a Marine Corps color guard at each of their home games at the Coliseum. Their front office sent eight tickets, one for each Marine and his guest, to the RS prior to each game.

We attended cocktail parties where well-known actors and actresses were present, and we were often called on for radio and television interviews. On one memorable occasion, I was asked if I'd like to make a film with Bing Crosby. A film company needed a Marine recruiter for a one-minute, color TV "trailer," as it was called, a commercial for the Marine Corps' annual Toys for Tots program. I reported to the Paramount Studio set where the 1966 remake of the classic *Stagecoach*, with Bing Crosby, Ann-Margret, Red Buttons, and many other notables, was being filmed. During a break in the filming, the cast brought out a barrel filled with toys and sporting a big "Toys for Tots" label. I stood on one side of the barrel, with Bing on the other side, as he did a one-minute monologue. The film was distributed to television stations throughout the country as a public service spot. Bing later autographed an 8 x 10 photograph, taken on the movie set, for me.

Following a year and a half at RSLA, I began trouble-shooting at certain RSSs that were having difficulty making their monthly quotas. I worked at each of these stations, some-times for a week to a month, to help the recruiters to locate and call prospects, and to mail information that would help with their recruiting efforts. Most recruiting stations had the current listing of graduating high school students in their areas, and these proved to be extremely valuable tools for finding prospects.

In early 1967, I was working at RSS Long Beach, Cali-fornia, when the word came from HQMC that all recruiters were frozen on the job. The Corps was looking for a few good men, and we recruiters would stay in place to find them. I had been on recruiting duty for three and a half years. The war in Vietnam was hot and heavy, and I wanted to get over there and see what was going on.

Lt. Col. Joseph Hennegan was stationed in San Francisco as OIC of the Marine Detachment at Hunter's Point Naval Ship-yard there. I had worked for "Crazy Joe," as he was affection-ately known to Marine tankers, when he was the 1st Tank Battalion S-4 and I was his logistics chief. Joe and I talked on the phone frequently. When he made occasional trips to southern California, we went out for dinner and tipped a beer or two. I gave the colonel a call to explain the freeze on recruiters and ask if he knew anyone at HQMC who could influence the action. He said that he'd see what he could do.

Less than two months later, orders transferring me to the 1st Marine Division in Vietnam came in. The manner in which I was informed of the orders, however, was quite an uncomfortable event. It began when I received a telephone call from Maj. Theodore J. ("Ted") Lutz, OIC at RSLA. A Navy Cross winner from his days in Korea, Lutz was a no-nonsense individual, and he told me to drop whatever it was I was doing and get over to his office as soon as possible. He gave no reason for his sudden summons, and I was at a loss for what I could have done to upset him. The hour's drive from Long Beach to Los Angeles gave me plenty of time to wonder and sweat.

When I reported to his office, he immediately began chewing me out for "going over his head." I still couldn't figure out what he was talking about. Finally, he told me that he had just received my orders to the 1st Marine Division. Because they had come to him by way of the 12th District, the people there also wanted to know what the hell was going on.

The major accused me of "working my bolt"—a popular Marine Corps expression indicating an effort on the part of an individual to achieve a desired goal, usually without going through proper channels. Then it dawned on me. Crazy Joe had come through! I played dumb and said that I couldn't imagine why I had received orders, but I also said a silent prayer and thanked both God and Crazy Joe Hennegan for looking out for me.

My orders were effective in June 1967. On the day I detached from RSLA, I had been on recruiting duty for exactly four years. I took a short leave, went to San Diego to say goodbye to the kids and Marion and Scotty, and then reported to Camp Pendleton for processing. In early July, I went to the Marine Corps Air Station at El Toro, California, to board a transport plane, and I was on my way to my third war.

# ═══ 17 ═══

# My Third War

ON 20 JULY 1967, I landed at Kadena Air Force Base on the island of Okinawa. Along with the rest of the Marines on the plane, I was bused north up the coast to Camp Hansen, where I had been a club manager several years earlier. The Marine Corps had set up a large transient facility at Camp Hansen, where all Marines going to or coming from Vietnam were administratively processed. Each man's service record book was checked; those who had missed or avoided their required inoculations were identified, rounded up, and given their shots; and transportation was arranged to the next destination.

The entire process had been massaged into a fast-paced, highly efficient operation. I was on Okinawa for only two days before I was booked, with a replacement draft of fellow Marines, on a Continental Airlines flight chartered for Vietnam. Departing from Kadena, we arrived at the port city of Da Nang, in what was then the Republic of South Vietnam, on 22 July. Marine liaison personnel from the 3d and 1st Marine Divisions were there and arranged further transportation to their units on the spot.

The 1st Tank Battalion CP was located less than two miles from Da Nang Air Base. On receiving word that a replacement had arrived, the CP sent a Jeep and driver to pick me up. As I was reporting in, the battalion's commanding officer spotted me, and I'll be damned if it wasn't Roughhouse Taylor, now a lieutenant colonel. We greeted each other warmly and had a

245

cup of coffee; the colonel lost no time in asking me if I wanted to be his battalion's sergeant major. Two other positions were also vacant, first sergeant of Headquarters and Service Company and battalion operations chief with S-3.

I explained to Colonel Taylor that it probably wouldn't be long before a new sergeant major would report in and be able to take over the assignment, and any first sergeant would be eager to assume the position with Headquarters and Service Company. As long as the operations and training position was still open, I told him, I preferred to work in my MOS, and I asked to be assigned to the battalion's S-3 shop. He agreed, and that's where I ended up. The position called for a master gunnery sergeant, but none was available. Because of my previous experience with the 1st Tank Battalion at Camp Pendleton, I had no difficulty in handling the job.

The battalion S-3, along with our battalion's communications section and the S-2 (intelligence) section, operated from a combat operations center (COC), a fairly well-fortified, three-tiered bunker covered with logs, sandbags, and earth. Although it was considered to be sufficient protection against small arms, mortars, and shrapnel, larger types of ordnance, such as the Soviet-made 122-mm rocket, could have easily penetrated it. The entrances to the bunker were covered by thick flaps of green canvas to provide for nighttime light discipline. They also did a good job of keeping any fresh air from circulating inside, especially the cool evening air. Our COC was a dark, muggy, and claustrophobic place in which to work.

It took me a while to get accustomed to the unusual living conditions at the battalion CP, and ours were no better than most of the sections in the battalion. We lived in six-man huts with plywood decks and corrugated tin roofs. Young Vietnamese girls, called "house girls," made up our bunks, kept the huts clean, and washed our clothes, all for four dollars per month. There was a small SNCO club located in the middle of the compound, and the officers' club was just a few yards away from ours. We also had a small PX, a barbershop, and even the luxury of an outdoor theater where movies were shown several times each week, invariably, it seemed, on rainy nights. All of this was unlike any wartime duty familiar to me during World War II or Korea. I kept asking myself, is this war?

The 1st Tank Battalion was not organic to the 1st Marine Division, which means that our battalion was not actually in the division. It was a Fleet Marine Force (FMF) unit under the division's operational and administrative control. Our CP had been at the same location for some time and would remain there, with no tactical displacement, because the 1st and 3d Marine Divisions were not taking real estate but merely trying to hold on to what they already had.

Generally speaking, our battalion's three tank companies were scattered to the winds, as they moved with the infantry regiments to which they were assigned. Only six Marine infantry regiments were operating in all of Quang Nam Province. Company B was assigned to the 7th Marine Regiment southwest of Da Nang, Company C was with the 5th Marine Regiment located just south of Marble Mountain, and Company A was operating with the 1st Marine Regiment located near Con Thien, not far from the Demilitarized Zone (DMZ) in the northernmost province of the I Corps Tactical Zone.

We had only the headquarters gun tanks, that is, the commanding officer's and executive officer's tanks, and the flame tanks with us at the battalion CP. We rarely saw any of the other tanks belonging to the battalion unless they came in for repairs.

The battalion commander, executive officer (XO), and S-3 officer went out to visit the companies when road conditions permitted; however, well-hidden enemy mines were a constant danger. The 1st Tank Battalion would record ninety mine incidents in one calendar year. The devices ranged from small antipersonnel mines, which normally did no real damage to a tank, to the large antitank mines that could completely sweep the track, sprocket, road wheels, and support arms from the side of any of our tanks. These large types of enemy mines could also cause serious injuries to crew members inside the tank.

Normally, the command relationship and our tactical situation were unlike anything that Marines had dealt with in previous wars. U.S. Army Gen. William C. Westmoreland, commander of the Military Assistance Command, Vietnam, known as MACV (pronounced Mac-Vee), commanded all U.S. forces in Vietnam. His headquarters was in South Vietnam's capital city of Saigon, located several hundred miles south of the city of Da Nang.

The five northernmost provinces of the Republic of South Vietnam were located in what was designated as the I Corps Tactical Zone (CTZ), commonly known as I Corps. All Marines in I Corps were under the command of the 3d Marine Amphibious Force (III MAF), referred to as "Three-MAF." Its commander at the time of my arrival was Lt. Gen. Robert E. Cushman, Jr., whose headquarters was located in Da Nang.

The 1st Marine Division CP, located at Hill 327, not far from Da Nang Air Base, was commanded at the time by Maj. Gen. Donn J. Robertson. The 3d Marine Division head-quarters, located north of Da Nang at Phu Bai, was com-manded by Maj. Gen. Bruno Hochmuth, who would die in a helicopter crash near Hue on 14 November 1967.

My boss, Roughhouse Taylor, wore two hats. In addition to commanding the 1st Tank Battalion, he was also commander of the Southern Sector Defense Command (SSDC), an area stretching from just below Hill 327 on the north to Highway 1-A on the east and south to the Cao Do and Tuy Loan Rivers, where the Tuy Loan took a sharp turn northward and to the west. SSDC units included the 1st Tank Battalion; an armored amphibian company, located in our camp; the U.S. Navy petroleum, oil, and lubricants (POL) dump; an artillery bat-talion; and Ammunition Supply Point One (ASP 1).

The SSDC formed the Provisional Rifle Company to be called out when needed. It consisted of one platoon each from tanks, the Marine artillery battalion, and the armored amphibian company. The rifle company, which trained period-ically, was made up largely of volunteers from the head-quarters of those units.

Capt. Richard McPherson, our battalion's S-2 officer, was designated as the Provisional Rifle Company's commanding officer (CO). One of the platoons was commanded by WO James ("Jim") C. Carroll, XO of our battalion's Headquarters and Service Company. Carroll held the rank of Marine Gunner with an 1802 MOS, a tank officer.

The primary enemy action that we encountered in our area was in the form of the Soviet-made 122-mm rockets that flew, sometimes nightly, over our camp. They were aimed at, and usually hit, the Da Nang Air Base. On 14 July 1967, only eight days before my arrival "in-country," the Viet Cong (VC) had fired more than fifty rockets at the base, killing eight Americans, wounding nearly two hundred, destroying millions of dollars worth of U.S. aircraft, and causing considerable damage to the barracks and a bomb dump.

After a month, I began going out on an occasional patrol just to get away from the confines of the COC. Our patrols were mostly intended to be night ambushes, but we usually didn't stray too far from camp and there wasn't much action. We knew the Viet Cong were sneaking around at night, but they were able to avoid us. Gunner Carroll occasionally took out a patrol. He, too, was looking for any reason to break up his routine as company XO.

The weather in Vietnam was extremely hot and humid, similar to that of Florida. The temperature during a normal summer's day ranged between 100°F and 106°F, with a humidity level of at least 90 percent. In August, we experienced severe rains, which helped to cool off things a bit. When it rained in "Nam," it really poured. Several inches per hour was not unusual. Luckily, several friends who were Vietnam veterans had recommended that I bring a good two-piece rainsuit along, and their sage advice helped me to keep dry.

During August, Gunner Carroll and I were assigned to a one-day M16 rifle class conducted by members of the division ordnance staff. We then had the job of conducting our own classes on the proper care and cleaning of this new rifle for every new battalion member armed with it

There had been one hell of a ruckus earlier in the year, particularly within the 3d Marine Division, because of stoppage problems experienced with the M16 during combat operations. All kinds of senior brass and civilians had come to Vietnam to study the situation, and the problem was quickly narrowed down to two factors: failure to keep the rifle properly cleaned

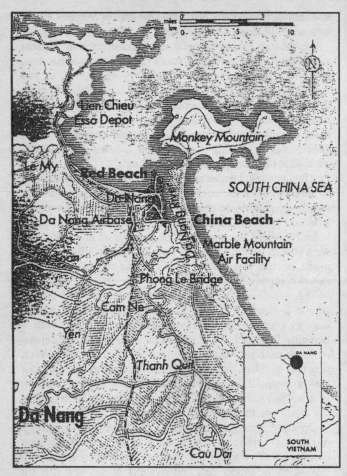

Da Nang and surrounding area, Quang Nam Province, South Vietnam, 1967. (Source: John Pimlott, *Nam: The Vietnam Experience—1965–1975* [New York: Mallard Press, 1988], 5. Used with permission.)

and pitting in the chamber that caused the weapon not to extract spent ammunition properly during the cycle of firing. The M16 had to be cleaned more frequently and much more thoroughly than did the M14 rifle because of the higher tolerances allowed in the manufacture of the new weapon. The M14 was similar to the M1 rifle in its bolt design. It was said that a Marine could throw an M1 into the sand or a mud puddle, pick it up, shake it off, and start firing. I had witnessed the truth of this claim many times during World War II. The M16's design was much different, but its problems were dramatically reduced after classes on proper care were conducted in both Marine divisions. The rifle chambers were subsequently refitted with chrome plating, and the problems associated with pitting soon ceased.

On the night of 28 August during a rocket attack on the Da Nang Air Base, Viet Cong divers set demolition charges against the pilings of the Phong Le bridge that spanned the Cao Do River on Highway 1-A, just south of our CP. There was one hell of an explosion—we could clearly hear the rumble.

I was on duty in the battalion COC bunker when Colonel Taylor walked in and said, "Well, they just blew up our goddamned bridge!" It was "ours" because it was in our area of responsibility and we had a guard detachment posted there. It would be a number of months before the bridge would be completely restored, but the combat engineers managed to install a temporary pontoon bridge that reconnected us with points south.

With the U.S. government's pacification program in full swing in Vietnam (an effort to win over the hearts and minds of the South Vietnamese people), the 1st Tank Battalion had responsibility for two civic-action programs. One was, of all things, a pig farm, where we purchased the livestock and attempted to encourage the local people to raise and market the four-legged product. Also, the program was intended to keep the VC from stealing the pigs. Overall, the program worked well.

The second civic-action endeavor was centered around a grammar school located south of our camp in the small village of Hoa Tho. Our battalion had supplied the money and materials to build it, and the local people really appreciated our efforts. A lot of dignitaries, both Vietnamese and U.S. military, were present when the school was dedicated. Brig. Gen. Foster C. Lahue, our assistant division commander (ADC), attended the ceremony, and, because it was our battalion's project, Colonel Taylor gave the keynote address, which was translated into Vietnamese. I took a number of photographs of the event and remember being surrounded by dozens of young, smiling children who would benefit from our efforts.

Our battalion had a rather good R&R program. Personnel were entitled to at least one trip during a thirteen-month tour, with priority going to those Marines who had been in-country the longest. They had the choice of some pretty exotic ports, such as Bangkok, Singapore, and Hong Kong. Married personnel were allowed to meet their wives in Hawaii. These R&Rs lasted five days, including travel time, with transportation paid by Uncle Sam.

When I had reported to the battalion, one of the first things that our S-3 officer told me was to take advantage of every R&R trip I could get—in his words, "To get the hell out of the country if the chance presented itself." I had told the company first sergeant that I had a tote bag packed and ready to go at a moment's notice. If there was a vacancy in our battalion's allotment of R&Rs that couldn't be filled, he could always give me a call.

One evening during the first week of October, the first sergeant came to my hootch and asked if I could go to Pinang, Malaysia, the following day. Not far from Singapore, Pinang was a popular R&R spot. I checked with our S-3 officer, who gave the go-ahead. The next morning, I left for what proved to be a great trip, complete with a fine selection of hotels, great exotic foods, cheap prices, and friendly people.

On 9 October, Colonel Taylor was detached and departed for home. Our new CO was Lt. Col. Vincent J. Gentile. Some of the tankers knew him, and I had served with him somewhere along the way when he was a major, but he was not as well known as Roughhouse, who was a legend among Marine tankers.

I had been in-country since July and had written to my children several times, but I had not received any mail from them. I couldn't excuse their ages anymore; they were fourteen, fifteen, and seventeen years old. I tended to blame their mother for not making them sit down and answer my letters, but their insensitivity left its mark.

The enemy rocket attacks continued on a regular basis. For some unexplained reason, Friday nights were always popular. The 122-mm rockets frequently came from just across the Cao Do River, and we could see the sparks trailing from them as they sailed over our camp. On many nights, one of our tank crews located right next to the river, on what we called outpost (OP) 47, could see the enemy rocket battery setting up in preparation for firing. Our tanks were equipped with infrared scopes, and the crew could observe the entire operation. Each time, they radioed the COC and requested permission to fire. Because of the ridiculous regulations concerning fire procedures, the duty officer was required to contact the division, which had to check with higher headquarters to ensure that there were no friendly patrols in the area! By the time clearance was received, if ever, the damage was done and the elusive enemy rocketeers were long gone.

With November came the incredible monsoon rains—several inches a day. The tank ramp was the only paved area in our compound, and the rains and resulting mud restricted our ability to move around.

On 18 December, Bob Hope and his USO troupe were scheduled to put on a show near the division CP. I happened to be in the area early in the morning and noted that the outdoor theater was already packed hours before the show was due to begin. The front rows were reserved for the senior brass. Anyone arriving at show time would have needed binoculars for even a glimpse of the performers on stage. I don't recall that anyone from our battalion bothered to attend the show.

The Marines were still recovering from the "scandal" of having booed Martha Raye off the stage during a show at the

3d Marine Division area when she showed up in the uniform of a Green Beret colonel. Although she was an honorary colonel of the Berets and her intentions were good, Martha didn't realize that the Marines were just not that impressed with the U.S. Army's Special Forces. Rumors floated around, however, that the division commander got up on the stage and berated his troops for this discourteous act.

I had been in Vietnam for six months before I saw the port city of Da Nang. Although we were positioned only several miles away, the city was off-limits to us except for official business. One day, I had a valid reason to visit Da Nang, and my Jeep driver, Corporal Welker, and I took a sightseeing ride. There wasn't much to see, however; the city was somewhat torn up, and troops of the U.S. Army and the Army of the Republic of Vietnam (ARVN) were everywhere. I took a number of photographs of Da Nang, and Welker had brought his camera along, too, but some little street kid grabbed it when we left the Jeep for less than a minute.

Because of our static situation, incoming mail was as regular as clockwork in our area, and I heard from my mother and most of the family frequently. Several packages arrived before Christmas, although I had asked that they not send anything because the camp PX and a larger one near the division CP were both well stocked. I especially appreciated the Gallo salami and a bottle of Galiano liqueur, however; these items simply were not available anywhere in Vietnam.

Christmas was fairly quiet. I attended Mass and then visited the POL dump next door. They had a fine enlisted club and usually had good stage shows there on Sundays and holidays, depending on the alert situation. There was a 24-hour truce for Christmas, and they had a really good show.

When I left the States for Vietnam, I had been dating several women. They were all good at keeping up with their correspondence, so I didn't want for mail. I took quite a ribbing from Gunner Carroll about the time I spent on writing letters during the evenings. I tried to pass it off to my popularity with the girls, which only brought on more ribbing. Jim was from San Diego, a former teacher and principal with the city schools, and had lived in Pacific Beach, my old stomping grounds. He was also single and familiar with a few of the local night spots there. Oddly enough, we had frequented the same places and knew some of the same people.

On the night of 2 January 1968, Da Nang Air Base was again hit hard by 122-mm rockets. I was duty officer in the COC when the firing started. A tank commander from OP 47 radioed in that he had the rocketeers under infrared observation and asked for permission to take them under fire. I had to refuse his request until I could relay it up the chain of command. The tank commander was so angry he was crying—I could tell by his voice. When I finally received approval, the enemy was far away. It was extremely frustrating to have our hands tied by military bureaucracy. Not far from camp that same night, two of our M-48 tanks were ambushed and attacked with rocket-propelled grenades (RPGs), which resulted in a staff sergeant being killed and four crewmen wounded.

The enemy rocket attacks continued, sometimes nightly and occasionally a few days apart. The rockets usually hit some part of the air base, but if they were overshot or undershot, they came down near the outskirts of Da Nang or slammed into an unsuspecting village and caused civilian casualties.

A new chaplain arrived at camp—a Protestant minister who was very enthusiastic about his work. When he found that we didn't have a chapel, he had a hootch dragged into camp and designated it as one. We even had a small dedication ceremony with some of the division brass in attendance. Because there were quite a few Catholics in the area, a Catholic chaplain was sent out to join us so that we no longer had to travel to the division area for services.

Our Protestant padre had another idea that proved to be interesting and educational. He organized a bus tour of several cathedrals and temples in the area, and a full busload of Marines, including myself, accompanied him to Da Nang one Saturday. Most of us knew little about the Vietnamese way of life. We visited a Buddhist temple, a Caoist temple, a Catholic cathedral, a girls' school, and two orphanages. We took dozens of photographs, but it seemed strange to visit places of worship in an area where the people never knew when they would experience the next rocket attack. We came away from Da Nang with admiration for their stoicism and composure under such conditions.

Things were fairly quiet for a couple of weeks. Then, on the night of 29 January, enemy rockets hit Marine Air Group (MAG) 11, located at Da Nang Air Base, and MAG 16, the Marine helicopter facility located to the southwest of us near Marble Mountain. We didn't realize it at the time, but this was a prelude to the 1968 Tet Offensive, the biggest enemy offensive of the Vietnam War.

Tet was the name given to the Chinese lunar new year, the most important of Oriental holidays, which was celebrated by all religious groups and social classes; 1968 was the year of the monkey. The Viet Cong had declared a seven-day truce, from 27 January to 2 February, in honor of the holiday, but the Allied forces had declared only a three-day truce period, 29 to 31 January.

There was to be no truce at all. The capital city of Saigon was heavily attacked by enemy forces that had been infiltrating for months. They were aided by those already living within the city and by Communist sympathizers. The American Embassy was attacked during the early morning hours of Wednesday, 31 January, when sappers blew a hole in the outer wall surrounding the embassy compound. Although the Marine Security Guard detachment in Saigon consisted of more than eighty Marines, only three were on duty at the time of the attack; however, they managed to defend the chancery itself. The Communist invaders were unable to gain entrance there, but two of them entered the quarters of a senior embassy official, Col. George Jacobson, U.S. Army (Ret.). Jacobson was unarmed, but he shot one of the enemy soldiers with a pistol thrown up to him by an MSG Marine on the ground. The other soldier fled and was quickly tracked down and killed. Because of the Viet Cong presence in and around the embassy compound, help was unable to reach the defenders for several more hours. It was necessary to wait until dawn to distinguish friend from foe. Finally, after almost seven hours of siege, a helicopter landed on the embassy roof with reinforcements and the embassy was secured. About fourteen Viet Cong had been killed on the grounds. Friendly KIAs numbered five, including one U.S. Marine.

During that same night, 30–31 January, the Da Nang Air Base and many surrounding installations were attacked by the Viet Cong with rockets, satchel charges, and mortars. As usual, the rockets aimed at the air base flew over our camp. Most of us thought it was the beginning of just another attack until we heard small-arms fire coming from a nearby military compound. For a short time, it sounded like our hootches were taking small-arms rounds, too, but the noise came from spent rounds falling on the tin roofs.

The alert was sounded. During the early morning hours, the SSDC rifle company received its first order to search the nearby villages for suspected Viet Cong and to chase the enemy rocketeers. Several weeks before, Captain McPherson had designated me first sergeant of the company. I took the Jeep, with Welker as my driver, and the troops boarded 6 x 6 trucks.

The search of the villages produced nothing, but we did find some signs that the Viet Cong had been there. Of course, the elusive enemy rocketeers were nowhere to be found. Our company stayed out in the bush for three days. Corporal Welker and I came in only for ammunition and chow resupply.

Soon, my job with the SSDC company was done. The brass decided that a "first shirt" wasn't needed because no administrative work was required and the company had the expert services of a gunnery sergeant. The rifle company stayed out in the bush for three more days and killed several Viet Cong, captured almost ninety of them, and brought in dozens of weapons.

Meanwhile, Hue, the ancient imperial capital of all Vietnam, had been completely overrun by North Vietnamese Army (NVA) and VC forces, which attacked and occupied most of the government installations. Hue had no U.S. military garrison, but it did have a large U.S. civilian population and some joint military advisers.

The 1st ARVN Division occupied the Citadel, and other ARVN units were located nearby. The Citadel, a huge, ancient

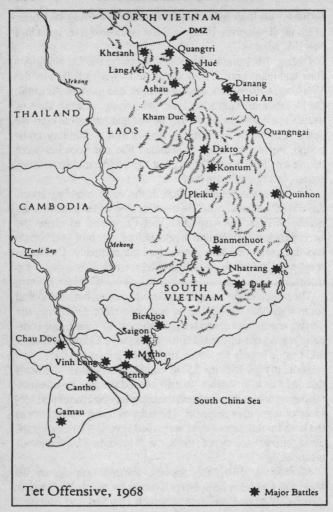

Tet Offensive, 1968     🟊 Major Battles

Battle areas during the Tet Offensive of the North Vietnamese Army and Viet Cong forces in South Vietnam, 1968. (Source: John Pimlott, *Nam: The Vietnam Experience—1965–1975* [New York: Mallard Press, 1988], 355. Used with permission.)

fortress with high walls and towers and almost three square miles in size, even contained a small airfield. Hue's attackers had lists of their enemies and sought out government officials, military personnel, political figures, and foreigners other than the French. The NVA and VC were particularly interested in Catholics, especially priests. Their captives were quickly executed, except for the priests, who were buried alive. The ARVN troops and local militia fought a bloody battle but could not withstand the Communists.

On the morning of 31 January, Company A, 1st Battalion, 1st Marine Regiment, was dispatched from Phu Bai to reinforce the MACV compound just south of the Perfume River. It was joined on the way by a platoon of tanks, and, two days later, Companies F and H of the 5th Marines also joined in the battle. In turn, they were reinforced by Company B, 1st Marines. The street fighting in Hue was reminiscent of that in Seoul in 1950.

The battle for Hue was the longest in the Tet Offensive—twenty-five days—and the bloodiest. The NVA and Viet Cong suffered more than 5,000 killed. The ARVN lost some 390 soldiers, and 142 U.S. Marines were killed in action.

The number of civilians executed by the invaders in the city of Hue has been estimated at more than 3,000 Vietnamese and foreign nationals, including Americans. Among the latter was senior American adviser Philip W. Manhard, a veteran Foreign Service officer, who was led away by the NVA and never seen or heard from again. More than 2,800 bodies were recovered during the next two years, some in graves of hundreds. Almost all bore the sign of execution—a single bullet hole in the head.

The Tet offensive was extremely costly to the Communists, who lost an estimated 55,000–80,000 troops killed. There was no general uprising of the South Vietnamese people, as the enemy had expected, and all territories occupied by the Communists were lost within a month. Not a single objective in Quang Nam Province, including Da Nang, was occupied. Despite all of this, the Communist offensive became a victory for NVA as a result of the American news media coverage. As usual, our own press and radio and television newscasters grossly exaggerated enemy gains and American losses. Two such examples were the report of heavy Marine causalities in Hue and the report of the first five floors of the chancery building—one that the enemy was never able to enter—at the American Embassy in Saigon being seized by the Viet Cong.

The effect on the American public was predictable. Antiwar agitators had a field day as they organized more riots and demonstrations and brought greater pressure on Washington and President Lyndon B. Johnson to bring an end to U.S. involvement in Vietnam. The Tet Offensive was considered a primary reason for President Johnson's decision not to seek reelection.

Following Tet, things in the Da Nang area quieted down somewhat. I was back in my bunker at my regular job when I received a call from the division's special services officer, Maj. Martin Young. "Marty" was a tanker, and I had known him when we served together at 1st Tanks at Camp Pendleton a few years back. One day when I saw him at CP, he had told me that his job included assigning all R&Rs, and I had jokingly remarked that, if he ever had an empty seat for Sydney, Australia, he should give me a call. Sydney had just opened up as one of the available cities, and my senior operations clerk, Sgt. James ("Jim") Sefrhans, had been on the first planeload of Marines to go. He came back with glowing reports of the city and its friendly people.

When Marty asked me if I could leave for Sydney the next morning, I told him I'd get back to him in a couple of hours. I cleared my request through Maj. Dwight Dickey, our new S-3 officer, and then went to Colonel Gentile, who, after a bit of grumbling, also approved it. Marty told me to be at Da Nang Air Base at 0700. I didn't want anyone changing his mind at the last moment, so, to be safe, I went next door to the Navy POL dump and, after a few drinks, spent the night in the chief petty officer's quarters. Early in the morning, the Navy gave me a ride to the air base. By 0730, I was on board a Pan American 707 bound for Sydney.

A beautiful city, Sydney reminded me very much of San Diego, harbor and all. The girls were friendly to the U.S. troops from Vietnam, as was the rest of the citizenry. A Marine's money was considered no good in Australia. The first day there, I met a businessman and his girlfriend at the bar of the R&R hotel. They rounded up a girlfriend for me, and we all spent several days together—sailing on the bay and touring local places of interest.

Also at the bar that first afternoon was Billy Daniels, a popular American singer who had gained fame with the 1945 hit tune, "That Old Black Magic." Billy was appearing at the hotel there and, during a performance that evening, interrupted a song to introduce me to the audience when my new friends and I walked in.

Here were 250 people wondering, "Who the hell is that?" When Billy mentioned Vietnam, however, they gave me quite a hand. Really great people, those Aussies!

My seven days were over much too quickly, and then it was back to Nam.

On my return, I was shocked and saddened to learn about what had happened a couple of days after I left. Our SSDC rifle company had been called out when a report came in that some NVA were in the area. The enemy ambushed the rifle company and killed nine Marines, including Sergeant Sefrhans, who had gone to the aid of a wounded buddy acting as radioman for his platoon. His buddy, a clerk in our company office, was also killed. Captain McPherson, the CO, was seriously wounded and would spend nearly a year in the hospital.

My Jeep driver, Corporal Welker, had gone to Sefrhans's aid as soon as he saw that Jim was hit, only to find him dead. Welker thought that he also had been hit. He checked himself over but found no wounds. When the firefight was over and everyone had returned to camp, Welker later related, he walked into the COC bunker and removed his cartridge belt. Two AK-47 rounds fell from the belt. He had been hit, but the rounds had lodged in his heavy belt.

In 1967, the Marines had adopted a new effort called the Chieu Hoi (open arms) Program, one of many ideas in U.S. attempts to win over the enemy. Viet Cong defectors were given an opportunity to learn a trade. Those who assisted our troops militarily were called hoi chanhs (ralliers) and knows as Kit Carson Scouts (KCSs). Often used as point men, the KCSs led U.S. infantry and reconnaissance patrols against their former comrades in VC-controlled territory.

The tank battalion was assigned a scout, and he went to work for us in the operations section. He was a gung ho little bastard, and I'll be damned if, within a week, he didn't discover a cave complex in the village just below OP 47, an area that I had walked over several times.

He routed out three Viet Cong and shot them all. Before they expired, the scout and an ARVN staff sergeant, also assigned to our S-3, interrogated them. The Viet Cong admitted that their mission was to reconnoiter our tank battalion's camp, as well as other sites in the area. Our KCS turned out to be a good tunnel rat. Armed only with a .45 pistol, he had gone right into the cave and flushed them out. He found three more Viet Cong a couple of weeks later. They were right on the river in front of OP 47. He had shot them and dragged their bodies out of a tunnel. Marines on the OP called the COC, and several of us went out to take a look at the results. One of the Viet Cong was, or had been, an attractive nurse.

One day in early March, the word came down that a Marine brigadier general, who had been a POW during the Korean War, would visit our camp. At battalion headquarters, I asked his name and learned that it was McLaughlin. I told Colonel Gentile that I would like to see the general while he was there.

The CO gave my message to the general. When he heard that it was from Maffioli, he said, "Well, let's go and see him." The general, of course, was former Maj. John N. McLaughlin from Task Force Drysdale and my Kanggye POW camp days. We hadn't seen one another since 1955. We had time for only a short visit, but we caught up on news about the whereabouts of some former POW friends and what they were doing.

Back in January, a message from division headquarters had stated that some 81-mm mortars were available for units that didn't have them on their table of equipment (T/E) allowance. Our unit didn't rate a mortar, but we wanted one because of its value in providing illumination. I talked about this situation with our battalion S-3. He didn't think that we stood much of a chance of getting one, but he said that I should try. About two months later, in mid-March, our supply chief walked into the COC and wanted to know if anyone in the battalion had ordered a mortar. I let out a great whoop and told him it was mine.

I had never been in the infantry or had any real experience with mortars, but I was determined to learn because it would provide good illumination for our bridge and OP 47. These positions were located about 2,000 and 3,200 yards distant, respectively. The 81-mm was good for about 4,000 yards, but the outpost at the west end of our sector was at least 5,500 yards away, well out of range.

Fortunately, Sgt. "Gunny" Budney, an infantry gunnery sergeant assigned to the battalion and in charge of the security platoon, had been a mortar man in his earlier days. Gunny Budney remembered his mortar training well. He supervised construction of the mortar pit and helped to train my Ops clerks and me as an 81-mm mortar crew.

Our next task was to find ammunition. Although ironic, it was not unusual that the division had made no provision for any allotment of 81-mm illumination rounds to support its mortars. ASP 1 was low on illumination rounds because the infantry got the majority of them.

As is often the case in the Marine Corps "family," however, I had a friend at the ammunition supply point. Now a lieutenant, he had served with me on Okinawa ten years earlier, when he was a young staff sergeant. He fixed me up not only with illumination rounds but also an M53 sight for the mortar, complete with telescope, although we really didn't need the sight to fire illumination rounds. We knew the ranges of our intended targets and relied on only two aiming stakes for our outposts at the bridge and OP 47 in order to cover them with illumination.

Inasmuch as my clerks and I were the mortar crew, I had our pit constructed just outside our bunker entrance. With our small compound, the pit was only fifty yards from the officers' club and not more than seventy-five yards from the SNCO club. We hadn't been in business more than a week when the first call came in one night. Our Marines manning the ridge announced movement in front of their position. The radio communicator who took the call came running down to my hootch to get me. I rounded up our gun crew, and we fired off two illumination rounds. The Marines at the bridge adjusted the mortar fire after our second round illuminated their area, then we let them have a few more rounds. They radioed back that it was good light—they had actually seen some figures hauling ass through the bush.

Unfortunately, no one had bothered to tell the patrons of the two camp watering holes that our new weapon was about to be fired. The firing of an 81-mm mortar can be quite loud, particularly in the still of night, and it can even sound like incoming fire. I don't know what happened in the officers' club, but I learned that, only moments after we had fired our mortar, all customers in the SNCO club were under tables, chairs, or whatever else provided cover. When they realized what the noise was, some uncalled-for name-calling and numerous references to my ancestry were screamed my way. From then on, during club hours, a runner was dispatched to the clubs to warn that the camp's mortar was about to be fired. After a few more fire missions, I got to where I could handle the mortar myself when a call came in. I broke open the ammunition, set the proper charge, and began firing.

Because of ASP 1's location in the SSDC and my dealings with them as I scrounged for ammunition, I had told the major who ran the operations section there about our mortar. He said that he would give me a call if he ever needed some illumination. Sure enough, he called several weeks later and said that they had some enemy movement outside their protective wire. I ran out to the mortar pit—the ASP was in my line of sight and I knew the range—and fired off one round. It was beautiful to watch. The canister popped open, and a small parachute deployed to slow the descent of the burning flare—right on top of a stack of ammunition boxes.

All I could muster was "Oh, my God!" as I imagined what havoc the burning flare could wreak on the entire area.

Fortunately, an alert sentry at the ammunition dump had also watched the illumination round drift downward. When he saw where it landed, he grabbed a bucket of water and quickly moved to extinguish it. Possibly he saved the ammunition dump, the surrounding area, and my ass.

Before I could get back into the bunker, the radio operator yelled out, "Call for you from ASP 1, Top." The major and I, right then and there, agreed that there would be no more illumination rounds fired from my mortar toward his ASP.

One day in late March, I was out in the pit with my crew when we heard a pop. We looked toward the POL dump and watched the canopy fly off of a low-flying jet. Seconds later, both pilot and copilot ejected and their plane crashed into a ravine that separated the two camps.

I ran inside the bunker and grabbed the keys to a gate in the barbed-wire fence at the end of the camp. By this time, nearly a dozen Marines from our camp were headed in the direction of the crash. The plane had exploded when it hit and was burning. We could hear the .50-caliber machine-gun ammunition cooking off, and we continued our approach carefully. When we got into the ravine, we saw that the aircraft had been a B-57 Canberra jet bomber.

The stricken plane had been flying so low that the pilot could have seen that, if he and his copilot ejected when the aircraft was level, it would most likely crash into the POL dump or the troop staging area across the road. So, just before they punched out, he banked the plane and headed it for the ravine, which put them at too much of an angle for their parachutes to have any chance of opening. Both men landed not far from the aircraft and were killed on impact. One hit a barbed-wire fence and was badly mangled; the other one landed in a heavy brush area.

A helicopter from Da Nang Air Base arrived within minutes, and some of us helped load the bodies aboard. A few minutes later, another helicopter came in with some Air Force officers who were looking for witnesses to the crash. They asked us to submit written statements on what we had seen.

A few days later, we learned the whole story about what had happened. The plane, from an air base far south of us, had been on a bombing mission to the north. It had taken small-arms fire that knocked out one of the two engines, so the pilot had tried to limp on toward the nearest runway, which was Da Nang, and radioed ahead that he had an emergency. Da Nang had cleared the plane for landing and diverted all other aircraft from the area. The pilot had brought the plane in for a landing with the proper approach and at the right altitude, but, for reasons that will forever remain unknown, he had gunned his engine in preparation for a second attempt at landing. That was when he had lost his second engine and attempted to bail out.

Several days later, when the Air Force came to retrieve the wreckage, I learned that the investigators found bullet holes in both engines. Apparently, they had been hit at the same time, but the crew had not realized it.

That tragic story had an ironic epilogue. About three weeks after the crash, one of my clerks who had been at the crash site received a letter from home that enclosed an article from his hometown newspaper. The story described an aircraft crash near Da Nang Air Base on that very date, with all of the details and also the shocking news that the plane's copilot was the clerk's cousin! The clerk hadn't seen his cousin for several years and, because of the condition of the bodies, did not recognize him.

Our former H&S Company commander, Major C. R. Casey, had been reassigned to take over Company A tanks, and Maj. Leo Gildersleeve, a well-known figure among Marine tankers, now commanded H&S. Gunner Jim Carroll also went with Company A as leader of its 3d Platoon. Operating up north in the 3d Marine Division's tactical area of responsibility (TAOR), in the Hue City area, the company was moving in and out of Phu Bai. Even though Tet was over, there was still plenty of offensive action within the I Corps northern provinces.

On 7 May 1968, the enemy launched a routine rocket attack against Da Nang Air Base. The 122-mm rockets, coming in just south of the Cao Do River, flew over us as usual. To us, it was just another shoot (we had been experiencing them almost every night) until one of the rockets landed short and exploded right at the main gate to our camp. Several Marine sentries were wounded.

I was duty officer that night, but it was hot and humid in the

COC bunker. I had told the communicators that I'd be catching some shut-eye outside on top of the bunker. When the rocket hit, the concussion knocked me off the top of the bunker. I fell onto the second tier, right onto some rocks. I landed on my knees, and one was pretty well banged up. The next morning at the division hospital, I had my knee X-rayed and ended up with a shot of hydrocortisone. I was on crutches for the next two weeks, but I was lucky not to have been seriously injured—no Purple Heart for me.

A few nights after my injury, the enemy gunners lowered their sights and managed to zero in on the artillery battalion camp just across the road from our compound. The battalion's sergeant major, who had been in-country only a few days, was killed. He had been over at our camp that very day to introduce himself to the staff. A Navy corpsman later told me that the sergeant major had been hit in the temple by a single piece of shrapnel.

Later, I heard that Lt. Col. Bill Fagan, my old OIC from our recruiting days in the Los Angeles area, was the new CO of the 1st Battalion, 7th Marines (1/7), and located only a few miles southwest of our location. I was able to get him on the phone and told him that I would be down to his area some day for a visit. In a week or so, I talked the S-3 into taking a Jeep ride, and we arrived at 1/7's area just after a daylight mortar attack. Colonel Fagan was out counting casualties, but we did get a chance to talk about old times.

The weather was getting hot again, now that the heavy rains had subsided. With the temperatures back up to 102°–105°F and a constant humidity of 90 percent, everyone was using salt tablets and drinking plenty of water.

I was due for rotation out of Vietnam in early August and, naturally, wondered where my next duty station would be. One thing was certain. The way that we had to fight this war—with our hands tied by absurd policy and prevented by politicians from fighting to win—I wasn't interested in extending my tour, although such incentives as an R&R trip anywhere in the Free World were being offered for those who agreed to remain in-country for six more months. Even this offer couldn't entice me to stay. Vietnam was not my kind of war.

When my orders arrived in late May, I received one hell of a surprise to learn that I would be going back to Marine Security Guard School. I had written a letter to CMC and requested MSG duty, but I viewed my request as a shot in the dark. NCOICs were seldom given a second MSG tour, but I had my orders in hand. I wondered why I had to go back to school. The reason, I learned later, was because so many policy changes had occurred during the seven years since my MSG duty. The course would be more than just a refresher. I was so pleased with my orders that I felt able to handle any required schooling while standing on my head.

Also in late May, we received word at the battalion CP that Gunner Jim Carroll had been wounded and evacuated to a U.S. Navy hospital ship off the coast of Da Nang. The report stated that his wounds were not too serious. He had been hit in the hand and buttocks by just one small-arms round and did not need to be hospitalized. When he reported back to our CP, I couldn't wait to ask him how and why his two wounds were made by one round. His reply was simple: "I was scratching my ass when I got hit!" Now it was *my* turn to get in some good kidding.

One evening during the first week of June, we witnessed a heavy rocket attack on Da Nang Air Base. Our OP 47 had spotted the enemy setting up the rockets and then leaving the area; I reported the grid coordinates to the division G-3 during the night. Early the next morning, we got a call saying that some division G-2 and G-3 personnel wanted to inspect the enemy's rocket-launching site. The Cao Do River was pretty wide at this time, and I suggested that we get a small aluminum boat and motor from the warehouse to ferry the party across the river. The S-3 agreed, and we put the plan into motion.

Our visitors arrived at the camp with two photographers from the PIO (public information office) and two EOD (explosive ordnance disposal) technicians. The addition of these four passengers meant two river crossings into what had been enemy territory only the night before. Despite the "ferry service," our trip to the site was uneventful.

It was interesting to see how the Viet Cong had set up their launch site. Deep pits, which had been uncovered, indicated that the rockets had been stored there for some time. In fact, one of the pits still contained two 122-mm rockets that had not been set up. The VC had dug a narrow mound of dirt, one foot high and about twenty-five feet long, on which they had set the rockets, their noses pointed in the direction of the target. A bamboo stake pounded into the ground in front of each rocket served as a crude aiming device. How the rocket was laid on the mound, that is, the attitude of the rocket's nose, determined the range.

The rockets were then electrically wired to one main circuit. After everyone else left the area, the battery firing officer set off the rockets and then jumped into a small boat to take him downriver. Reportedly, he sometimes jumped into the river and swam away from the area.

While we were looking over the site and marveling at the simplicity of the set up, a captain from G-3 picked up a rolled-up shirt that he had found in the middle of the launch site. Until that moment, everyone had been smart enough not to touch anything.

I had just turned away from the captain when he screamed, "Grenade!" We all hit the deck.

An old U.S. Mark-II fragmentation grenade, with the pin removed, had been wrapped up in the shirt to prevent the spoon from flying off the grenade—a simple but deadly booby trap.

We all laid there on the deck for at least a full minute, when one of the EOD Marines said, "Hell, if it ain't gone off by now, it ain't going off." We got up to take a look. Thankfully, the grenade, old and weathered, was a dud.

The captain was standing around, looking foolish, and well he should have. A major started chewing his ass. One of the young photographers had landed directly on his camera when he hit the deck, and it was smashed to pieces. The EOD Marines, both senior enlisted men, also voiced their opinions about picking up suspicious objects in an enemy area.

The EOD men destroyed the grenade and the remaining 122-mm rockets in place, and I again ferried everyone across the river to our camp. Several weeks later, when I happened to be in the division G-3 section, I saw the major who had been on our inspection trip and asked him about the captain. He replied that the captain was no longer with the division, and hadn't been since a few days after the grenade incident.

We sometimes went for as long as a week without a rocket attack, then with renewed effort, they hit III MAF. Several Marines were killed and their barracks destroyed. The rocket attacks continued through July, although they now seldom came from the other side of the Cao Do River, opposite OP 47. After nearly a year, we had finally worked out a system with the higher echelons that allowed us to fire at our enemies when we saw them, once we had notified the division.

I was scheduled to fly out of Vietnam on 8 August 1968, nearly twelve and a half months after my arrival in-country. One day I happened to be in the battalion's administration office talking with our adjutant. He was an old friend who had served with me at Camp Del Mar in 1953 when we were both young staff sergeants. On his office wall, he had a large board with the rotation dates of personnel leaving Vietnam during the next thirty days. I noticed that a Marine, scheduled to depart on 4 August, had been placed on legal hold for some unknown reason. I asked the adjutant if that meant the Marine's seat was open. He said, "Yeah, you want it?"

This would allow me to leave four days early. While we were discussing the situation, Lt. Col. Harry Hite, the CO who had replaced Vincent Gentile, asked what we were talking about. He said that if my boss, the S-3, had no real objections, I could take the open seat. When I went back to the COC bunker, I mentioned the 4 August departure date to the major who had replaced Major Dickey as our S-3.

I'll be damned if he didn't remind me that I was supposed to read the citation for a Silver Star medal to be awarded to one of our tank lieutenants on 6 August during a battalion formation. The Commandant of the Marine Corps was going to be in-country and was scheduled to present the award personally. (I had been reading citations at our battalion awards ceremonies for several months.) I was surprised and a little confused that the major would even bring up the issue. I said, "Major, I'm not the only Marine in the battalion who is capable of reading a citation."

I guess he didn't like my response one bit. We had never

been on the best of terms. I had known him at Camp Pendleton when he was a shavetail (second) lieutenant assigned to Company B tanks; in my opinion, he hadn't changed much since then.

He said, "Well, if you feel you should go, then go ahead."

That statement was good enough for me. For the past two weeks, I had been snapping in my relief, Gunnery Sergeant Barnett, and we were starting to get in each other's way inside the COC. Even "Gunny" Barnett had casually suggested that I should check out a few days early. He was ready to assume my duties and didn't need any additional help from me.

I turned in my weapon and all of my equipment, went through the age-old process of checking out, and said my good-byes. On the morning of 4 August 1968, I departed Da Nang Air Base for Okinawa. As our "freedom bird" roared down the runway, an enormous cheer reverberated from all hands on board that aircraft. The plane's nose lifted, and we severed physical contact with Vietnam and the war.

Perhaps everyone on board felt the same way that I did—what a hell of a way to fight a war. Good-bye, Vietnam!

# ═18═

# Fair Winds and Following Seas

AFTER COMPLETING THE administrative process at Okinawa to get me out of the war, I was booked on a flight bound for Marine Corps Air Station, El Toro, California, the same base from which I had left the States one year earlier. The plane landed at El Toro on 6 August at dusk. Many of us were not shy in kneeling down and kissing the warm tarmac when we stepped off the ramp. Never had it felt so good to be back on the firm soil of the USA.

I called my mother in Anaheim, and she was thrilled to know that I had come home safely and early. She was still keeping Mike, my German shepherd. While talking to her, I decided to play a trick on Mike. I told my mother that I would take a cab to her house, twelve miles from El Toro, and be home in about thirty minutes. I asked her to put Mike in the backyard before I arrived.

I went in the front door of my mother's house and placed my suitcase on the floor in the middle of the living room. My mother let the dog in while I watched through a window from outside. I had never seen a dog go as nutty as that German shepherd when he came into the living room and caught my scent on the suitcase. He jumped all over it and then went from room to room in search of me. He began to howl when he couldn't find me. Then, I opened the door and walked in. He damn near knocked me down when he greeted me. Mike wouldn't leave me for the rest of the evening, and he slept alongside my bed that night.

My mother, of course, was equally glad to see her son return home from his third war. She let me know, in no uncertain terms, that she was getting too old to go through this type of thing every so many years. I assured her that my volunteering days were now over.

I had left my car, a 1964 Plymouth Barracuda, with a friend, but it was at my mother's house when I arrived. As I made the usual round of welcome-home parties and saw old friends and acquaintances, I finalized several social commitments by notifying certain female friends that I was headed back to Virginia and, from there, overseas. Despite several semi-serious romances, I was not ready to consider the institution of marriage. I had been a bachelor for ten years, and being single certainly had its advantages, particularly so when I was on recruiting duty or service with the State Department.

After spending some time with my brother Sonny and his family, which now included my nephew Steve and niece Gina, in Orange, I headed for San Diego for a visit with my sister Marion and Scotty. We enjoyed a few trips on the *Marstan* and even managed to catch some fish. I also spent some time with my children, but, sadly, they were more like total strangers to me than members of my family. As was always the case, my leave ended too quickly, and it was time to head for the East Coast.

I decided to give myself a few extra days and drive east. My car was in good shape, with low mileage. I had traveled the southern route back in 1963, so I drove across the middle of the country this time. Taking the back highways, I saw something of several states that I had never been through before. Although it was early in September and the fall scenery was beautiful, I was pleased that the car was air-conditioned.

As had happened the first time that I reported to the Marine Security School, I just missed the convening of a class. I worked in the school's operations section until a new class began. Those of us who were there early were allowed weekends off, and this gave me the opportunity to visit the Washington, D.C., area, where there was always so much to see and do.

One day, I walked across the road to the Navy Annex, which

housed Headquarters Marine Corps, and asked permission to view my official file. Usually, a career Marine's file is a thick folder containing service records, any correspondence between the Marine and CMC, and copies of every fitness report that a Marine has received during his or her career. At the time, fitness reports were submitted to every officer and staff NCO on a semiannual basis, as well as at each change of duty station and after completion of schooling. Each report was written by the Marine's immediate superior at the time.

During the late 1960s, the standard fitness report was a comprehensive, one-page "report card" indicating how well the individual Marine performed throughout the period under review. It covered every facet of the Marine's character, personality, and leadership ability. The majority of the report was graded on a scale ranging from unsatisfactory to outstanding, but Section D allowed for a handwritten evaluation by the reporting officer. In those days, the fitness report was graded by the reporting senior and then forwarded through the chain of command to Headquarters Marine Corps. The individual Marine never saw his or her report, unless it was graded unsatisfactory, in which case the Marine was entitled to write a rebuttal. The system has since undergone several changes, including the addition of several new evaluations. Also, each Marine now reviews his or her report before it is sent to HQMC.

Seated in a private viewing room at the Annex, I opened my official record. Sitting right on top of the pile of papers was my last evaluation report, written by the former operations officer (S-3) of the 1st Tank Battalion, which he had submitted when I was detached from the battalion in August. The fitness report had arrived at HQMC at a good time.

The report itself was not all that bad, but Section D contained the following remark: "This senior Staff NCO was so anxious to leave Vietnam that he failed to properly break in his replacement," or words to that effect. When I read that sentence, I almost hit the ceiling. I was livid. It was a damned outright lie. Gunnery Sergeant Barnett and I had agreed that he was thoroughly briefed on the responsibilities of his new job, and the major had concurred. I could think of no other reason for this insult than the fact that I hadn't volunteered to remain in-country just to read a Silver Star citation in the presence of the Commandant of the Marine Corps.

What really ticked me off was that I had always prided myself on receiving good fitness reports. I had reviewed my file a few years earlier, and many reporting seniors had shown me completed fitness reports before they were forwarded, so I knew what my record contained. More important, the promotion board would be meeting while I was attending school, and I wondered what the hell the board members would think when they saw the major's unfounded remark.

I returned to the school and mentioned the situation to the school's executive officer. I told him that I was thinking of writing a rebuttal. He asked me who the reporting senior was, and, when I told him, he smiled and said, "Oh well, I wouldn't worry about it if I were you. The major's reputation is well known."

Although I decided to let the matter drop, I was still angry. I could honestly say that his observation was the only lie ever entered on my fitness reports.

The time for our class to convene finally arrived. Much to my surprise, I was the senior student of the seventy Marines reporting in. This gave me the dubious distinction of being designated class commander, which came to be something of a pain in my backside. Every time a student screwed up, I was called by the school's senior instructor to explain who, what, when, where, and why, as well as to suggest a possible solution to the problem. Luckily, the senior instructor was M.Gy.Sgt. William ("Bill") Rappold, a man of exceptional character and fine sense of humor. His experience and personality made it easy for me to do my job, both as a student and as the senior Marine in the class. Bill was also single, and, as our professional friendship progressed, the two of us visited SNCO clubs located in and around Washington on several occasions.

During the second week of school, the first screening board (to determine suitability for duty) was conducted. I was the first Marine to be interviewed by the board, which consisted of several senior Marine officers and State Department officials. A major, who had my jacket (official file) in front of him, looked at me and asked, "Master Sergeant Maffioli, have you ever been so anxious to leave a combat zone that you failed to properly snap in your replacement?"

The point behind his question was a little more than obvious. I replied, "Sir, if you are referring to the remark in Section D of that fitness report written by Major——, it's a damned lie!"

Some of the seniors raised their eyebrows, and some even smirked a bit. The major merely stated, "I see," and that was the end of it.

There were few changes in the school's curriculum. A little more emphasis was placed on weapons training and security procedures, including the protection of VIPs, but the course was still six weeks long. At least half of the students were veterans of Vietnam.

Sometime during the fourth week of school, I received word to report to Rappold's office, now something of a common occurrence. As I walked in, he had a grin on his face.

"How does it feel not to have to sweat fitness reports anymore?" he asked.

At first, I didn't understand him and thought he might be referring to the major's report. Before I could answer, he extended his hand and said, "Congratulations! I just got a call from across the street [referring to HQMC], and you were selected for master gunnery sergeant!"

I had made it. The one invidious fitness report had not affected my chances for selection. I could put that behind me, but I would always remember that major, and not in a kind way.

During the second screening board, the panel brought up the fact that I had previously been on MSG duty as an NCOIC and stationed in Munich and Vienna. One of the Marine board members said, "I hope that you don't expect a plum like you had on your first tour."

When I said that I didn't hope to be that fortunate again, he said, "Good, because you're going to Calcutta, India."

Good God! All I could think about was the gruesome story about the "black hole of Calcutta." I had read the post reports on what would be available to the current graduates, and, as I recall, Calcutta didn't read very well. There was one consolation. Dhahran, Saudi Arabia, was also open for duty, and it was considered to be far worse—no socializing with the local population, no use of alcohol, no nothing. Dhahran was a small consular post with only five Marines assigned to it. I guessed that I could count my blessings.

Graduation day came, and, after the ceremonies, several of us went to the SNCO club to celebrate. G.Sgt. "Mac" Hildebrand, the poor soul who had been assigned to Dhahran, was with us. We were sitting around and discussing the merits of our assignments when the MSG battalion clerk came in. He said, "Top Maffioli, the commanding officer wants to see both you and Gunny Hildebrand in his office, right away." Gulping down our beer, we wondered what was up.

We reported to the colonel, and he greeted us with the announcement that our assignments had been switched. Mac was going to Calcutta, and I had been assigned to Dhahran. If the colonel gave any further explanation, it was lost within my stunned brain.

Our seabags, trunks—everything that was to be shipped—had been stenciled and now had to be changed. New visas had to be requested. Most of the class departed within a few days, but Mac and I were sitting around and waiting for new orders and documents.

When I learned that it would be more than a week before I would have my orders, I decided to take leave and drive my car back to California. I could get a good price for the car there; the East Coast used-car sharks didn't want to give me anything close to its value. I headed home, where I left the car with Scotty, who sold it within a few weeks.

I flew back to Washington and picked up my orders. On the last day of 1968, I boarded a commercial flight at New York City's John F. Kennedy Airport that was bound for Saudi Arabia. Going out with me were two watchstander replacements, Corporals Bud Cook and Rex Burbank. We were about halfway across the Atlantic Ocean when the New Year came in. The pilot ordered the plane's liquor cart rolled out and left for everyone's enjoyment.

After stops at Rome, Athens, and Cairo, we finally landed,

twenty jet-lagged hours later, at Dhahran International Airport, where the NCOIC, S.Sgt. Norman Jennings, met us. We were fairly well beat and only wanted to find a place to sleep.

Dhahran was truly a lonely post. Its only saving grace was the presence of the Arabian-American Oil Company (ARAMCO), located about a mile from the consulate compound. In fact, the only reason for the consulate was to handle the passport and other consular business of American employees at the oil company.

A few single women were employed there, but they were the exception to the rule. ARAMCO had a commissary, swimming pool, restaurant, bowling alley, and other such comforts, and consular employees, including Marines, were afforded the use of these facilities. There were no other such amenities in the area.

Alcohol was prohibited in this strict Moslem country, with no nightclubs or bars of any kind. Interestingly, both ARAMCO personnel and the Marine House operated small stills. The products from these illicit facilities were powerful medicine and not all that bad in taste. After a few drinks, no one really cared what they tasted like, anyway. Some regular brand-name liquors were brought into the country as administrative supplies, whenever possible, but resupply missions were infrequent.

The consulate owned two British Land Rovers, four-wheel-drive vehicles, that were available to us for weekend trips into the desert. The only drawback was that, with the exception of an occasional oasis and countless miles of sand, there wasn't much to see, but the trips provided a welcomed break in the routine. Additionally, the island nation of Bahrain, located less than twenty miles off the coast in the Persian gulf, had a number of modern hotels and accommodations. Occasionally, some of us flew out there for a day of relaxation.

The temperatures and humidity of this part of Saudi Arabia made Vietnam seem like a balmy version of Hawaii. I believe that it and Subic Bay in the Philippines rank as the two most humid places on earth.

Despite the lack of recreational activity, the months began to slip by quickly. I made two trips to Kuwait, one by borrowed automobile and the other by commercial air. An MSG class-mate, M.Sgt. Edward ("Ed") Teague, had ended up in Kuwait as the NCOIC. Kuwait placed few restrictions on visitors, and the Kuwaiti-American relationship was exceptionally good.

In September, after nearly nine months on post, I received notice that I was being transferred, three months early, to become the NCOIC at the American embassy at Kabul, Afghanistan. The senior Marine at the embassy was having trouble handling a detachment of seven Marines, and the ambassador wanted him out of the country as soon as possible. Here, again, was another case of an unqualified SNCO slipping through the MSG screening board prior to assignment.

I had a hurried departure, with no time to get an Afghan visa. I flew to Tehran, Iran, and spent a week there with the Marines at the U.S. embassy while its consular section obtained the proper visa for me to enter Afghanistan.

The NCOIC met me at Kabul International Airport and took me to my quarters. He departed Afghanistan less than twenty-four hours later. I hardly knew my way around the embassy, and he hadn't even provided me with the combination to the NCOIC's safe where the pistols were stored. Fortunately, the combination was on file in the embassy's communication section.

Because my predecessor lacked leadership ability, the morale and discipline of the detachment had deteriorated to an unacceptable level. Several "playboys" seemed to think that they could do as they pleased. During the next fifteen months, I would relieve six Marines as unsuitable and succeed in forming a sharp MSG detachment.

Kabul turned out to be an interesting post. The city is located at a 6,000-foot elevation and has little annual rainfall. Winters are cool, with light snowfall, and summers are warm and dry.

At that time, Robert G. Neumann was the American ambassador to Afghanistan. He had been a professor of political science at the University of California, Los Angeles, for nineteen years before he was appointed to this post. Born in Austria, he had escaped the Nazi occupation and had served with the U.S. Office of Strategic Services during World War II.

Deputy chief of mission (No. 2 official) was L. Bruce

Laingen. He would become well known during the late 1970s when he was charge d'affaires at the U.S. embassy in Tehran, Iran. Laingen and most of the embassy staff, including the MSG detachment, were held captive by Iranian fundamentalists for 444 days.

Afghanistan is a landlocked country, bordered on the north by the former Soviet Union and a small portion of Red China, on the east and south by Pakistan, and on the west by Iran. American presence in the country was fairly extensive. In addition to the embassy staff, there was a large U.S. Agency for International Development (USAID) contingent, a U.S. Information Agency (USIA) staff, and Peace Corps personnel. The latter were a source of irritation for some of the other Americans, particularly the Marines, because they tended to look, dress, and act like a band of hippies. Whether they did any real good in Afghanistan was a matter of personal opinion, but it was my belief that they were there only because of the availability of what was considered to be the world's finest and cheapest hashish.

I purchased a used Volkswagen Bug so that I could take some weekend trips around the country. There was so much to see and learn. Kabul itself was often called "The Crossroads of Asia." Large camel caravans had been passing through the city for more than three thousand years and continued to do so. I was particularly impressed with the scenery and history of the nearby Kyber Pass, made famous by Rudyard Kipling.

The social situation in Afghanistan was a 100 percent improvement over that in Saudi Arabia. The Americans hosted cocktail parties, get-togethers, and dinners several times each week. Thursday nights were "open house" at the Marine House bar. We worked a split weekend. The embassy was closed on Friday and Sunday, but Saturday was a normal workday. The Marines occupied a two-story house only three blocks away from the embassy. I had my own quarters in a house situated in the block behind the embassy compound.

As in Saudi Arabia, absolutely no fraternization with the local population was tolerated, and the women were veiled at all times. Single U.S. and other foreign women worked at our embassy, USAID, and other English-speaking embassies, however, and my watchstanders did not want for dates.

Working for USAID, on the other side of town, was a young, single, very cute secretary, Canadian by birth but a naturalized U.S. citizen. Donna Moore had been with the USAID program for three years. She had been stationed in Pakistan before coming to Afghanistan. I met her at a football game one Friday afternoon and saw her again that evening at Staff House, USAID's restaurant and bar, which was the Americans' social club. I asked her to have a drink with me and then lost no time in inviting her to be my guest at the upcoming Marine Corps Birthday Ball. She said that she had already promised to go with a young soldier assigned to the embassy.

I explained that no girl should attend the Marine Corps Birthday Ball with a soldier when she could go with a Marine. Luckily, she relented, and this was the start of a beautiful friendship. She became the love of my life, and, before my tour was up, I would ask her to marry me.

We held the 1969 Birthday Ball, which was, without doubt, the social event of the year, at the new Intercontinental Hotel in Kabul, the finest and most modern facility in the entire country. Although the balls were traditionally funded by the Marines, the other Americans in Kabul customarily provided the liquor and the beer, and this reduced our expenses greatly.

A large Soviet embassy staff was also in Kabul because the Afghan Army was equipped and trained by the Soviet Union. Always hungry for information about Americans, the Soviets made a couple of attempts to compromise one of my guards, which resulted in the Marine's transfer to MSG Battalion for reassignment. The Soviets, of course, were not above offering liquor or women in their efforts to gain access to our embassy.

The Christmas season was always a busy time for us, with some party to attend almost every evening of the week. Donna and I were now seeing each other regularly, and we were invited as a couple to most of the social functions. We sometimes found ourselves with two or three invitations for the same evening and dropped in at all of them so that we could decide which one would be the most fun.

The year 1970 passed quickly. I took leave and went to

Beirut, Lebanon, for about a week. Our MSG company head-quarters was located there, and Capt. Robert M.S. Slater was the company's executive officer. He had visited Kabul while he was conducting a semiannual inspection, and we had become friends. When I checked in at company headquarters, he took off a few days to show me Beirut. Captain Slater had been awarded the Navy Cross, Silver Star, and many other decorations for his service during the Vietnam War. I used to needle him for having the same number of ribbons and decorations for one war as I had for three.

While I was in Beirut, I had an engagement/wedding ring custom-made for Donna, and I surprised her with it when I returned to Kabul. I had asked her to marry me, and she had accepted, but we decided to wait until we returned to the States to get married. Her contract with USAID would not expire until several weeks after my departure, and getting married in Kabul was a difficult process that required two wedding ceremonies.

My orders arrived in late November. I was assigned to the 2d Tank Battalion, FMF, at Camp Lejeune, North Carolina. These orders really amused me. I had been in the Marine Corps for more than twenty years and had never seen Camp Lejeune. I had contacted my monitor at HQMC and asked about the possibility of a West Coast assignment. He said that absolutely no master gunnery sergeant 1811 billets were open on the West Coast. I accepted my fate and looked forward to some new surroundings.

I departed Kabul in February 1971 and had a twenty-day leave in southern California. During this time I visited the 1st Tank Battalion at Camp Pendleton and discovered that a gunnery sergeant was filling the billet of the S-3 chief. Two more master gunnery sergeant billets were also open, chief instructor at the tank unit leaders course and the inspector-instructor staff at the 4th Tank Battalion, USMCR, at San Diego. So much for believing my monitor.

I flew from Los Angeles to Washington, D.C., and picked up a new Dodge Monaco ordered from Kabul. Because I was eligible for a diplomatic discount, I had been able to save a great deal of money on the car. I then headed south for "Swamp" Lejeune, as it was sometimes called, and found that it was aptly nicknamed. It has lots of waterways, wetlands, and inlets, and all of it is on low, flat land.

The 2d Tank Battalion was surprised when a master gunnery sergeant reported for duty. The battalion hadn't had a Marine with an 1811 MOS at that rank for years. Operations chief was the billet, of course, but there were only seven master gunnery sergeants in the entire Marine Corps.

Donna joined me a month later, and we were married in the Catholic Chapel at Camp Lejeune, on 25 March 1971. Mac Hildebrand, now home from Calcutta, and Ed Teague, home from Kuwait, were also stationed at Camp Lejeune, and they attended the wedding.

I had been operations chief for only two months when the battalion's sergeant major was called away on emergency leave. He was due for transfer soon, so I was reassigned and took over his position.

Because I had expected at least a three-year tour of duty, Donna and I started looking at homes for sale in the area. Some fine brick homes, not too distant from the main gate, were available at reasonable prices. I called my monitor at HQMC to ask how long we could expect to remain at Camp Lejeune, and I mentioned our desire to buy a home.

He immediately said, "Don't buy anything. You're going back on recruiting duty!"

When I reminded him of just how much independent duty I had had during the past few years, he told me that he had my file right in front of him and was well aware of my situation. HQMC, however, was recalling master sergeants and master gunnery sergeants with former successful recruiting tours because of the continuing buildup for Vietnam. With the war becoming more and more unpopular at home, all recruiters, particularly Marines, were hard-pressed to find quality personnel to fill their ranks.

I asked the monitor if I had any choice of location for my next assignment. He replied that he would give me any district I wanted, so I chose the 12th Marine Corps District, headquartered in San Francisco, which included the seven western states. After only five months at Camp Lejeune, Donna and I packed up our belongings and headed for the West Coast in our new Dodge. As it turned out, that was my last tour of duty with a Marine tank battalion.

My assignment was Recruiting Station, Los Angeles, again. With my entire family located in southern California, this was really my preference. When I reporting to RSLA, I found that it already had a chief recruiter and I was being assigned to RSS Van Nuys. Except for a Budweiser brewery there, Van Nuys wasn't much of an area. I had a talk with the OIC and managed to get assigned to RSS Downey, my old recruiting station from 1963 to 1965. This was much closer to Orange County, where Donna and I intended to purchase a home. We had moved in with my mother temporarily and were looking for a condominium. In September, we found a new one in the city of Orange, not far from my brother and his family.

After a year of recruiting in Downey, I moved up to RSLA, where I was assigned as chief recruiter. The position kept me on the road quite a bit because I had to inspect numerous recruiting substations. In the meantime, RSS Santa Ana had been redesignated as a recruiting station. Upon my request, I was reassigned there as chief recruiter.

As I approached the end of my fourth year as a Marine recruiter, I called my monitor to see what might be in store for me. He said that I was slated for duty at Camp Pendleton, where I would probably end up as the division's career planner, a fancy title for the reenlistment NCO. I had had my fill of the personnel procurement business, however, and called HQMC, where General McLaughlin was now assigned. Over the years, I had seen the general on several occasions. He always said that I should give him a call if there was anything he could do for me, but I never thought that I would ever take advantage of his offer. Now, I decided to take him up on his promise. When I called him, I said that I would like to do my last tour of duty in the Marine Corps where it all began, in my hometown of San Diego. He said that he would take care of it, and, a few weeks later, I had orders to the Marine Corps Recruit Depot, San Diego.

I reported at the depot in February 1975. Two jobs were

open, depot operations chief and inspections chief in the office of the depot inspector, both master gunnery sergeant billets of any MOS. The G-3 and the depot inspector interviewed me and gave me a choice. I opted for the latter. It was a busy time to report in for duty. The depot was preparing for an inspection by the Marine Corps Inspector General, and I was expected to get my feet wet in a hurry.

Less than a month after I reported in, the infamous McClure incident became national news. A young recruit had been fatally injured while undergoing pugil stick training—simulated rifle and bayonet fighting between recruits. Our office was heavily involved in the resulting investigation. When it was over, a drill instructor was court-martialed and a senior officer relieved of duty and reassigned.

Donna stayed in Orange for several months until we sold our condominium. We purchased a mobile home and placed it in a park near the town of Alpine, about a twenty-mile commute from the depot. We attempted to see more of my children, now that we lived in the area, but I usually had to initiate any contact. My son Jim (Leonard, Jr.) had married; in May 1971, my first grandchild, Jason, was born. He was also my mother's first great-grandchild.

In February 1973, my daughter Marsha married a young Coast Guardsman, who was stationed at President Richard Nixon's "Western White House" located in San Clemente, California. Donna and I attended the wedding and reception.

My oldest child, Debby, was a student at San Diego State College. When she received her degree, she became the first member on the Maffioli side of the family to become a college graduate.

The job of inspections chief was interesting and challenging. As the mission description read, the depot inspector was the principal adviser to the commanding general on inspection and request matters. The inspector planned, coordinated, and conducted the general's inspection programs; reviewed complaints of discrimination, fraud, waste, and abuse; investigated allegations of misconduct and mismanagment; handled matters of congressional and special interests; and conducted special investigations as ordered by the commanding general. In other words, this was one hell of a busy position, and the inspection chief was his righthand man. We used an electric scooter to take us throughout the base as we observed the training of recruits and other day-to-day depot operations.

About one month after I reported in, Maj. Gen. Kenneth J. Houghton relieved Maj. Gen. Joseph Fegan, Jr., as commander of the depot. General Houghton placed more importance on the office of the inspector than did some other commanding generals. He assigned a colonel to the billet, vice a lieutenant colonel who had been there when I first arrived.

General Houghton also suggested adoption of a performance evaluation system similar to the one used by the 3d Marine Division, which he had recently commanded. Our office went right to work to set up the new system. I wrote letters to the 3d Marine Division, still located on Okinawa, for information about its system and received photographs and documents related to how it functioned. There was just one major problem—our office might just as well have had a revolving door on it. Inspectors came and went quickly. Some colonels stayed for only a few months before other billets opened for them, and others came to the job when they were close to retirement. In fact, during my four-year tour, I served under six depot inspectors. (One of the six stated that he didn't *believe* in inspections!)

Despite the lack of continuity, I continued to march with the program and set up a quarterly inspection program for all units within the command. It covered almost every facet of the operation of the depot's organizations, from administration to troop inspection and personnel performance on the job. The personnel conducting these inspections were specialists in their fields. They usually came from depot headquarters or were temporarily borrowed from other commands.

When a new inspector checked in (for short periods, I was often acting depot inspector), I briefed him on the inspection system. We operated our office with just one clerk-typist, and I did a good deal of the typing when the workload was heavy. Occasionally, we had a young junior officer to help out with the legwork.

The performance evaluation system, when fully implemented, generated reports that kept the depot's commanding general apprised of the command's status and provided a basis for any necessary corrective action. Under the system, the depot functioned extremely well, and problem areas were identified while the problems were still minor.

Two colonels stayed in the inspector's billet long enough to give some continuity to the job, Col. Bernard B. ("Barney") Brause and Col. Franklin P. ("Pete") Eller. Both of these outstanding officers were Vietnam veterans who had seen considerable action. They took the job seriously by supporting the inspection program, and it was my pleasure to work for and with them. Another source of professional support came from Col. Richard D. ("Mick") Mickelson, who was the depot's chief of staff during the establishment of the evaluation system. Colonel Mickelson was the guiding hand and a source of sound advice during those periods when no inspector was on board.

The Marine Corps Recruit Depot was a beautiful base and a great duty station. As is always the case in that type of environment, the years passed by too quickly and I was soon nearing the end of my enlistment. I was considering the possibility of putting in a request for retention or reenlistment. My physical condition was still reasonably good, and I was training for a marathon that all of the depot's sergeants major and I intended to run.

John Massaro, Sergeant Major of the Marine Corps, was an occasional visitor to the depot when he accompanied Commandant Louis H. Wilson. I came to know Sergeant Major Massaro fairly well, and we went for a noontime run whenever he was on board the depot. I broached the subject of my extension to him one day, and he told me that General Wilson was personally against Marines remaining on active duty for more than 30 years. He said that during his three and a half years as Sergeant Major of the Marine Corps, the Commandant had approved no sergeants major and only a few master gunnery sergeants who were in critical MOSs for service beyond 30 years. My MOS of 1811 was not considered critical. General Wilson's policy was 30 years of active duty or 55 years of age, whichever came first.

Although I was only 53 years old at the time, I already had more than 30 years of service and the handwriting was clearly on the wall. It was going to be "Sayonara, Marine Corps," and I submitted my letter for retirement.

I requested a two-month extension so that I could assist the depot in the upcoming Inspector General's inspection, and it was granted. During that time, I completed my retirement physical examination and was given a retirement date of 1 March 1979.

Marine Corps Recruit Depot, San Diego, retired me in a grand style that left me with memories that I shall always cherish. I reviewed a parade of several hundred recruits with Maj. Gen. R. C. Schulze, the commanding general who had relieved General Houghton when he retired the year before. General and Mrs. Houghton also attended my retirement ceremony and the reception that followed.

Several days before, the depot senior SNCOs had presented me with a beautiful, velvet-covered awards showcase board. Mounted on it are my medals in miniature and the insignias for each of the enlisted ranks I held during my service to Corps and country. It is also adorned with a large Marine Corps emblem and an engraved plaque indicating appreciation for my service.

The best surprise, however, occurred during the retirement ceremony when I received the Meritorious Service Medal for my four years as the depot's inspection chief. The accompanying citation noted my efforts in establishing and maintaining the performance evaluation system (see appendix F).

My aunts, uncles, and cousins from all over northern California gathered for my retirement, and we had the largest family reunion ever. We were saddened, however, by the absence of my dear mother, who had suddenly passed away in her sleep in December 1978, just two and a half months before I retired. Although eighty years old and frail, she had not been ill. Her passing came as a shock to all of us. She had been truly looking forward to the day when she could finally watch her son retire and know that he no longer would be "going off to war."

My daughters attended the ceremony, but my son Jim was

not there. He had joined the Air Force and was stationed overseas.

The day was sad and emotional for me—leaving the Corps that I loved so much and that had been so good to me. Before the parade, the depot's bandmaster had contacted me and asked if I had any music preferences.

"Anything, but 'Aulde Lang Syne'!" I replied. I had seen too many retirees break down and cry when that song was played.

On the day of my retirement, I was the last Marine in the Corps on active duty who had been a prisoner of war in Korea, and the last on the depot who had seen combat during World War II. I was also the oldest Marine on board the depot, a legacy from General Houghton when he retired.

My retirement did have an interesting epilogue. Three months afterward, General Wilson retired. Gen. Robert H. Barrow, the new Commandant of the Marine Corps, rescinded the retirement policy of "30 years or 55 years old." He stated that if a Marine was still fit, he or she could continue to serve.

During an interview at my retirement, however, I had told a reporter from the depot's newspaper, *The Chevron*: "You've gotta go, sooner or later, and somewhere out there is an 1811 Marine master sergeant who is going to be damned happy to hear that he's finally got a chance to move up!"

# Epilogue

Lt. Gen. John N. ("Jack") McLaughlin, USMC (Ret.), resides in Savannah, Georgia.

Lt. Col. Charles L. ("Charlie") Harrison, USMC (Ret.), resides in Grass Valley, California.

Lt. Col. Mercer R. ("Dick") Smith, USMC (Ret.), resides in La Jolla, California.

Gy. Sgt. Ernest E. ("Ernie") Hayton, USMC (Ret.), resides in Moncks Corner, South Carolina.

Sfc. Saburo ("Sam") Shimomura, USA (Ret.), resides in Salt Lake City, Utah.

Andrew ("Chief") Aguirre resides in Colorado Springs, Colorado.

Former Royal Marine Kenneth J. T. ("Kenny") Williams resides in Sheering, Essex, England.

Of the three other Service Company, 1st Tank Battalion, truck drivers captured with me, Charles W. Dickerson and Theron L. ("Leon") Hilburn are since deceased, and I have been unable to locate Clifford R. ("Roy") Hawkins.

# Appendix A

*PRESIDENTIAL UNIT CITATION, 1ST MARINE DIVISION, 1951*
*THE SECRETARY OF THE NAVY*
*WASHINGTON*

*The President of the United States takes pleasure in presenting*
*PRESIDENTIAL UNIT CITATION to the*
*FIRST MARINE DIVISION, REINFORCED*
*For service as set forth in the following*
*CITATION:*

"FOR EXTRAORDINARY HEROISM and outstanding performance of duty in action against enemy aggressor forces in the Chosin Reservoir and Koto-ri area of Korea from 27 November to 11 December 1950. When the full fury of the enemy counterattack struck both the Eighth Army and the Tenth Corps on 27 and 28 November 1950, the First Marine Division, Reinforced, operating as the left flank division of the Tenth Corps, launched a daring assault westward from Yudam-ni in an effort to cut the road and rail communications of hostile forces attacking the Eighth Army and, at the same time, continued its mission of protecting a vital main supply route consisting of a tortuous mountain road running southward to Chinhung-ni, approximately 35 miles distant. Ordered to withdraw to Hamhung in company with attached army and other friendly units in the face of tremendous pressure in the Chosin Reservoir area, the Division began an epic battle against the bulk of the enemy Third Route Army and, while small intermediate garrisons at Hagaru-ri and Koto-ri held firmly against repeated and determined attacks by hostile forces, gallantly fought its way successively to Hagaru-ri, Koto-ri, Chinhung-ni and Hamhung over twisting, mountainous and icy roads in sub-zero temperatures. Battling desperately night and day in the face of almost insurmountable odds throughout a period of two weeks of intense and sustained combat, the First Marine Division, Reinforced, emerged from its ordeal as a fighting unit with its wounded, with its guns and equipment and with its prisoners, decisively defeating seven enemy divisions, together with elements of three others, and inflicting major losses which seriously impaired the military effectiveness of the hostile forces for a considerable period of time. The valiant fighting spirit, relentless perseverance and heroic fortitude of the officers and men of the First Marine Division, Reinforced, in battle against a vastly outnumbering enemy, were in keeping with the highest traditions of the United States Naval Service."

*The following reinforcing units of the First Marine Division participated in operations against enemy aggressor forces in Korea from 27 November to 11 December 1950:*

ORGANIC UNITS OF THE FIRST MARINE DIVISION: First Marine Division (less Detachment Headquarters Battalion; Detachment First Signal Battalion; Detachment First Service Battalion; Detachment Headquarters and Companies A & C, First Tank Battalion; Automotive Supply Company, First Motor Transport Battalion; Automotive Maintenance Company, First Motor Transport Battalion; Detachment First Ordnance Battalion; Detachment Headquarters and Company A, First Medical Battalion; First Shore Party Battalion; 4.5" Rocket Battery and Service Battery, Fourth Battalion, Eleventh Marines).

ATTACHED MARINE CORPS UNITS: Companies A and B, Seventh Motor Transport Battalion; Detachment Radio Relay Platoon.

ATTACHED ARMY UNITS: Provisional Battalion (Detachments, 31st and 32nd Regimental Combat Teams); Company

D, 10th Engineer Combat Battalion; Tank Company, 31st Infantry Regiment; Headquarters Company, 31st Infantry Regiment; Company B, 1st Battalion, 31st Infantry Regiment; 2nd Battalion, 31st Infantry Regiment (less Company E); 185th Engineer Combat Battalion (less Company A).

*For the President,*
*R. B. Anderson*
*Secretary of the Navy*

# Appendix B

*MEDAL OF HONOR CITATION,*
*Lt. Col. Don Faith, Jr., USA*

RANK AND ORGANIZATION: Lieutenant Colonel, U.S. Army, commanding officer, 1st Battalion, 32nd Infantry Regiment, 7th Infantry Division. PLACE AND DATE: Vicinity Hagaruri, Northern Korea, 27 November to 1 December 1950. ENTERED SERVICE AT: Washington, Ind. *Born:* 26 August 1918, Washington, Ind. G.O. No.: 59, 2 August 1951. CITATION: Lt. Col. Faith, commanding 1st Battalion, distinguished himself conspicuously by gallantry and intrepidity in action above and beyond the call of duty in the area of the Chosin Reservoir. When the enemy launched a fanatical attack against his battalion, Lt. Col. Faith unhesitatingly exposed himself to heavy enemy fire as he moved about directing the action. When the enemy penetrated the positions, Lt. Col. Faith personally led counterattacks to restore the position. During an attack by his battalion to effect a junction with another U.S. unit, Lt. Col. Faith reconnoitered the route for, and personally directed, the first elements of his command across the ice-covered reservoir and then directed the movement of his vehicles which were loaded with wounded until all of his command had passed through the enemy fire. Having completed

*Source:* U.S. Senate, *Medal of Honor Recipients, 1863–1978* (Washington, D.C.: Government Printing Office, 1979), 742–43.

this he crossed the reservoir himself. Assuming command of the force his unit had joined he was given the mission of attacking to join friendly elements to the south. Lt. Col. Faith, although physically exhausted in the bitter cold, organized and launched an attack which was soon stopped by enemy fire. He ran forward under enemy small-arms and automatic weapons fire, got his men on their feet and personally led the fire attack as it blasted its way through the enemy ring. As they came to a hairpin curve, enemy fire from a roadblock again pinned the column down. Lt. Col. Faith organized a group of men and directed their attack on the enemy positions on the right flank. He then placed himself at the head of another group of men and in the face of direct enemy fire led an attack on the enemy road-block, firing his pistol and throwing grenades. When he had reached a position approximately 30 yards from the roadblock he was mortally wounded, but continued to direct the attack until the roadblock was overrun. Throughout the 5 days of action Lt. Col. Faith gave no thought to his safety and did not spare himself. His presence each time in the position of greatest danger was an inspiration to his men. Also, the damage he personally inflicted firing from his position at the head of his men was of material assistance on several occasions. Lt. Col. Faith's outstanding gallantry and noble self-sacrifice above and beyond the call of duty reflect the highest honor on him and are in keeping with the highest traditions of the U.S. Army. (This award supersedes the prior award of the Silver Star [First Oak Leaf Cluster] as announced in G.O. No. 32, Headquarters X Corps, dated 23 February 1951, for gallantry in action on 27 November 1950.)

# Appendix C

*INTERVIEW WITH*
*Col. Mercer R. Smith, USMC (Ret.)*

During an interview with the authors in November 1995, Col. Mercer R. ("Dick") Smith, USMC (Ret.), offered the following information about his captivity in North Korea:

> On the first day of May 1951, I was flying one of two F9F Panther jets on an armed reconnaissance mission in the central part of Korea. The Marines and Chinese Communist Forces (CCF) were engaged in heavy fighting in this particular sector, and our two jets were to attempt to seek and destroy any enemy forces they might discover.
>
> My aircraft was struck by heavy-caliber antiaircraft fire and burst into flames. I was able to use my ejection seat successfully to leave the burning aircraft and descended in my parachute. I was captured, shortly after landing, by North Korean soldiers and suffered some superficial bayonet wounds.
>
> The North Koreans moved me around the local area rather aimlessly, and I actually escaped once just by walking out of a mud hut, just before dawn, while my guards slept. I was returned later that day by villagers who saw me hiding

*Note:* Colonel Smith was released on 3 September 1953, after more than twenty-eight months of captivity.

in some brush. Within the week, I was joined by a U.S. Navy pilot who had been shot down and was severely burned. Neither of us was provided any medical attention and provided for ourselves with warm water whenever possible.

Late one day, while in the company of some South Korean prisoners, the two of us were with just one guard, and lagging far behind the main group, when we set upon our guard, killing him and throwing his body over a cliff and into a river. The next day, we were recaptured by villagers and soldiers and were both severely beaten.

The North Korean soldiers had walked us for several days when we came into a village that the Chinese Communists were using as a holding point for several hundred U.S. Army personnel. A Lt. Henry Land, one of the Army prisoners, told me that there were some Marines in another part of the village. I was able to make my way through a cornfield and while doing so came upon Lieutenant Cold and Corporal Maffioli making their way, bent on the same endeavor, and looking for me.

This was a most fortuitous meeting. For when I was captured, I was rendered unconscious and the U.S. rescue helicopter crews reported from their visual sighting that the North Koreans had apparently killed me. When Lieutenant Cold and Corporal Maffioli returned to U.S. forces control, they were able to correct this earlier information.

# Appendix D

*AMERICAN POWs WHO ESCAPED FROM*
*THE CHINESE COMMUNISTS, 25 May 1951*

| NAME | UNIT* |
|------|-------|
| 1st Lt. Frank E. Cold, USMCR | Headquarters and Service Company, 3d Battalion, 7th Marines |
| M.Sgt. Gust H. Dunis, USMC | Military Police Company |
| S.Sgt. Charles L. Harrison, USMC | Military Police Company |
| S.Sgt. James B. Nash, USMC | Military Police Company |
| Sgt. Charles W. Dickerson, USMC | 1st Tank Battalion |
| Sgt. Morris L. Estess, USMC | 1st Signal Battalion |
| Sgt. Paul M. Manor, USMC | Company A, 7th Motor Transport Battalion |
| Cpl. Clifford R. Hawkins, USMC | 1st Tank Battalion |
| Cpl. Ernest E. Hayton, USMC | 1st Tank Battalion |
| Cpl. Frederick G. Holcomb, USMC | 11th Marines |

*All Marine units listed were part of the 1st Marine Division.

| | |
|---|---|
| Cpl. Leonard J. Maffioli, USMCR | 1st Tank Battalion |
| Cpl. Theodore R. Wheeler, USMCR | 1st Service Battalion |
| Cpl. Calvin W. Williams, USMCR | Headquarters Battalion |
| Cpl. Saburo Shimomura, USA | 163d Military Intelligence, X Corps, U.S. Army |
| Pfc. John A. Haring, USMCR | 7th Marines |
| Pfc. Theron L. Hilburn, USMCR | 1st Tank Battalion |
| Pfc. Charles M. Kaylor, USMCR | Weapons Company, 2nd Battalion 7th Marines |
| Pfc. Paul J. Phillips, USMCR | A Company, 7th Motor Trans. Battalion |
| Pfc. Charles E. Quiring, USMC | 5th Marines |

# Appendix E

HEADQUARTERS
1ST MARINE DIVISION (REINF) FMF
C/O FLEET POST OFFICE
SAN FRANCISCO, CALIFORNIA

*In the name of the President of the United States, the*
*Commanding General, 1st Marine Division (Reinf) FMF, takes*
*pleasure in awarding the BRONZE STAR MEDAL to*
*CORPORAL LEONARD J. MAFFIOLI,*
*UNITED STATES MARINE CORPS RESERVE,*
*for service as set forth in the following*
*CITATION:*

"FOR HEROIC ACHIEVEMENT in connection with operations
against the enemy in Korea on 24 May 1951. Corporal Maffioli, having spent approximately six months as a prisoner of
war, had escaped from his captors along with several other
Marines. Although unarmed and with no means of self protection behind enemy lines, he volunteered, with four other men,
to carry out a dangerous plan of escape. He assisted in stripping
wall paper from a Korean house and, even though subjected to
intense enemy small arms fire from nearby hills, began con-

structing a rescue message in a rice field for friendly aircraft. Before the message was completed, he was subjected to heavy artillery fire but, with complete disregard for his own personal safety, continued to work until the message was completed. Subsequently, the message was sighted by a friendly aircraft which, in turn, directed friendly tanks to the rescue of the Marines. His timely actions and coolness under fire contributed materially to the rescue of his group and served as an inspiration to all who observed him. Corporal Maffioli's initiative and courageous actions were in keeping with the highest traditions of the United States Naval Service."

Corporal Maffioli is authorized to wear the Combat "V".

*G. C. Thomas*
*Major General*
*U.S. Marine Corps*

Temporary Citation

# Appendix F

COMMANDANT OF THE MARINE CORPS

*The President of the United States takes pleasure in*
*presenting*
*the MERITORIOUS SERVICE MEDAL to*
MASTER GUNNERY SERGEANT LEONARD J. MAFFIOLI
UNITED STATES MARINE CORPS
*For service as set forth in the following*
CITATION:

FOR OUTSTANDING MERITORIOUS service as Inspection Chief
in the office of the Depot Inspector, Marine Corps Recruit
Depot, San Diego, California, from February 1975 through
February 1979. Instrumental in establishing a Performance
Evaluation System, Master Gunnery Sergeant Maffioli directly
contributed toward achieving an improved level of efficiency
within the Command. This System generated reports which
kept the Commanding General apprised of the Command
status and provided a basis for appropriate corrective action.
Demonstrating a high degree of resourcefulness and initiative,
he planned and coordinated the many details associated with
periodic formal and informal inspections. Illustrative of his
loyalty was his decision to postpone his retirement in order to

assist the Command in preparing for the Inspector General Inspection conducted in January 1979. Master Gunnery Sergeant Maffioli's untiring efforts to carry out the duties of his demanding tasks with unfailing good judgment, effectiveness, and total devotion to duty were in keeping with the highest traditions of the Marine Corps and the United States Naval Service.

*For the President,*
*Louis H. Wilson*
*Commandant of the Marine Corps*

# Bibliography

Appleman, J. *East of Chosin*. College Station: Texas A&M Press, 1987.

Bartley, Whitman S. *Iwo Jima: Amphibious Epic*. Washington, D.C.: Historical Branch, G-3, Headquarters Marine Corps, 1954.

Department of Defense. "Transfer of U.S. Korean POWs to the Soviet Union." Report of Department of Defense Prisoner of War/Missing in Action Office (DPMO) to U.S. Senate Committee on Foreign Relations, 25 August 1993.

Garand, George W., and Truman R. Strobridge. *Western Pacific Operations*. Vol. 5 of *History of U.S. Marine Corps Operations in World War II*. Washington, D.C.: Historical Branch, G-3, Headquarters Marine Corps, 1971.

Goulden, Joseph C. *Korea: The Untold Story of the War*. New York: McGraw-Hill Book Co., 1982.

Gugeler, Russell A. *Combat Actions in Korea*. U.S. Army Historical Series. Washington, D.C.: Office of the Chief of Military History, U.S. Army, 1954.

Hastings, Max. *The Korean War*. New York: Simon & Schuster, 1987.

Kozlenko, William. *Men at War*. New York: Wings Books, 1942.

MacDonald, James Angus, Jr. *Problems of U.S. Marine Corps Prisoners of War in Korea*. Washington, D.C.: History and Museums Division, Headquarters Marine Corps, 1988.

Montross, Lynn, et al. *U.S. Marine Corps Operations in Korea, 1950–1953*. 5 vols. Washington, D.C.: Historical Branch, G-3, Headquarters Marine Corps, 1954–72.

Moran, Lord. *Anatomy of Courage: The Classic Study of the Soldier's Struggle against Fear*. New York: Avery Publishing Group, 1945.

Moskin, J. Robert. *The U.S. Marine Corps Story*. Rev. ed. New York: McGraw-Hill Book Co., 1987.

Norton, Bruce H. *Sergeant Major, U.S. Marines: The Biography of Sergeant Major Maurice J. Jacques*. New York: Random House, 1995.

Proehl, Carl. *The Fourth Marine Division in World War II.* Washington, D.C.: Infantry Press, 1946.

Thomas, Peter. *41 Independent Commando Royal Marines—Korea—1950–1952.* London: Royal Marine Historical Society, 1990.

U.S. Congress. House Committee on Foreign Affairs. *Examination of U.S. Policy toward POW/MIAs,* 85th Cong., 1st Sess., 1991.

White, William Lindsay. *The Captives of Korea.* New York: Charles Scribner's Sons, 1957. (Unofficial white paper on the treatment of war prisoners.)

# Index

Aguirre, Andrew "Chief," xvi, 81, 99, 156–57, 170, 174, 175, 179, 191, 211, 290

Aircraft, Japanese: "Betty," 42–43, 45–46; "Zero," 44, 46, 207

Aircraft, U.S.: B-24 Liberator, 14, 27–28; B-29, 138, 148; B-57 Canberra, 265; "Enola Gay," 55; F4U Corsair, 106; OY Spotter, 197, 198; P-38 Lighting, 25; P-51 Mustang, 202; R4D "Gooney Bird," 229; XB-32, 28

Aldridge, Dennis, 101, 206

Alford, Art, 6, 58, 208

Alford, Don, 6, 58

Alford, Gene, 6

Anderson, Edward N., 202

Antonis, "Nic," 155

Arabian-American Oil Company, 278

Army, U.S., 1–2, 13, 14, 18, 131–32; 1st CAV Division, 190; 9th Corps, 189; 10th Corps, 102; 25th Infantry Division, 187; 31st Infantry Regiment, 138; 32d Infantry Regiment, 138; Baker Company, 31st Regiment, 7th Infantry Division, 90, 93, 97, 101; Reconnaissance Company, 7th Infantry Division, 199

Ascom City, South Korea, 73

Bangkok, Thailand, 252

Bardello, Italy, 1

Barnett, "Gunny," 271

Barrow, Robert H., 289

Beall, Olin L., 68

Biesterveld, Thomas, 184

Billingsley, V. L., 21, 22–23, 24, 26, 31

Bodies Not Recovered (BNRs), 213–14

Boot camp, San Diego, 20–35

Brause, Bernard P. "Barney," 287

Brutsche, Fred, 71–72

Buck, John "Jack," 109–10

Budney, John, 263

Burbank, Rex, 277

Burnette, Lowell, 68

Buttons, Red, 243

Cabanatuan, Philippine Islands, 228

Cabrillo Cleaners & Laundry, 13–14

Cao Do River, Vietnam, 253, 266, 270

Capraro, Michael, 109–10

Carroll, James C. "Gunner," xvi, 248–49, 254, 266, 268

Casey, C. R., 266

Casualties: from Korean War, 210; from Task Force Drysdale, 108

Chambers, Justice M. "Jumping Joe," 47

Chase, Lester, 74

Chidester, Arthur A., 100

Chinese Communist Forces (CCF), 88, 98, 100, 101–21, 148–50, 154, 162, 171, 183, 196, 201

Chinese People's Volunteer Army (CPVA), 129

Chinhung-ni, North Korea, 89, 155, 291, 292

Chosin Reservoir, North Korea, 85, 88, 138, 148, 213

Christmas Day 1950, 132–33

Chunchon, South Korea, 190, 198, 200–202, 215–16

Civilians, North Korean, 154, 158, 167

Clarke, Bruce W., 93–94, 140

Claunch, John "Jake," 41, 52

Coast Guard, U.S., 25

Code of Conduct, U.S., 215

Cold, Frank, 170

Cole, Paul M., 213

Commandant of the Marine Corps, 207, 220, 222, 224, 268, 275

Communism, interpretation of, 147

Consolidated-Vultee Aircraft Corporation, 28

Control methods, used by Chinese Communist Forces, 161–63

Cook, Bud, 277

Corwin, Mac, 88, 89, 109

Courts-martial, 131–32, 215

Craig, Edward A. "Eddie," 110

Crosby, Bing, 242–43

Cushman, Robert C., 248

Da Nang, Vietnam, 245, 247, 248, 249, 251, 255–56, 257, 259, 260, 265–66, 268, 271

Daniels, Billy, 261

Danneker, Michael, 52

Dean, William F., 135–36

Delano, Clifford, 241

Desert Field Exercise (DESFEX), 225

Dickerson, Charles W., 88, 124, 134, 170, 290

Dickey, Dwight, 270

Dingalan Bay, Philippines, 228

Dirst, Lloyd, 97

Dix, Don, 59, 61

Dolby, Robert, 81, 99, 155, 156

Drysdale, Douglas B., 87, 89, 90, 94

Dulles, John Foster, 158

Dunis, Gust H. "Gus," 195, 207

Dysentery, 136, 159, 160, 188, 214

Eisenhower, Dwight D., 215

Eller, Franklin P. "Pete," 287

English, "Max," 72, 78, 223

Escape, from the Chinese, 183–99

Estess, Morris L., 198

Evans, Holly, 203

Explosive Ordnance Disposal (EOD), 268–69

Fagan, William, 267

Faith, Don C., 138, 294–95

Fegan, Joseph Jr., 286

Forrestal, James V., 62

Frankfurt, Germany, 233, 237

Freedom Village, South Korea, 210

Frostbite, effects of, 121

Funchilin Pass, North Korea, 85, 155

General Classification Test (GCT), 224

Gentile, Vincent J., 252

Gildersleeve, Leo, 266

Glasgow, James, 155

Goon-zo-yeh, 143

Grahl, Hans, 174

Grant, John "Hook," 51–52

Haberlie, Douglas, 203

Hagaru, North Korea, 85, 90, 91, 101

Hamhung, North Korea, xi
Haneda Air Force Base, Japan, 206
Hargett, Ernest, 156
Harrison, Charles L. "Charlie,"
    163–64, 170, 174, 181,
    195–97, 198, 202, 290
Harrison, William, 97, 102, 106,
    109, 140
Harshman, Earl R., 67
Hasha, Bob, 30, 58, 60–61
Hawkins, Clifford R. "Roy," 94, 97,
    124, 170, 187, 290
Hayton, Ernest E. "Ernie," 97, 106,
    120, 124, 137, 140, 159,
    170, 198, 207, 290
Headquarters Marine Corps
    (HQMC), 140, 141, 274
Hell Fire Valley, North Korea, 103,
    109, 206
Helms, John, 54–55
Henderson Hall, Arlington, Virginia,
    230
Hennegan, Joseph, 243, 244
Herlong, Richard, 71, 81
Hibbing, Minnesota, 1
Hilburn, Theron L. "Leon," 94, 102,
    124, 140, 170, 187,
    206–207, 290
Hilderbrand, McKinley "Mac," 277
Hiroshima, Japan, 55
Hite, Harry, 270
Hoa Tho, Vietnam, 252
Hochmuth, Bruno, 248
Holcomb, Fred G., 198
Home Guard, North Korean Unit,
    117
Hongchon, South Korea, 189,
    200–201
Hong Kong, 229–30, 252
Hope, Bob, 82, 253
Houghton, Kenneth J., 286, 288,
    289
Howells, William "Heavy," 54
Hubberts, James, 2
Hubberts, Jane, 2
Hubberts, Leonard, 2
Hubberts, Lillian, 2

Hue City, Vietnam, 257, 259–60,
    266
Hungnam, North Korea, 86, 87, 157

Inchon, South Korea, 72
Iwo Jima, Volcano Islands, xiv,
    47–54

Jacobson, George, 256
Jennings, Norm, 278
Jones, Jennifer, 204
Junior Reserve Officers Training
    Corps (JROTC), 9, 22

Kabul, Afghanistan, 279–82
Kaechon, North Korea, 168
Kadena Air Force Base, Okinawa,
    231, 245
Kanggye. See Prisoner of War
    camps, in North Korea
Kanner, Harry, 1
Kanner, James, 2
Kanner, Lillian, 2
Kanner, Mary Skelly, 1
Kelly, Guy, 219
Kimpo airfield, near Ascom City,
    South Korea, 73
Kōbe, Japan, 67, 69, 204
Kojo, North Korea, 82
Kolbeck, Farris, 6, 58, 208
Koontz, Willy O., 223
Koto-ri, North Korea, xi, 85, 90,
    101–103, 110, 155
Kumhwa, North Korea, 186

Lahue, Foster C., 252
Laingen, L. Bruce, 279–80
Lane, Offie, 71–72
Lice, 164–65
Lindbergh Field, San Diego, 16, 25
Liu, Lieutenant, CCF-POW
    instructor, 153, 169, 171,
    179, 180, 191, 193, 216
Lottig, Crystal M., xvi
"Lucky 60," 169
Lutz, Ted, 244

MacArthur, Douglas, 72, 88, 129, 158, 202

Maffioli, Carl, 1–3, 6, 15, 18, 57, 209, 217, 237

Maffioli, Carl Jr., "Sonny," 3, 57, 237

Maffioli, Deborah Lynne, 66, 205, 207–209

Maffioli, Dominico, 1

Maffioli, Donna Moore, xvii, 281–85

Maffioli, Ethel Kanner, xvi, 1, 2, 6, 18, 57, 209

Maffioli, Gina, 273

Maffioli, Jason, 285

Maffioli, Leonard J., Jr., 222

Maffioli, Margie Pearson, 238

Maffioli, Marion Rose, 2, 18, 57, 208, 232

Maffioli, Marsha Jeanne, 225

Maffioli, Rosa, 1

Maffioli, Sharon, 139–41, 205, 207–209, 217–19, 222, 228

Maffioli, Steven, 273

Majon-dong, North Korea, 85, 93

Majon-ni, North Korea, 83, 84

Manchuria, China, 121

Manhard, Philip, 259

Manpojin, North Korea, 135

Margaret, Ann, 243

Marine Corps, U.S.: air station, El Toro, 244; Fifth Amphibious Corps, 46; First Provisional Marine Brigade, Korea, 220; Reserve(s), 18; tanks, A-1-1, 83

—Bases: Camp Pendleton, 36, 39, 56, 57, 209, 219; San Diego, 5, 28, 209, 219

—Battalions: Eleventh Tank, 63, 65, 67–69; First Engineer, 85; First Marines, 90; First Motor Transport, 52, 68; First Provisional Guided Missile, 223; First Tank, 65, 69, 85, 86, 109; Fourth

Motor Transport, 67; Third, First Marines, 90

—Camps: Elliot, 13, 32–34; Hansen, Okinawa, 228–29; Las Flores, 226; Las Pulgas, 220; Lejeune, 282–84; Matthews, 29–30

—Companies: Amphibious Reconnaissance, 156; D, 1st Tank Battalion, 109; E, 1st Medical Battalion, 203; G, 3d Battalion, 1st Marines, 90, 93, 94, 101; Service, 1st Tank Battalion, 109

—Divisions: 1st Marine, 91; 2d Marine, 46–47; 3d Marine, 228, 266; 4th Marine, 38–39, 40–41, 43–46, 47, 52–53, 56; 5th Marine, 52

—Regiments: 1st Marine, 101; 5th Marine, 72–74; 7th Marine, 74, 101, 109; 14th Marine (Artillery), 41; 25th Marines, 47

Marine division cemeteries: on Iwo Jima, 52; on Saipan, 44–45

Marine Memorial Club, 207

Marine Security Battalion, 235

Marine Security Guard School, 230–33

Marines, Republic of Korea, 75, 77, 81

*Marstan* (cabin cruiser), 237–38, 273

Martin, Dick, 61

Marxism, 161

Massaro, John, 287

Mathis, Chester, 191, 211

Mathis, Phyllis, 16, 18, 36–37, 50, 55, 61

Maxwell, Marilyn, 82

McCool, Felix, 114, 211

McLaughlin, John N., xii, 102–103, 114, 118, 136, 145, 170, 211, 262, 290

McMakin, Richard A., 28

McPherson, Richard, 248, 257

Medals: Bronze Star, 206, 300–301; of Honor, 47, 294–95; Meritorious Service, 302–303; Navy Cross, 206, 223; Purple Heart, 206; Silver Star, 206, 275

Mexico: Mexicali, 61; Tijuana, 61

Military Amateur Radio System (MARS), 205

Military Assistance Command Vietnam (MACV), 248, 259

Military Police, 27–28

Mickelson, Carlan F., xvi

Mickelson, R. D. "Mick," xvi, 287

Milne, Harry T., 85, 203

Missiles: Hawk, 224; Terrier, 224

Morell, Philip R., 65, 203

Mortar, 81-mm., 262–63

Motoyama airfield No. 1, Iwo Jima, 50

Mougenkoff, Igor, 221–22

Mount Suribachi, Iwo Jima, 48, 50

Munchon, North Korea, 83–84

Munich, Germany, 233–35

Nagasaki, Japan, 55

Nash, James B. "Smokey," 207

Navy, U.S., 17–18, 223–24; submarine service, 59–60

—Bases: Destroyer, San Diego, 3; Naval Air Station, Coronado, 3; Naval Hospital Balboa, San Diego, 208–209, 218; Naval Station, San Diego, 3; Naval Training Center, San Diego, 3

—Ships: *Fanshaw Bay*, 56; *Haven*, 204; *Hercules*, 53–54; *John Land*, 42–43; LSTs and LSDs, 38, 67, 69, 70, 83; LCVPs and LCMs, 43, 53; *M. C. Meigs*, 66–68; *Missouri*, 174; *Nereus*, 59;

*Pickaway*, 82; *Sanborn*, 47; *Sperry*, 59

Neumann, Robert G., 279

*New Life, The*, POW newspaper, 157–58

New Year's Day 1951, 139

Nichols, Rueben, 170

Noel, Frank, xi, 102, 114, 170, 211

North Korean People's Army (NKPA), 64, 72, 73, 74, 75, 83, 104, 161

Norton, Bruce H. "Doc," xi, xv, xvi

Norton, Darice T., xvi

Okinawa, Japan, 228–30

Operations: Big Switch, 211–12; Little Switch, 210–12; Ripper, 189; Rugged, 190; Strongback, 228; Yo-Yo, 82

Orr, Elizabeth Kanner, 2

Pan, Lieutenant, CCF-POW instructor, 145–46, 147, 153, 158, 161, 163–64, 169, 171, 172, 179–80, 191–92, 216

Paoletti, Angela, 3

Paoletti, Dominic, 3

Paoletti, John, 3

Pearl Harbor, 12, 54

Pearson, Margie, 238

Peiping, China, 143

Perfume River, Vietnam, 259

Phong Le Bridge, Vietnam, 251

Phillips, S. W. "Bill," xvi

Pinang, Malaysia, 252

Pistols: American .45 ACP, 101; Russian (Tokarev) 9-mm., 80, 111

Pomeroy, William, 73, 77, 78, 79

Presidential Unit Citation (PUC), 291–93

Prisoners of War (POWs): American: 140–41, 143, 159, 210–16; British: 170; Colombian, 215; Turkish, 215

Prisoner of War camps, in North Korea: Chonsong, 170; Chorwon, 186; Kanggye, xi, 121, 122, 133, 138, 141, 142, 153, 157, 160–66, 168, 169, 171, 183, 185, 193, 213, 216, 262; Pyoktong, 170
Public Information Officer, 144–45, 268
Pugh, Marvin E., 108
Pukhan River, South Korea, 190, 195
Puller, Lewis B. "Chesty," 74, 77, 93
Pusan, South Korea, 72
Pyongyang, North Korea, 83, 168, 186

Quang Nam Province, Vietnam, 247, 250, 259

Rand Corporation, 213
Rappold, William "Bill," 275, 276
Raye, Martha, 253–54
Recruiters School, Parris Island, South Carolina, 238
Recruiting Stations, 239
Red Cross, American, 203–204
Rhodes, Tiny, 78
Rifles, American: M-1 Carbine, 30; M-1 Garand, 24–25, 30, 89, 149; M-2 Carbine, 100; M-14, 251; M-16A1, 249, 251; '03 Springfield, 5, 149–50; recoilless, 75-mm., 99, 111
Roberts, Albert, 191, 211
Robertson, Donn J., 248
Roebuck, Leon, 173–74
Roi-Namur, Marshall Islands, 38
Roosevelt, Franklin D., 12
Rosenthal, Joe, 50
Rowan, Dan, 61
Royal Marines, 130; Four-One Independent Commando, 87–93, 101, 206
Royal Navy, 88, 90

Saigon, Vietnam, 248, 256
Saipan, Mariana Islands, xiv, 42–46
San Francisco, California, 2
Sapyong-ni, South Korea, 189
Saxon, Joe, 155
Schulze, R. C., 288
Scott, Marion, 16, 30, 57, 208, 232
Scott, Stan "Scotty," 16, 23, 30, 32, 37, 55, 57, 208, 232
*Scout, The*, Camp Pendleton newspaper, 221
Seeley, Henry "Pop," 110
Sefrhans, James, 260, 261
Seoul, South Korea, 80–81, 189–90
Shepherd, Lemuel C., 72
Shimomura, Saburo "Sam," xvi, 174, 191, 197, 202, 216, 290
Silva Family, on Hawaii, 54
Singapore, 252
Slater, Robert, 282
Smith, Holland M. "Howling Mad," 46
Smith, Mercer R. "Dick," 184, 290, 296–97
Smith, Oliver P., 88, 94, 190
Sorghum, 127, 152
Soyang-ni, North Korea, 85
Soyang River, North Korea, 195
Stearns, Lloyd, 38
Stiles, Sharon, 61
Stockholm Peace Appeal, 163–64
Submachine gun, Thompson .45-caliber, 79
Sullivan, Robert, 6, 58
Suyuhyon, South Korea, 77, 79, 80, 81
Sydney, Australia, 260

38th Parallel, Korea, 129–30, 190, 200
Tanks, American: M-4A3 (Sherman), 63, 69, 199; M-26 (Pershing), 69, 72, 74, 155–56; used in Vietnam, 245–71
Tanks, Russian, T-34, 72–73

Task Force Drysdale, xiii, 87, 93–103, 108–10, 138, 140, 156, 173

Task Force Faith, 138

Taylor, Richard M. "Roughhouse," 74, 83, 220, 245–46, 252

Teague, Edward, 279

Tehran, Iran, 279

Tet Offensive, 1968, xiii, 256–60

Thomas, Gerald C., 202–203

Tinian, Mariana Islands, xiv, 46–47

Tokchon, North Korea, 171

Toktong Pass, North Korea, 91

Travis Air Force Base, California, 207

Treasure Island, San Francisco, 207

Truman, Harry S., 62, 64, 129, 158

Turner, Herbert B., 114

Tuy Loan River, Vietnam, 248

Typhoons: Jane, 67; Kezia, 69

Uijongbu, South Korea, 80, 189

Uniform Code of Military Justice, 222, 233

University of California, San Diego, 29

U.S. Agency for International Development (USAID), 280–81

Van Fleet, James A., 202

Vehicles: Ontos (anti-tank armored vehicle), 227; truck, 2¹/₂ ton, 6×6, 105; truck, 2¹/₂ ton, wrecker, 69, 71

Vienna, Austria, 235–36

Viet Cong, 249, 251

Vietnam: The Citadel, 257, 259; DaNang Air Base, 245, 255–56, 265–66; First CTZ, 248; I Corps in, 248, 266; III MAF in, 270; Military Assistance Command in, 248, 259

Viverios, Eugene, 223

Wake Island, 207

Webb, Johnie E., Jr., xvi

Welker, Dale, 261

Westmoreland, William, 248

Wheeler, Theodore R. "Ted," 67, 107, 192

White, Bill, 6–7

Wilkinson, Bud, 6, 61, 208, 217

Wilkinson, Dave, 6, 61

Williams, Bruce, 74

Williams, Calvin W., 198

Williams, Kenneth J.T. "Kenny," xvi, 89, 94, 96, 107–108, 290

Wilson, Louis H., 287, 289

Winker, Fred R., 50

Wisda, Martin, xvi

Wolmi-do Island, South Korea, 70–72

Wonsan, North Korea, 82–84

Yalu River, North Korea, 121, 135, 136, 138, 148, 160, 170

Yangdok, North Korea, 171

Yesko, Daniel, 191, 211

Yokohama, Japan, 67

Yokosuka, Japan, U.S. Naval Hospital at, 204

Young, Martin, 260

Yudam-ni, North Korea, 91

**FORCE RECON DIARY, 1969**
by Bruce H. Norton

FORCE RECON DIARY, 1969 is the riveting, true-to-life account of survival, heroism, and death in the elite Marine 3rd Force Recon unit, one of only two Marine units to receive the Valorous Unit Citation during the Vietnam War. Doc Norton, a 3rd Force Recon medic and retired Marine major, recounts his unit's experiences behind enemy lines during the tense patrols, sudden ambushes, and acts of supreme sacrifice that occurred as they gathered valuable information about NVA operations right from the source.

Published by Ivy Books.
Available in bookstores everywhere.

**FORCE RECON DIARY, 1970**
by Bruce H. Norton

Operating beyond the artillery fan of friendly forces, in the thick of a jungle war, the Marines of 1st and 3rd Force Recon companies understood that the only things keeping them alive in "Indian Country" were their own skills and courage and the loyalty they had to one another. Here is the continuing saga of life behind enemy lines by a former member of these fearless and peerless Force Recon companies.

Published by Ivy Books.
Available in your local bookstore.

# SERGEANT MAJOR, U.S. MARINES
by Maurice J. Jacques and Bruce H. Norton

Maurice Jacques served for thirty years with the U.S. Marine Corps from the razorback hills of Korea to the steamy jungles of Vietnam and beyond. As an accomplished infantryman, recon Marine, record-setting drill instructor, and regimental sergeant major who was awarded two Bronze Stars and a Purple Heart, Jacques reveals the sacrifice and valor, combat and comradery that have made the Marines legendary around the world. This is his story—a story of the pain, pride, and triumph that is the USMC.

# ONE TOUGH MARINE
### The Autobiography of
### First Sergeant Donald N. Hamblen, USMC
by Donald N. Hamblen and Bruce H. Norton

In September 1962, during a routine parachute jump at Camp Pendleton, Marine Staff Sergeant Don Hamblen suffered injuries that cost him a leg. To most people, that would have been a ticket to early retirement. But Don Hamblen fought his way back into 1st Force Recon company. Then in 1965 he was reassigned to Vietnam, where he was part of a small Marine detachment assigned to SOG as advisers to South Vietnamese commando teams fighting in North Vietnam. ONE TOUGH MARINE is the amazing story of the courage, spirit, and self-determination of a Marine who fought the toughest battle of all and won.

Published by Ivy Books.
Available in a bookstore near you.